THE WORLD OF TH

BOOK OF MORMON

PAUL R. CHEESMAN

Deseret Book Company
Salt Lake City, Utah
1978

©1978 by Paul R. Cheesman
All rights reserved
Printed in the United States of America

Library of Congress Cataloging in Publication Data

Cheesman, Paul R
   The world of the Book of Mormon.

   Bibliography: p.
   Includes index.
   1. Book of Mormon. 2. Indians — Antiquities.
3. America — Antiquities. I. Title.
BX8627.C477   289.3'22   77-18772
ISBN 0-87747-649-7

Appreciation is given to my assistants who helped in the preparation of this manuscript: Ivy Berry, Kirk Magelby, Wayne Hamby, Bryson Jones, Elizabeth Shaw, William Clauson, Jim Vandygriff, Kenneth Slater, Dwaine Yearsley, Leonard Carter, Karen Wirkus, John Wilson, and Kathryn Schellenberg.

CONTENTS

Preface vii

Origin of the American Indian 1

Indian Traditions 5

The Bearded White God 7

The Chroniclers 12

The Conquerors 18

Geography of the Book of Mormon 21

Theories on the Book of Mormon Geography 28

Pre-Columbian Cultures and Ruins 35

Ancient Civilizations in Mexico 42

Pre-Columbian Ruins in Guatemala 53

Ancient Ruins in Honduras 56

Ancient Cultures and Ruins in Peru 58

Possible Phoenician Influence 64

Ancient Writing and Language 68

Baptism and Sacrament 74

Stone Boxes 77

Highways 80

The Wheel 84

Arts and Crafts 87

Horses 91

Calendar Systems 93

Medicine 97

Conclusion 101

Bibliography 103

Index 106

To my family and all those
whose love for the Book of Mormon
strengthens their dedication to
The Church of Jesus Christ of Latter-day Saints
and the building up of
the kingdom of God.

PREFACE

The question often arises: Have there been any archaeological discoveries in Central and South America that sustain or support the Book of Mormon?

The Book of Mormon was not written with the intention of providing a full historical account of the people involved. Rather, Mormon, Moroni, and Nephi (the three principal authors) wrote an abridged spiritual record that contains only enough historical data to bring continuity to the very lengthy time span involved. Any external evidence, therefore, would be important primarily for the book's historicity, not its spiritual message. Since the record contains spiritual lessons, the reader would need to have a spiritual experience in order to verify its validity. The formula for gaining that testimony is found in the record itself in Moroni 10:4-5. Proof of the authenticity or truthfulness of the Book of Mormon thus remains within the spiritual realm and is not obtainable from the singular study of archaeology.

Joseph Smith made the greatest archaeological discovery of all time when he was led to the ancient metal plates and translated and published them as the Book of Mormon.

The acquisition of mummies and documents from the Old World is further indication of his interest in archaeology. Speculating on the location of Book of Mormon sites, he expressed his opinion concerning archaeological findings in an article in one of the Church's periodicals: "It would not be a bad plan to compare Mr. Stephen's ruined cities with those in the Book of Mormon. Light cleaves to light and facts are supported by facts. The truth injures no one. . . ." (*Times and Seasons* 3:927.)

Elder LeGrand Richards of the Council of the Twelve related an interesting story regarding the Book of Mormon. He said that he once heard Elder Charles A. Callis, also an apostle of the Church, declare: "When Joseph Smith received the plates he got down on his knees and said, 'O, God, what will the world say,' and the voice of God came to him, 'Fear not. I will cause the earth to testify of the truth of these things.'" (*Conference Report*, October 1946, p. 125.)

It need not be supposed that the Book of Mormon is the only evidence that will come forth out of the earth. In the Pearl of Great Price we read:

"And the day shall come that the earth shall rest, but before that day the heavens shall be darkened, and a veil of darkness shall cover the earth; and the heavens shall shake, and also the earth; and great tribulations shall be among the children of men, but my people will I preserve;

"And righteousness will I send down out of heaven; and truth will I send forth out of the earth, to bear testimony of mine Only Begotten; his resurrection from the dead; yea, and also the resurrection of all men; and righteousness and truth will I cause to sweep the earth as with a flood, to gather out mine elect from the four quarters of the earth, unto a place which I shall prepare, an Holy City, that my people may gird up their loins, and be looking forth for the time of my coming; for there shall be my tabernacle, and it shall be called Zion, a New Jerusalem." (Moses 7:61-62.)

Modern scripture sheds interesting light on the subject of proving God's words:

". . . the Book of Mormon . . . contains a record of a fallen people, and the fulness of the gospel of Jesus Christ to the Gentiles and to the Jews also;

"Which was given by inspiration, and is confirmed to others by the ministering of angels, and is declared unto the world by them—

"Proving to the world that the holy scriptures are true, and that God does inspire men and call them to his holy work in this age and generation, as well as in generations of old;

"Thereby showing that he is the same God yesterday, today, and forever. Amen.

"Therefore, having so great witnesses, by them shall the world be judged, even as many as shall hereafter come to a knowledge of this work." (D&C 20:8-13.)

Although a testimony is gained only by a prayerful study of this record, there are many external evidences that would sustain or support (though not necessarily prove) the Book of Mormon. It must be remembered also that the Book of Mormon does not claim to be a record of *all* the inhabitants of the American continent and the ancestors of *all* of the American Indians. It does, however, claim to be a spiritual record of three groups that came to America: (1) the Lehi colony, which divided into the Nephites and Lamanites; (2) the Mulekites, who merged with the Nephites; and, (3) the Jaredites, who were the first of the three groups to arrive. The bulk of the Book of Mormon is a history of the Nephite-Lamanite-Mulekite cultures.

The Nephite-Lamanite narrative in the Book of Mormon commenced in 600 B.C. and ended in A.D. 421. Mormon and Moroni abridged ancient records and compiled a set of metal plates which, when translated, became the present Book of Mormon, 522 pages in length.

The fields of anthropology, archaeology, and ethnology have provided much evidence concerning the ancient inhabitants of America. Many terms are used to describe these natives who lived prior to the time of the Spanish conquerors, but the term used here will be *pre-Columbian*, which refers to the groups found on the North and South American continents prior to the arrival of Columbus.

In attempting to recreate scientifically the story of the pre-Columbian peoples of America, a variety of methods have been utilized, such as ancient hieroglyphs, translation of oral traditions, and study of artifacts and buildings (archaeology). Some hieroglyphs and records were made anciently by the natives. Much of their writing was destroyed by the Spanish conquerors, but a few manuscripts, or codices, have been found thus far. Some hieroglyphs on stone and other materials are also available but as yet have not been translated. Natives learned the Spanish language after the conquest and translated some of their manuscripts and oral traditions into the tongue of their conquerors. One such record is the writings of an Indian named Ixtlilxochitl.

Certain early Spanish priests and scholars likewise learned the language of the natives to gain an understanding of the culture of their ancestors. Their writings are known as the chronicles.

Artifacts from the material remains of these great ancient civilizations, such as potsherds, jewelry, clothing, metal objects, musical instruments, and surgical tools, have been assembled, correlated, compared, and dated to produce hypotheses concerning the pre-Columbian civilization. All of these investigations are part of a new science known as archaeology, which emerged at the turn of the century. Many mysteries still exist as attempts are being made to determine the origin and environment of the early inhabitants of the American continent.

The findings of the scientific world today reveal that prior to the arrival of the Spanish, part of the civilization on the American continent was highly developed. Some of the people achieved in architecture, engineered intricate agricultural irrigation systems, became masterful goldsmiths and silversmiths, and participated in well-planned civic, political, and religious communities. In almost every facet of living, their civilization was equal to or surpassed the majesty and grandeur of Rome and Greece. Would not these findings be supportive evidence, then, of the Book of Mormon accounts of large cities with temples and a highly cultured civilization rich in gold, silver, and fine textiles?

Evidences of a high civilization are also revealed in the ancient Americans' knowledge of mathematics, astronomy, and such religious practices as sacrifice, baptism, sacrament, and belief in immortality. All of these, and many other evidences, certainly would sustain and support the Book of Mormon.

It may be noted that there are still some historical and cultural concepts mentioned in the Book of Mormon that have not been sustained by the study of archaeology. This is understandable, since this discipline is a relatively new science and new discoveries are being reported constantly. Time will undoubtedly provide supportive evidence for the few remaining claims in the Book of Mormon that now lack archaeological parallels. This, therefore, is the purpose of my writing—to share with the reader more than twenty years of research regarding pre-Columbian ruins, artifacts, and findings that may help us fit together some of the pieces of this mysterious puzzle called ancient America. One may say with certainty, however, that nothing in the Book of Mormon has been proven to be false through the findings of archaeology. In my research on ancient America, as I have concurrently studied the Book of Mormon, I have found hundreds of evidences that substantiate this remarkable record.

The Book of Mormon centers around a strongly religious group who were constantly at war with those who opposed their teachings. Academic research reveals that religion seemed to be the underlying influence among many of the early Americans. The Book of Mormon's central figure of influence is Jesus Christ, whose visits to the American continent are recorded therein. All through ancient American legend, and even today in the various tribes living in the Americas, we still hear one of the most enduring of ancient legends—the story of "big brother," who came to their ancestors, taught them, blessed them, and promised to return. One cannot help but note these similarities.

The early inhabitants of the land we now refer to as America were as civilized and cultured at their peak as any group living in any place upon earth during the same time period. Many scholars conclude that the peak of the pre-Columbian civilization was co-existent with the time of Christ. Studying the present Indian cultures, one would wonder what has happened to the majestic civilization which once existed upon this continent. Where are the people who produced the magnificent highways that carried travelers to temples and palaces as great as those in the Old World? The story of some of these peoples, as told in the Book of Mormon, provides some interesting parallels with modern archaeological discoveries and oral Indian traditions.

A just God who is not a respecter of persons would certainly visit, instruct, and leave a record of his dealings with the millions of people in this new world as well as the old. Translations of ancient Indian histories, as well as the Book of Mormon, bear this out. Many Indian traditions reveal a knowledge of the flood, the ark, the dividing of the waters, and other biblical occurrences, all told to the Spaniards when they arrived in the New World.

Many concepts in the Book of Mormon emerge in man's study of archaeology and ethnology. Among those that do sustain and support the Book of Mormon record are those listed in the accompanying chart.

Other miscellaneous traits indigenous to the Mesoamerican culture (possibly the central Book of Mormon area) that correspond to the ancient Near East before and after Lehi's day include the following:

1. Development of agricultural methods, including irrigation and fertilization, cotton and the gourd.

2. A highly organized, graded priesthood, which was frequently the controlling force in a theocratic government.

3. Symbolism, including the Tree of Life, the serpent as a sign of wisdom, and the cat as a frequent artistic and religious symbol. The Tree of Life motif, which occurs in the ancient arts of the Old World, has also been found in Central America and South America. Stela 5 Izapa, found in Chiapas, Mexico, seems to have similarities with the Tree of Life symbol as found in the Book of Mormon as well as in ancient Mesopotamia. Dr. Ross T. Christensen, professor of archaeology at Brigham Young University, has said that the Stela 5 Izapa discovery is "the most direct and striking evidence in support of the Book of Mormon which has yet come forth from the science of Archaeology. I do not know who carved this sculpture—whether the artist was a Nephite, a Lamanite, or of some other lineage—but whoever did it was beyond any doubt familiar with the story of Lehi's vision of the Tree of Life as recounted in 1 Nephi, Chapter 8." (*Instructor*, November 1968, p. 432.)

4. Historical and genealogical records, often on paper.

Archaeological Evidences	Book of Mormon
Buildings in Meso- and South America	2 Nephi 5:15 Mosiah 8:8 Mosiah 9:8 Mosiah 11:8
Cement of unusual strength	Helaman 3:7, 9, 11
Towers seen by Cortez in his explorations	Alma 48:1 Alma 50:4
Highways up to 9,000 miles in length criss-crossing South America	3 Nephi 6:8 Helaman 14:24
Wheels found on many wheeled toys	2 Nephi 12:7 Alma 18:9
Weapons similar to Old World construction	Alma 23:13 Alma 25:14 Jarom 8
Metallurgy, including gold, silver, and copper	Helaman 6:9 Ether 10:23
Practice of medicine and surgery	Alma 46:40

5. Precious stones as a common form of wealth.

6. The umbrella as a symbol of divinity or rank.

7. Manufacture and use of purple dye from shellfish and scarlet dye from the cochineal insect.

8. Turbans in great variety.

9. Advanced chronological and mathematical reckoning.

10. The use of the true arch. An example of this is found in LaMuneca. The reason the ancient Americans did not often use the true arch is apparently not because they did not know about it, but because of other factors we do not understand at present.

11. Large stature. The Jaredites in the Book of Mormon are described as "large and mighty men." Among the first civilized inhabitants of this continent were people whom the chroniclers called giants. Large skeletons have been found in Kaminaljuyu, Guatemala.

12. Knowledge of pottery and textiles.

13. Bearded men with Semitic features. Some of the Book of Mormon people were white. Evidences of bearded men with Hebrew noses have been found.

14. Temple buildings in the form of pyramid structures or ziggurats, terminating in a flat area atop which a place of worship was built. Examples of these stepped pyramids are in evidence in Mesopotamia. The use of the pyramid of Egypt to bury the honored dead is also duplicated in the structures found on the American continents. Sunbaked bricks were basic building materials in both areas.

15. Cement, which was of a very high quality and similar in nature to the lime cement used today.

16. Other similarities discovered as a result of archaeological research, including: (a) hair composition, (b) skull measurement, (c) aqueducts, (d) burial methods, (e) tattoos, (f) walls around cities, (g) use of gold and silver, (h) building tools.

The findings of scholars in archaeology have taken much time, knowledge, patience, and money. The surface has only been scratched, and the present conclusions may be altered with new information.

The student of the Book of Mormon should maintain an open mind and remember that he has much to look forward to. More complete archaeological evidences of the truth of the Book of Mormon will be found sooner or later, and as these truths are offered for study, it is well to remember:

1. There is a great deal of evidence in archaeology that coincides with the history of the Book of Mormon, but there are a great many other findings that are not yet clearly defined, and we must be very cautious in accepting them.

2. As far as the writer has been able to determine, there are no non-Latter-day Saint archaeologists at the present time using the Book of Mormon as a guide in archaeological research.

3. Latter-day Saint archaeology is concerned with correlating the historical precepts of the Book of Mormon, not the theological philosophies.

4. We do not know how many groups prior to Columbus came to the areas now known as North America and South America. The Book of Mormon does not claim to identify all of the ancestors of the American Indian; it is a record of only three major groups.

5. A testimony of the truth of the Book of Mormon does not come from scientific findings alone. The spiritual confirmation of the Holy Ghost is a more sure source of truth, as testified to by the many persons who have put Moroni's challenge (Moroni 10:4-5) to a test.

This book provides information concerning the cultures and peoples who lived during Book of Mormon times. I have therefore researched the works of as many non-Latter-day Saint scholars and archaeologists as possible— not to prove the Book of Mormon from these sources, but rather to stimulate study and reinforce the claims made within the pages of this ancient record, and hopefully to challenge the world to read this history of a magnificent people whose cultures once spanned the area of the New World.

Paul R. Cheesman,
Director, Ancient Scripture Studies
Brigham Young University

ORIGIN OF THE AMERICAN INDIAN

One of the great historical questions of our time concerns the origin of the American Indian. Some evidence points to a route from Asia across the Bering Strait and then stretching south through North and South America. Experts theorize that some migrants who took this route stayed in Canada, some in the United States, others traveled to Central America, and the remainder pressed on toward South America. According to modern dating methods, there is indication that someone was in Tierra del Fuego at least eight thousand years ago.

There is also evidence of Oriental blood in the ancient peoples, but that alone did not make them what they were. Their carvings in wood and stone, pottery, and designs are reminiscent in style to those of Egypt, Greece, and Assyria, as well as Japan and China. They were a virile people, ingenious and hardy, with high morals and intelligence.

They were self-made. They learned from observation and reasoning. Indeed, in the world of their time there seemingly were no teachers—and even if they could have secured them, who could have taught them much about astronomy or mathematics? The Chinese had not yet devised numerical place value nor the zero symbol, and these ancient Indians are credited with being first in the use of the zero. (Lorang, *Footloose Scientist in Mayan America*, pp. 184-85.)

"It would have been a joy to tell from whence the peoples of Mayan America came. We can be certain some came from Asia, but from where did the Olmecs come? And where did they go? Why are sculptures from thirteenth-century Cambodia similar to Veracruz Olmec heads, older than 600 B.C.? Why do carved stones from Tiquisate, Guatemala, have a laughing and sad side, reminiscent of Greek stage decorations? Why do statuettes from fifth-century Oaxaca resemble Shakespearean jesters? Why do figurines from the Gulf coast make one think of effervescent movie actors? Is Dr. Sidney Edelstein right in thinking the similarity of dyes used in Mexico and Israel (I might add, in Pliny's Rome) has a bearing on Mayan migration? If so, which way did the migration go, from Israel and Rome to Middle America or vice versa?" (Ibid., pp. 279-80.)

Paul Rivet has concluded: "Physically, it is difficult for us to relate the Maya to an Asiatic group. 'The cranial deformation is absent from the northeast of Asia, with people who can be classed as Mongoloid, and the prominent nose with convex bridge is incompatible with the complete development of the Mongoloid physical characteristics.' 'Neither those flattened heads nor those "Proboscoden" noses are at home in Mongoloid Asia,' and Ernest A. Hooton, from whom I have borrowed these phrases, adds that he is inclined to think that the ancestors of the ancient Maya were not very different from the Armenoid type from the plateaux of Iran, with hooked noses, and from the Alpine type with round heads, and that they acquired certain Mongoloid traits in their hair, pigmentation, shape of cheekbone, etc., in the course of time." (*Maya Cities*, p. 227.)

Sir Grafton Elliot Smith, a chief spokesman and anatomist, writes that he has "traced all civilization back to Egypt, whence it was carried all over the world by sun-worshipping, gold-seeking Egyptians . . . spreading out from Egypt, they came first to Mesopotamia, where they built or taught the natives to build ziggurats in imitation of their own pyramids, later repeating the performance in Cambodia and finally in Central America." (Sprague and de Camp, *Ancient Ruins and Archaeology*, p. 167.)

Sources of culture favored by other diffusionists include Brazil, the Ohio Valley, the Arctic, and "Atlantis."

Some diffusionists have observed resemblances between the vast mausoleums built to guard the mummies of Egyptian pharaohs and the pyramid temples of ancient Mexico. In a tomb beneath the pyramid of the Temple of the Inscriptions in Palenque were found the jewel-adorned remains of an exalted personage, placed there some 1300 years ago. This finding demonstrates that, in some cases, the pyramid temples of Middle America did serve as tombs. Another princely interment was found beneath a pyramid at Tikal, Guatemala, thus establishing the custom of pyramid burial in the lowland Maya area. Samples of bacteria entombed there for more than a thousand years are being studied by microbiologists and may provide a clue to the mysterious decline of the Maya culture.

Middle-American contact with Asia is a theory that has been argued by such scholars as Gordon F. Ekholm and Robert von Heine-Geldern. The late artist-archaeologist Miguel Covarrabias, commenting upon the design of Mayan objects of polished jade recovered from the depths of the Well of Sacrifice at Chichen Itza, said, "It would be hard not to share the belief in stringent and more direct ties with the East." (Reed, *The Ancient Past of Mexico*, pp. 7-8.)

Artist and Egyptologist Joseph Lindon Smith observed that he found striking features common to the cultures of the Egyptians and of the Maya, among them the "flowing vase," symbolizing one of the earliest astral myths. With its undulating streams, flowing in opposite directions, it is a symbol of the Milky Way, regarded by ancient peoples as the seed, or life-power, of deity, and known as early as 2400 B.C. to the Mesopotamians as well as to the astronomers of pre-Columbian Mexico.

Another symbol shared by the Egyptians and the Mayans was the serpent, hailed as the river of the sky and the source of rain, as well as a symbol of life, rebirth, and resurrection. The Tree of Life design, a motif found in ancient Sumerian, Egyptian, Assyrian, Hittite, and Hebraic cultures and mentioned in the books of Genesis and Revelation, may also be seen in the Mayan area. Dr. Matthew W. Stirling has dated its appearance on a stelae at Izapa in Chiapas at about the beginning of the Christian era. A Tree of Life design appears in bas-relief on the lid of a sarcophagus in a chamber deep within the heart of the pyramid of the Temple of the Inscriptions at Palenque. (Ibid., p. 11.)

In South America stories are told similar to the following from Father Jose de Acosta concerning the origin of their civilization:

"It is no matter of any great importance to know what the Indians themselves report of their beginning, being more like unto dreams than to true histories. They make great mention of a deluge which happened in their country. . . . The Indians say that all men were drowned in this deluge, and they report that out of the great Lake Titicaca came one Viracocha, who stayed in Tiahuanaco, where at this day there are to be seen the ruins of ancient and very strange buildings, and from thence came to Cuzco, and so began mankind to multiply. They show in the same lake a small island, where they feign that the sun hid himself and so was preserved; and for this reason they make great sacrifices unto him in that place, both of sheep (i.e., llamas) and men.

"Others report that six, or I know not what number of men, came out of a certain cave by a window, by whom men first began to multiply; and for this reason they call them Paccaritambo. And therefore they are of opinion that the Tambos are the most ancient race of men. They say also that Manco Capca, whom they acknowledge for the founder and chief of their Incas, was issued of that race and that from him sprang two families or lineages, the one of Hanan Cuzco and the other of Urin Cuzco. They say moreover that when the King Incas attempted war and conquered sundry provinces they gave a colour and made a pretext of their enterprise, saying that all the world ought to acknowledge them for all the world was renewed by their race and country; and also that the true religion had been revealed to them from heaven." (Osborne, *South American Mythology*, p. 61.)

Robert Wauchope, a well-known scientist, summarized the feelings of the diffusionists concerning the origin of the civilization of the New World:

"Perhaps the most popular theory about American Indian origins derives the famous ancient civilizations of Mexico, Central America, and the Andes from Egypt. There were pyramids in both America and Egypt, there were mummies in Peru and Egypt, sun worship was practiced in many parts of the New World as well as in Egypt, and both areas produced hieroglyphic writing, royal tombs, bas-relief sculpture, and a number of other similar customs and cultural traits. To most people the word 'archaeology' conjures up but one picture: towering pyramids, the brooding Sphinx, King Tut's tomb, and the Valley of the Nile. It is only natural that when they see ancient relics like these somewhere else, even in faraway America, they see a connection with the classic expression of ancient civilizations—Dynastic Egypt." (Wauchope, *Lost Tribes and Sunken Continents*, p. 7.)

The Aztecs thought of themselves not as natives of America, but as people whose ancestors had migrated to America. Four significant teachings of the Book of Mormon concerning the peoples who are the ancestors of the American Indian indicate that they (1) were from Jerusalem, (2) were white, (3) came in ships, (4) were taught by God the concept of a promised land. Many writings and discoveries of recent years seem to point out similarities to these teachings.

Cortez records: "Montezuma replied that they were not natives of the land but had come to it a long time since—and were well prepared to believe that they erred somewhat from the true faith during the long time since they had left their native land." (Cortez, *Five Letters 1519-1526*, p. 91.)

The Aztecs taught that their ancestoral father and mother, with their fifteen children, came to the Americas by way of a boat. (Powell, *Latest Aztec Discoveries*, p. 45.) Andres De Tapia added that Montezuma related to Cortez how the people we know as Indians had come from ships. This general tradition among Montezuma's people indicates that the early arrivals were white men from a civilization founded in the Mediterranean area, with traditions that we today could scarcely fail to assign to Phoenicians, Egyptians, and Greeks, since there are indeed traces of all these influences in them. (Kelley, *Blood-Drenched Altars*, p. 38.) The Aztecs indicated that they had been wandering from place to place for many years seeking the promised land their deity had offered them. (Enock, *Mexico*, p. 21.)

One writer told of an old Indian chief who said he did not know the origins of his people, but that their most ancient legend said their fathers came from "where the sun rises; that they were a long time on their journey and were on the point of perishing on their journey." He claimed also that they reached their destination "without any effort on their part, inferring that some power other than their own brought them here." (Sperry, *Science, Tradition and the Book of Mormon*, pp. 64-65.)

An ancient Hopi creation myth says that "the Hopis came to America from the west, crossing the sea on boats or rafts from one 'stepping-stone' or island to the next." And a legend of the ancient Quiche Maya relates that "the waters parted and the tribes crossed on stepping stones placed in a row, over the sand." (Waters, *Book of the Hopi*, p. 31.

Concerning the religious views of the Cherokees, we read:

". . . from time immemorial the tribes had been divided in sentiment . . . while the greater part had been idolatrous—worshipping the sun, moon, stars and other objects—a small portion denied that system and taught that there were three beings above who created all things and will judge all men; . . . they fixed the time and manner of death. Their names were: U-ha-he-ta-qua, the great head of all power; A-ta-no-ti; and U-squa-hu-la. Are not these comparable to the Father, Son, and Holy Ghost? They sit on three white seats and are the only objects to which worship and prayers should be directed. The angels are their messengers and come to earth to attend to the affairs of men.

"They claim that Yehowa was the name of the great king. He was a man, yet a spirit; a great and glorious being. His name was never to be mentioned in common talk. This great king commanded them to rest every seventh day. They were told not to work on this day and that they should devote it to talking about God.

"Yehowa created the world in seven days at Nu-ta-te-qua, the first new moon of autumn, with the fruits all ripe. God made the first man of red clay and he was an Indian, and made woman of one of his ribs. All people were Indians or red people before the flood. They had teachers and prophets who taught the people to obey God and their parents. They warned the people of the approaching flood, but said that the world would be destroyed by water only once, and that later it would be destroyed by fire, when God would send a shower of pitch and then a shower of fire which would burn up everything. They also taught that after death the good and bad would be separated; the good would take a path that would lead to happiness, where it would always be light; but evil led to a deep chasm." (Spence, *Myths and Legends: The North American Indians*, p. 3.)

Golden R. Buchanan, who spent many years living among the Indians, wrote that when he was on the Papago Reservation, a convert to the Church told him the following story:

"I had never joined any church because the ministers and priests did not teach the Bible as I read it. I couldn't read it and make it say the same things the other churches said it did. I speak the Papago language. I have lived among them all my life. I know their story and their traditions. And as I read the Book of Mormon that was placed in my hands by missionaries, I recognized the stories of the Papagos, and I knew the book was true. Your missionaries read the Bible the same way I did. These are the reasons I joined the Church. The Papagos believed they crossed the ocean and came to this land, that in the ships and on the trails they were guided by a ball. In this ball was a needle that pointed the direction they were to go. In the Papago language yet today, the name of this ball is 'Liahona.'" (*Improvement Era*, April 1955, p. 241.)

Regarding the Navajos, Buchanan wrote:

"Navajo tradition tells that a man and his wife and four sons came to this land a long time ago. They have, in their native language, the names of these four sons, but I cannot write them. The oldest two of these sons rebelled against the youngest two who were appointed leaders. The older sons and their children lived in the

Seventeenth century drawing of Hernando Cortez, who lived from 1485 to 1547. This Spanish conqueror and his armies marched through Mexico in 1519, capturing city after city until they reached Tenochtitlan. There they were received by Montezuma, ruler of the Aztec empire, as descendants of Quetzalcoatl — messengers from heaven. Taking advantage of this superstition, Cortez made Montezuma his hostage and attempted to rule through him. War ensued, with the Aztec empire falling at last to Cortez and the Spanish.

forest. They made their living by hunting and by the use of the weapons of warfare. They warred and preyed upon their two younger brothers. They covered their bodies with mud and thus became a dark people. The two younger sons became builders and built cities and houses of stone. They planted gardens and fields. They did not place mud upon themselves and thus remained white. For generations there were fightings, wars, and difficulties, the children of the older sons being the aggressors.

"There came a night in which the sun didn't go down, and it was light all night, and the people were much disturbed and distressed. But still there were troubles. Some years after this, came an extended period of darkness." (Ibid.)

Another researcher, Sigvald Linne, has presented the following observations:

"Archaeologists and ethnologists in America have been seized by the general tendency to eliminate all distances. Detailed studies are continued with increasing intensity and with more efficient methods, but at the same time remote associations are made, so daring that they would have been considered as jokes a score or so years ago. It is considered that traces of a primitive arctic culture can be traced from the most northerly part of Norway across northern Asia, over Bering Strait and far south in North America. Heyerdahl's incomparable Kon Tiki expedition showed that certain elements of American culture may have reached Polynesia. Once cautious scientists now arrive at increasingly daring conclusions, especially with regard to the art of Mexico and that of the Far East (so daring that the similarities become proof of direct contact, an immigration of bearers of culture from China). Indeed, the similarities are sometimes so striking that it is difficult to deny the possibility of Asiatic culture elements having reached the ancient cultures of Mexico." (Linne, *Treasures of Mexican Art*, p. 14.)

An interesting observation was made by Fray Diego Duran: "In order to discuss the real and truthful account of the origin and beginnings of these Indian nations, so mysterious and remote to us, and to discover the real truth about them, some divine revelation or spirit of God would be needed. However, lacking this, it will be necessary to make conjectures and reach conclusions through the many proofs that this people give us with their strange ways and manner of conduct and their lowly conversation, so like that of the Hebrews." (Duran, *The Aztecs—The History of the Indies of New Spain*, p. 3.)

Thor Heyerdahl's transoceanic crossing of the Atlantic in 1969 proved that such voyages were technically feasible. Certain other substantiative facts indicate that not only were these voyages feasible, but they actually did occur. Dr. Cyrus H. Gordon, of Brandeis University, has said that a shipload of Phoenicians from Sidon actually landed in Brazil in 531 B.C. It is his opinion that enough evidences are available now to confirm the theory that Middle America produced a meeting ground for people coming from both seas and across both oceans. The Valdivia pottery found in Ecuador is definitely Jomon pottery from Japan, and it is Heyerdahl's contention that this connection was made around 3000 B.C.

Ruth Underhill has decided that America has been discovered at least three times. She claims that Leif Ericson landed in what we know as Massachusetts. Columbus came later, also from the East. However, she believes streams of migration from the west over the Bering Strait accounted for the ancestors of most of the Indians.

Dr. Gordon also reminds us that in 1885, the Smithsonian Institution sponsored an expedition to Tennessee, where an untouched tomb was unearthed. The group excavated it and found undisturbed skeletons. Under the head of one man was a pure Hebrew inscription, which has since been declared authentic. Here is an excellent example of a finding made under professional supervision and strengthening the belief as to how Hebrew-writing people once visited that area long before Columbus. (Lecture, Brigham Young University, October 1970.)

John Lear describes the similarity of Minoan writing of the Old World to inscriptions found in the New World on the Metcalf stone. He too concludes that an American tribe may have ancestors common with the Hebrews of the Bible. ("Ancient Landings in America," *Saturday Review*, July 18, 1970, pp. 18-19.)

Briefly summarized, ideas of the origin of the American Indian advanced by scholars over the years include the following:

1. The American Indian originated in America.

2. Japan, China, and possibly the Polynesian islands were the homes of the first transoceanic voyagers from America.

3. They were from the lost Ten Tribes of Israel, guided to the Americas by some divine power.

4. The ancestors of the American Indian came across the Bering Strait.

5. There existed an island between Africa and South America. This island became the bridge affording travelers a better way to get to America. The island was known as Atlantis.

6. The Mormon theory is that three groups came to America by marine navigation, the first group arriving in the third millennium B.C.

These explanations represent possibilities and perhaps there are others. Latter-day Saints claim a spiritual confirmation of their particular historical record and therefore assume a state of satisfaction regarding the authenticity of the Book of Mormon. Some misunderstanding might also arise here. This ancient record claims to be a record of only three groups of people who came to the New World, commencing with the third millennium B.C. and ending the fifth century A.D. Many other groups may have come, and probably did, either before or after. It is also possible that other groups could have lived on the North and South American continents, without communication or contact or any written history. The Book of Mormon even attests to this possibility, since the Mulekites and the Nephite-Lamanite groups were living close, yet did not discover each other for several hundred years. (See the book of Omni in the Book of Mormon.)

INDIAN TRADITIONS

The history of the American Indian—and indeed, of any people—has a way of emerging upon the written tablet or page. Some histories are more accurate than others. Often today we tend to maintain a biased attitude regarding acceptance of written documents over oral legends. We have no assurance that written history is any more true than verbal, but we persist in giving the written word more veracity. Yet there are certain peoples, including the American Indians, who prefer that their histories be preserved through word of mouth. Some of these legends and oral traditions have endured through many generations.

Golden R. Buchanan, who studied Indian legends and stories that had been handed down through the years, wrote: "As I have lived and worked among the Indian people, I have about come to the conclusion that the story of the race, as we know it from the Bible and the Book of Mormon, can be found in their legends. This story would have to be pieced together—a little from one tribe, a little from another." (*Improvement Era*, April 1955, p. 240.)

Some Indian tribes believed in a premortal existence. For example, Ernest Thompson Seton, in his book *The Gospel of the Red Man* (pages 68-69) writes: "All creatures, including man, were spirits. They moved about in space between the earth and the stars (the heavens). They were seeking a place where they could come into a bodily existence."

One of the most interesting traditions among the Indians concerns the creation of the earth and of man. Two authors, Ellen R. Emerson and James W. LeSueur, have written about this subject as follows: "The Cherokee Indians relate that a number of beings were employed in constructing the sun, which planet was made first. It was the intention of the creators that men should live always; but the sun, having surveyed the land, and finding an insufficiency for their support, changed this design, and arranged that they should die. The daughter of the sun was the first to suffer under this law. She was bitten by a serpent, and died. Immortality fled; men must die." (Emerson, *Indian Myths*, p. 82.)

God the Father and his Son, Jesus Christ, figure prominently in Indian legends and histories. (See Chapter 3.) For example, we read:

"A chief in Guatemala related the following to a priest: 'They knew and believed in God who dwells in the heavens, and that God is Father, Son, and Holy Ghost. The Father's name was Ieona, and he created man and all things. The Son had for a name Bacab, and he was born from a maiden always a virgin, called Chibirins, that lives in the heavens with God. The Holy Ghost they called Fchauc. They say that Ieona means the Great Father; of Bacab, who is the Son, they tell that Eopuce put him to death, had him scourged, and placed a crown of thorns on his head, and hung him with extended arms. There he finally died, and remained dead three days, and the third day he came to life again and ascended to Heaven, where he is now with the Father. Immediately after came Fchuac, who is the Holy Ghost. . . .'" (De Roo, *America Before Columbus* 1:373.)

That the native Americans had knowledge of scriptures and of divine writings is well attested to in some of their legends. Among the many statements in books on Indian history and legends that affirm this are the following:

"They, the American aborigines, assert that a book was once in possession of their ancestors; and along with this recognition they have traditions that the Great Spirit used to foretell to their fathers future events; that angels once talked with them; that all the Indian tribes descended from one man who had twelve sons; that this man was a noble and renowned Prince, having great dominions; and that the Indians, his posterity, will yet recover the same dominion and influences. They believe by tradition that the spirit of prophecy and miraculous interposition once enjoyed by their ancestors will yet be restored to them and that they will recover the book, all of which have been so long lost." (McGavin, *Mormonism and Masonry*, pp. 154-55.)

"'Divine Book,' an account of the Otomis Indians: 'The Indian narrated to him how, long ago, the Otomis were in possession of a book, handed down from father to son and guarded by persons of importance, whose duty it was to explain it. Each page of that book had two columns, and between these columns were paintings which represented Christ crucified, whose features were the expressions of sadness; and such is the God who reigns, they said. For the sake of reverence, they did not turn the leaves with their hands, but with a tiny stick kept along with the book for that purpose. The friar having asked the Indian what the contents of the volume were and its teachings, the old man could not give the details, but said that, were it in existence yet, it would be evidence that the teachings of that book and the preaching of the friar were one and the same. But the venerable heirloom had perished in the ground, where its guardians had buried it.'" (De Roo, *America Before Columbus*, p. 425.)

Joseph Merrick tells of some parchments he found while ploughing. These were said to have Hebrew writing, and a certain Sylvester Larned took them to Cambridge and examined them. He said the translation compared to certain parts in Deuteronomy and Exodus. (Smith, *View of the Hebrews*, pp. 199-200.)

William H. Prescott wrote: "After this we may be prepared for Lord Kingsborough's deliberate confession that the Aztecs had a clear knowledge of the Old Testament and most probably of the New, though somewhat corrupted by time and hieroglyphics!" (Prescott, *History of the Conquest of Mexico* 2:287.)

There are many traditions that the people of the earth at one time became so wicked that the Great God thought it necessary to destroy the earth. Albert B. Reagans' research among the Pima Indians tells how the flood came and the marks where the water touched a woodpecker may still be seen on his feathers. (Reagans, *Pima Flood Myth* 3:97-99.)

According to Buchanan, "The story

Common among the traditions of many ancient American tribes is the biblical account of the great flood. Each group tells its own version of the water that covered the land and destroyed the wicked people. One Ohio Indian told a researcher of a few people who were saved in "a great canoe" such as that which is shown above in this early European drawing.

of the flood is common among many tribes. Men and women, these stories tell, were destroyed because of wickedness. Water covered the land. Men, beasts, and the fowls fled to the tops of the highest mountains to escape the wrath of an angry sea." (*Improvement Era*, April 1955, p. 241.)

Ethan Smith, an early historian, has written: "An Ohio Indian told a Dr. Beatty one of their traditions was 'once the waters had overflowed all the land, and drowned all the people then living, except a few, who made a great canoe and were saved.' . . . 'A long time ago the people went to build a high place; that while they were building, they lost their language, and could not understand each other. . . . Dr. Boudinet assures us that two ministers of his acquaintance informed him, that they being among the Indians away toward the Mississippi, the Indians there (who never saw a white man) informed him that one of their traditions was—a great while ago they had a common father, who had the other people under him: that he had twelve sons by whom he administered his government; but the sons behaved illy. . . .'" (Smith, *View of the Hebrews*, p. 116.)

Hasteen Klaw tells a Navajo legend: "It rained forty-two days and water covered the whole earth, except the tops of the mountains. Then a great rainbow appeared and in top of it stood Great Creator with his hands spread out in gladness." (Klaw, *Navajo Creation Myth*, Bulletin No. 1, p. 75.)

James Adair, a trader among the Indians in the eighteenth century, listed a number of reasons why he thinks the Indians were descendants of the Israelites:

"1. Their division into tribes; 2. Their worship of Jehovah; 3. Their nation of a theocracy; 4. Their beliefs in the ministration of angels; 5. Their language and dialects; 6. Their manner of counting time; 7. Their prophets and high priests; 8. Their festivals, fasts, and religious rites; 9. Their daily sacrifice; 10. Their ablutions and anointings; 11. Their laws of uncleanness; 12. Their abstinence from unclean things; 13. Their marriages, divorces and punishments of adultery; 14. Their several punishments; 15. Their cities of refuge; 16. Their purifications and preparatory ceremonies; 17. Their ornaments; 18. Their manner of curing the sick; 19. Their burial of the dead; 20. Their mourning for their dead; 21. Their change of names adapted to their circumstance and times; 22. Their raising seed to a deceased brother; 23. Their own traditions; the accounts of the English writers; and the testimonies given by Spanish and other writers of the primitive inhabitants of Mexico and Peru." (Smith, *View of the Hebrews*, pp. 142-43.)

Another interesting Indian legend concerns their belief in marriage. Ethan Smith reports:

"Long ago, before ever a white man stepped his foot in America, the Delawares knew there was one God; and believed there was a hell, where bad folks would go when they die; and a heaven, where good folks would go. . . . The missionaries reported that 'he believed there was a devil, and he was afraid of him. These things (he said) he knew were handed down by his ancestors long before William Penn arrived in Pennsylvania. He said, he also knew it to be wrong if a poor man came to the door hungry and naked, to turn him away empty. For he believed God loved the poorest of men better than he did proud rich men. Long time ago, (he added) it was a good custom among his people to take but one wife, and that for life. But now they had become foolish, and so wicked, that they would take a number of wives at a time; and turn them away at pleasure. These things he assures us came down from their ancestors, before even any white man appeared in America.'" (Ibid., p. 104.)

Ernest Seton tells of high standards of chastity among many tribes. Of the Sioux, he quotes Major James McLaughlin as saying "they hold nothing more sacred than the purity of a maiden." (Seton, *The Gospel of the Red Man*, p. 22.)

Louise Grant, who lived among the Indians all her life, interviewed twenty persons from nine tribes at Brigham Young University in July 1970 and wrote concerning the modern Indians' philosophy of the future:

1. There will be more self government.
2. The young people will tend to forget traditions.
3. They will intermingle with whites more.
4. There will be more college education and more professionals.
5. The reservations will change.
6. The people will not be as backward and shy, becoming more like white men.
7. Through intermarriage many Indians will lose any physical characteristics of the Indian.
8. All Indians are waiting and expecting something unusual to happen.
9. Some feel they will maintain their identity.
10. The Indians will not be exploited, but will be in control of all they can grasp and become the powerful Indian nations and tribes of days past. The Indian is going to affect the whole world in days to come.

THE BEARDED WHITE GOD

The bearded white God is one of the most universally taught and accepted legends of the Indians of North and South America. Virtually all tribes teach of him. Tribal songs, dances, and sacred rituals are dedicated to his name. Who was this fair god who appeared so mysteriously among them centuries ago, and what could be the significance of this legend in their lives?

Although his name varies from tribe to tribe, his description and teachings are basically the same. In each tribe, in song and story, he was described as white and fair, with long brown hair and a beard. He wore a loose-fitting robe and sandals. His palms were scarred. His message was of love and peace. He announced to the people that he was born of a virgin. And, last of all, he promised to return.

The supreme god, Tonacatecu, and his wife, Tonacacihuatl, were believed by the Aztecs to be the original gods. The people also believed that these two were self-created and that they would always dwell in the highest heaven, which to the Aztecs was the thirteenth heaven. (Leon-Portillia, *Aztec Thought and Culture*, p. 35.)

Of their great god Sahagun said: "Quetzalcoatl—he was the wind, the guide and roadsweeper of the rain gods, of the masters of the water, of those who brought rain. And when the wind rose, when the dust rumbled, and it crackled and here was a great din, and it became dark and the wind blew in many directions, and it thundered; then it was said: 'Quetzalcoatl is wrathful.'" (Sahagun, *A History of Ancient Mexico* 1:3.)

Hubert Howe Bancroft, a famous historian of the past century who gathered legends from the Indian tribes of the New World, wrote: "Although bearing various names and appearing in different countries, the American culture-heroes all present

Of all the legends and traditions circulating through pre-Columbian America, perhaps the most universally taught is the story of the bearded white God. Known as Itzamna to some, Viracocha to others, and Quetzalcoatl to still others, this deity came to the ancient Americans, clothed in a long robe, to teach them principles of love and peace. Book of Mormon students recognize in the legends the description and deeds of Christ when he appeared on this continent.

Quetzalcoatl was often represented, as in the above sculpture from the Temple of Quetzalcoatl in Teotihuacan, Mexico, in the form of a plumed serpent ("quetzal" signifying a bird and "coatl" meaning serpent.) Many archaeological ruins carry this symbol of the white God who left ancient America with the promise that he would someday return.

the same . . . characteristics . . . all described as white, bearded . . . clad in long robes, appearing suddenly and mysteriously upon the scene . . . at once set about improving the people by instructing them in useful . . . arts, . . . exhorting them to practise brotherly love and other Christian virtues, . . . introducing a milder and better form of religion; having accomplished their mission . . . disappeared as mysteriously . . . as they came." (Bancroft, *The Native Races* 5:23.)

Dr. Daniel Brinton, another scholar of the nineteenth century and a student of native Indian customs, recorded this statement:

"[The bearded white God] personally appeared among the ancestors of the [Indian] nation and taught them the useful arts, gave them food . . . initiated them into . . . their religious rites, framed the laws which governed their social relations and . . . left them. . . . It was expected that some time he would return . . . [and] whenever the personal appearance of this . . . god is described, it is . . . that of one of the white race, a man of fair complexion, with long, flowing beard, . . . abundant hair, and clothed in ample and loose robes." (Brinton, *American Hero-Myths*, p. 27.)

The impact of this figure of deity was such that he is considered by historians to be the greatest single influence in the New World in ancient times. Just as our history is dated before and after the appearance of Christ, the Aztecs and their ancestors commenced their history with the bearded white god whom some called Quetzalcoatl. Long before the arrival of the white man, pyramids and religious centers were erected to the memory of this god.

The Temple of Quetzalcoatl in Teotihuacan, Mexico, is located in one of the oldest ruins in Mexico. Teotihuacan means "the city of the gods," and this site, which is over eight square miles in size, was constructed in relation to the sun. Archaeologists who have compared the architecture and ancient artifacts in this ruin with similar cultures have concluded that this must have been a very important center of civilization.

Some of the ancient symbols of the white god were the quetzal feathers, the plumed serpent, jade, and the color green. The word *quetzal* signifies a beautiful bird with long undulating green tail feathers, and *coatl* means *serpent*. Even today these symbols are woven into blankets and clothing, and in Guatemala the quetzal bird is stamped on the country's money. The quetzal bird and the serpent are seen everywhere:

1. On the calendar stone at Tikal, Guatemala.
2. On the Bonampak murals dating back to A.D. 600.
3. On the carving of the ancient plumed serpent in the National Museum in Mexico City.
4. On the plumed serpent's head at the base of the pyramid of Kukulcan in Chichen Itza, Yucatan, Mexico.
5. In Chichen Itza, in the walls of an ancient ball court.
6. In Xochicalco's famous temple.

When the Spanish padres first arrived in Yucatan, they learned that the people worshiped a white god bearing a remarkable resemblance to Quetzalcoatl, whom they called Itzamna. Father Bernardo de Lizana, a devout priest who wrote a history of Yucatan in 1633, recorded this description: "[Itzamna] cured the sick by placing his hands on them. He was a king, a priest, a legislator, a rule of benevolent character, like Christ. . . . He came from the east and founded the Itza civilization." (Willard, *Kukulcan the Bearded Conqueror*, pp. 131-33.)

The Incas first immigrated to Peru and Bolivia. They told their Spanish conquerors that they had obtained their traditions from their ancestors, who in turn had been taught by a white bearded god known as Viracocha, which means "white man." Sarmiento de Gamboa, a Spanish writer of the sixteenth century, wrote: ". . . all agree that Viracocha was the creator of these people. They have the tradition that he was a man of medium height, white and dressed in a white robe . . . and that he carried a staff and book in his hands." (Gamboa, *History of the Incas*, p. 247.)

The description of the bearded white god appears to be the same up and down the Americas—from the Haida Indians' "fair god" atop a totem pole north of Ketchikan, Alaska, to the

Incas' white god on the southern continent. There are works of art and ancient structures too numerous to mention that attest to the influence of the bearded white god. Bishop Diego de Landa, who arrived in Yucatan shortly after Cortez, wrote that he was surprised to learn the ancient Americans of pre-Columbian times practiced baptism:

"We have not been able to find its origin, more than it is a custom that has *always existed*." (Landa, *Landa's Yucatan 1549-79*, pp. 42-43.)

If, as ancient legend indicates, this bearded white god came from across the waters, it would be even more sensible to admit to other similarities in the Old and the New World. One of the striking similarities scholars have discovered is the Mayan script, as compared to Phoenician characters. Both scripts have simple symbols in common, such as the circle, cross, hand, and eye. Diego de Landa indicated that the Maya themselves said it was the white god who gave them their script, and de Landa even went so far as to draw up a comparative chart of the two scripts. (Honore, *In Quest of the White God*, p. 38.)

One of the tragedies of the Spanish conquest was the utter disregard for the natives' manuscripts and histories, which they burned by the bundle. The few records that have been salvaged are valued as great treasures. One of the most outstanding records was found as late as 1823 in a stone box buried in a hill in Palmyra, New York. Translated by Joseph Smith, it is known as the Book of Mormon. It stands alone today as the most accurate and complete history of ancient cultures that existed before Columbus came to the New World from western Asia and that developed as great nations through the power and influence of the bearded white god.

The spiritual leaders of these ancient civilizations were dedicated historians who recorded their wars, their spiritual experiences, and the causes of their destruction. One of the most impressive segments in the Book of Mormon is a detailed account of the visit of the bearded white god. The people knew of him through their spiritual leaders. They even knew that he was resurrected. They knew him as Jesus Christ.

They also recognized the signs of the tempest, earthquake, whirlwind, and fire that occurred during the three-day period when Christ lay in the tomb. The face of the whole land became changed, according to this record. Darkness covered the hemisphere, with mists so intense that no fire or candle could be lit. The Book of Mormon records:

"And now it came to pass that there were a great multitude gathered together, . . . round about the temple which was in the land Bountiful; and they were marveling and wondering one with another. . . .

". . . conversing about this Jesus Christ, of whom the sign had been given concerning his death.

"And . . . while they were thus conversing one with another, they heard a voice as if it came out of heaven . . . not a harsh voice, neither was it a loud voice; nevertheless . . . it being a small voice it did pierce them that did hear to the center, insomuch that there was no part of their frame that it did not cause to quake. . . .

"And it came to pass that again they heard the voice, and they understood it not.

"And again the third time they did hear the voice, and did open their ears to hear it; and their eyes were towards the sound thereof. . . .

"And behold, the third time they did understand the voice which they heard; and it said unto them:

"Behold my Beloved Son, in whom I am well pleased, in whom I have glorified my name—hear ye him.

"And . . . they cast their eyes up again towards heaven; and behold, they saw a Man descending out of heaven; and he was clothed in a white robe; and he came down and stood in the midst of them; and the eyes of the whole multitude were turned upon him, and they durst not open their mouths, even one to another, and wist not what it meant, for they thought it was an angel that had appeared unto them.

"And it came to pass that he stretched forth his hand and spake unto the people, saying:

"Behold, I am Jesus Christ, whom the prophets testified shall come into the world. . . .

"And it came to pass that when Jesus had spoken these words the whole multitude fell to the earth; for they remembered that it had been prophesied among them that Christ should show himself unto them after his ascension into heaven.

"And it came to pass that the Lord spake unto them saying:

"Arise and come forth unto me, that ye may thrust your hands into my side, and also that ye may feel the prints of the nails in my hands and in my feet, that ye may know that I am the God of Israel, and the God of the whole earth, and have been slain for the sins of the world.

"And . . . the multitude went forth, and thrust their hands into his side, and did feel the prints of the nails in his hands and in his feet; and this they did do, going forth one by one until they had all gone forth, and did see with their eyes and did feel with their hands, and did know of a surety and did bear record, that it was he, of whom it was written by the prophets, that should come.

". . . And they did fall down at the feet of Jesus, and did worship him." (3 Nephi 11:1-17.)

He also told them: "And verily I say unto you, that ye are they of whom I said: Other sheep I have which are not of this fold; them also I must bring, and they shall hear my voice; and there shall be one fold, and one shepherd.

"But behold, ye have both heard my voice, and seen me; and ye are my sheep, and ye are numbered among those whom the Father hath given me." (3 Nephi 15:21, 24.)

Jesus taught the people many things. He chose one to be their leader and gave him power to baptize the people into his church. He also chose twelve disciples to represent him in power and authority. After he had anointed his disciples and blessed the children, ". . . a cloud . . . overshadowed the multitude that they could not see Jesus. And while they were overshadowed he departed from them, and ascended into heaven. . . ." (3 Nephi 18:38-39.)

This is only a small segment of a

most impressive experience as recorded in the Book of Mormon. So great was the impact of this marvelous visitation that for more than two centuries these people lived in peace—without war, without poverty, without hate and greed. And because of their faithfulness to the teachings of Jesus Christ, they prospered and developed culturally beyond our power to comprehend.

Gradually, after two centuries of peace, the children of these ancient Americans began to forget the traditions of their fathers. They became divided into separate groups, forgetting their God, who had blessed and prospered them. Eventually there came a final struggle between the Christians and the nonbelievers, which resulted in the destruction of this once-glorious civilization, leaving only a remnant of a noble race to wander upon the land. When such men as Columbus sailed to this continent, they found a dark-skinned race already inhabiting it. Columbus wrote:

"The natives . . . received (my messengers) . . . with great ceremony, lodged them in the most beautiful houses, carried them around on their arms, kissed their hands and feet, and . . . tried to make clear to them in every possible way that it was known the white men came from the gods. About fifty men and women asked my messengers to be allowed to travel back with them to the Heaven of the eternal gods." (Thacher, *Christopher Columbus* 2:22-23.)

Recently a study was made comparing the many stories and legends of Quetzalcoatl to the possible relationship they might have to Jesus Christ.

One of the observations of this study was the fact that not all Quetzalcoatl stories refer to the same personage nor to the same period of time. A tenth century culture hero known as Topiltzin Ce Acatl took upon himself the name of Quetzalcoatl, and many legends have been attributed to him, making it difficult to separate him from the deity Quetzalcoatl. The author of this study, Joseph Allen, concludes that there is enough evidence to suggest that the myth of Quetzalcoatl was related to Jesus Christ both in time and space. A comparison of the other gods in North, Central, and South America with Jesus Christ seems to confirm this conclusion. (Allen, *A Comparative Study of Quetzalcoatl.*)

Constance Irwin states: "Quetzalcoatl in addition to being a culture-god was also god of the air, the healing air, and some of the ancient Mexican legends specifically state that he brought a knowledge of medicine. Itzamna, the Mayan god of medicine and knowledge, is often depicted as an ugly old bearded man with a protruding tooth and a nose that outnoses Cyrano's; and then again, particularly on the monuments in the old cities toward the south, we see Itzamna represented as a serpent with scales and rattle, whereas the serpent representation of Kukulcan is covered with feathers. Even the natives who transmitted the legends of Itzamna and Kukulcan to the Spanish chroniclers shortly after the conquest sometimes confused the two serpent gods, for both were also gods of medicine." (*Fair Gods and Stone Faces*, p. 100.)

The relationship of Quetzalcoatl and Itzamna is pointed out by Daniel Brinton:

"Chief of the beneficent gods was Itzamna. He was the personification of the east, the rising sun with all of its manifold mythical associations. His name means dew or moisture of the morning. He was said to have come in his boat across the eastern waters. One of his titles was Lakin-Chan, the serpent of the East. . . .

"As light is synonymous with life and knowledge, he was said to have been the founder of the culture of the Itzas and the Mayas. He was the first priest of their religion; invented writing and books. He named all of the localities in Yucatan and divided the land among the people.

"As a physician he was famous, not only knowing the magic herbs but possessed of the power of healing by the laying on of hands whence came his name Kabul, the Skillful Hand, under which he was worshipped in Chichen Itza. For his wisdom he was spoken of as the royal or noble master of knowledge. In the Maya language, this is Yax-coc-ah-mut, which means that he was the first man of great fame." (Cited in Hunter, *Christ in Ancient America* 2:40.)

The early religious leaders of Peru told legends of a man who landed on the shores of what is now Brazil and who slowly made his way westward preaching the gospel until he reached the shores of the Pacific Ocean. Some think this was St. Thomas.

The appearance of a bearded white man near Lake Titicaca long before the time of the Incas has been recorded. A mighty man, he taught the people about law and civilization. The creator of all things, he commanded men to be good to one another and to live without violence. His name was Tiki Viracocha, also called Tuapaca and Arunau.

This bearded white god built a great city with temples that contained many statues of himself, as did all the other temples in the country. Later he left the people, admonishing them once more to follow his teachings. Legends made him the god who created the sun and stars, for before him darkness had reigned upon the earth. (Honore, *In Quest of the White God*, p. 16.)

Legends tell of a Quetzalcoatl who lived in Tula, Mexico, a ruin that does not date back to the first century A.D. This Quetzalcoatl may be a man who took upon himself the name of deity. He also, however, claimed a virgin birth. Veytia, an early writer, describes this Quetzalcoatl as "a full grown man, tall of stature, white of skin, full bearded, barefooted and bareheaded, clothed in a long white robe, strewn with red crosses and carrying a staff in his hand." (Braden, *Religious Aspects of the Conquest of Mexico*, p. 31.)

It appears that there were two distinct representations of Quetzalcoatl: one a legendary heroic man, the leader of Tula, and the second, a god about whom there is a mass of legends.

Sahagun says that Quetzalcoatl departed in this manner: "When he arrived at the edge of the sea, he ordered a boat to be made of serpents, and entering into it, as into a canoe, he sailed away over the sea and it is not known how he arrived." (Sahagun, *A History of Ancient Mexico* 3:12-14.)

From the following references note

the similarity to those points about Christ's appearance on the American continent as told in the Book of Mormon. The Book of Mormon teaches us the following:

1. Christ was Jewish and therefore was white and likely had a beard.
2. He was clothed in a long robe.
3. He taught peace.
4. He started a period of prosperity.
5. He taught of stewardship.
6. He left with a promise to return.

Speaking of Quetzalcoatl, "They figured him tall, big, and of a fair complexion, with an open forehead, large eyes, long, black beard, dark hair. From the love of decency he wore always a long robe." (Clavigero, *The History of Mexico* 2:11.)

Hernando Cortez states: "Our nation was led by a certain Lord to whom all were subject and who then went back to his native land where he remained so long delaying his return that at his coming those whom he had left had married the women of the land and had many children in which they lived, so that they would in no wise return to their own land for they acknowledged him as Lord upon which he left them." (Cortez, *Five Letters 1519-1526*, p. 70.)

After a long conference the people concluded unanimously that he who had landed upon that shore with so great an army could be no other than Quetzalcoatl, the God of Air, who had been expected for many years. There prevailed among those nations an ancient tradition of such a deity who, after having acquired the esteem and veneration of the people in Totlan, Cholula, and Onohualco, disappeared, promising to return after a certain period to govern peace and render the people happy. The kings of those countries considered themselves the viceroys of that god and trustees of the crown, which they were to cede to him whenever he reappeared. (Clavigero, *The History of Mexico* 2:267-68.)

One of the names that God was known by was "Ipalneomani," which means "He by whom we live." Another name by which he was called was "Tloque Nahuaque," which means "He who has all in himself." (Clavigero, *The History of Mexico* 2:2.)

The Aztecs and even the Haitians and the Araucanians talked about their god in such words as "endless," "omnipotent," "invisible," "adorable," "Maker of All," "the mother and father of life," "the one god complete in perfection and unity," "the Creator of all that is," and "the Soul of the world." (Brinton, *American Hero-Myths*, pp. 74-75.)

Pierre Honore states: "The legend of a particular White God has survived to our day from all the ancient civilizations of Central and South America. The Toltecs and Aztecs of Mexico called him Quetzalcoatl, the Incas called him Viracocha. To the Maya he was Kukulcan, who brought them all their laws, also their script, and was worshipped like a god by the entire people. To the Chibchas he was Bochica, the 'white mantle of light.' To the Aymara of Peru he was Hyustus, and to this day they will tell you that he was fair and had blue eyes." (Honore, *In Quest of the White God*, pp. 15-16.)

Constance Irwin writes: "In all of America's past no figure is more exciting, more tantalizing, or more frustrating than that of the Fair God Quetzalcoatl. A stranger, a bearded white man dressed in a flowing robe, he is said to have come from afar and from the east. According to the many legends that surround his name, he appeared in Mexico of a sudden and lingered long in several places, dispensing a vastness of information, for which he was called the bringer of knowledge, 'the traditional master-builder of American civilization.' He disappeared as mysteriously as he had come with the promise that he would return." (Irwin, *Fair Gods and Stone Faces*, p. 33.)

The use of the serpent and the quetzal bird feathers seems unusual as symbols of the deity, which has been claimed by some to represent the Old World God of the Bible. Yet, the winged Sun-disk of Egypt, which is the symbol of the sun-god, is pictured with the sacred snake Uraeus on each side of the falconlike wings. (Unger, *Archaeology and the Old Testament*, p. 130.)

The feathered serpent was a very old symbol for the rain-god among the Indians. Everything depended on the rain; it governed all the natural powers: the sea, the water, the sky, the clouds and the lightning, the whole world of plants and animals. The feathered serpent is the symbol for water, rain, and vegetation, for everything that makes things sprout. Among the ancient Indian peoples the white God was the pioneer who made civilization "sprout." (Honore, *In Quest of the White God*, pp. 108-9.)

Some call the Indian the vanishing American, yet he is far from vanished. The testimonies in stone and precious metal that speak mutely of ancient days of glory are a far cry from the image of the Indian warrior we read of today. These evidences of a perished civilization are an unfinished chapter of American history. The Indians of today hold in great reverence the stories of the bearded white god who taught their people great truths, who healed the sick and raised the dead. His symbol is woven into blankets, carved upon the walls of canyons, sculptured into pottery, and danced in sacred rituals. It is the story of Jesus the Christ, whose hands performed miracles of healing, whose lips spoke of love and peace, and whose visionary eyes foresaw the vistas of the future.

THE CHRONICLERS

The Chroniclers were early priests, scholars, or educated natives who recorded the history of the pre-Columbian people and whose sources were ancient books (codices), traditions, and legends. Most of the material was of necessity obtained from secondary sources, yet they contain some valuable information.

The material may be classified as follows:

1. Historical writings by early Spanish authors, including Diego de Landa, Bernardino de Sahagun, Juan de Torquemada, and Fray Diego Duran.

2. Historical works in Spanish by native authors, such as Ixtlilxochitl.

3. Writings by native authors in their native language. These include (a) *Popol Vuh*, written in Quiche, the Mayan language of the Guatemalan Highlands; (b) *Chilam Balam*, written in the Mayan of Yucatan; (c) *Annals of Cuauhtitlan*, written in Nahuatl, the Aztec language of central Mexico; (d) *Title of the Lords of Totonicapan*, written in Quiche Mayan in 1554 in the village of Totonicapan, Guatemala; and (e) *The Annals of the Cakchiquels*, written by several Indians at the end of the sixteenth century in the native language and using Spanish characters. The first Spanish translation was published in 1873.

Many of these chroniclers seem to be in agreement, which tends to strengthen their authenticity. They agree that the first settlers were giants, or large in stature, and that they came after a flood. Another group, according to these records, came in ships from the east. This group of people united with yet another group. A great destruction caused by earthquakes and storms was reported to have taken place about the time of the crucifixion of Jesus Christ. Later, divisions of the people resulted in groups settling in various areas of central Mexico. The Chroniclers substantiate a strong religious belief among the people, with faith in a divine God who was born of a virgin mother.

HISTORICAL WRITINGS BY SPANISH AUTHORS

Fray Bernardino de Sahagun arrived in Mexico in 1529, eight years after the forces of Hernando Cortez conquered Mexico City. His first job was converting the Aztec language into a phonetic alphabet, after which he spent the rest of his life questioning the natives living before and after the Spanish conquest, recording their history and culture from the stories he had collected. The original manuscript of Sahagun's work was discovered in 1793 in the Laurentian Library in Florence, Italy; it consisted of some 1300 handwritten pages, with several watercolor illustrations by an Aztec artist.

Sahagun spent twenty-five or more years gathering this information. He wrote part of the work himself, and also had the Indians write. After editing all the information at least once and usually twice, he asked groups of Indians to recheck the work for accuracy. Finally he collected this into what was to become twelve volumes, written in both Spanish and Aztec.

Sahagun was born in 1499 of a Portuguese family, Ribiera, from Sahagun, Portugal. He studied at the University of Salamanca until he left to become a Franciscan monk. Nothing more is known concerning his life until he came to the New World.

In 1529 he was one of nineteen Franciscan monks led by Fray Antonio de Ciudad Rodrigo to New Spain (Mexico). On board ship were Mexican Indians whom Cortez had taken to Spain and presented in the Spanish court and who were now returning to the New World under order of the emperor.

Sahagun became one of two great masters of the Nahuatl or Aztec language; he is credited with a vocabulary in Aztec, as well as many other writings. He died in Mexico City in 1590.

Dr. Charles E. Dibble and Dr. Arthur J. O. Anderson undertook the arduous task of translating Sahagun's entire manuscript, entitled *Historia General de las Cosas de Nueva Espana: Florentine Codex*. Dr. Dibble's conclusion, after translating the manuscript, was that the ancient inhabitants of America were very highly civilized.

HISTORICAL WORKS IN SPANISH BY NATIVE AUTHORS

Fernando de Alva Ixtlilxochitl, a grandson of the last native king of Tezcoco, compiled the "Annals of Ixtlilxochitl," a historical document written in the sixteenth century that contained the history of his ancestors taken from the legends and stories gathered from his people. His history of Middle America began with the creation of the world by the supreme god, Tloque Nahuaque. The next great event in this history was the flood, which he places 1716 years later. He tells how the world was populated after the flood by giants, most of whom were destroyed by calamities. He describes the next era as the coming of the Olmecs and Xicalancas, who lived in Cholula and who later migrated eastward to the present state of Tabiasco, in southeastern Mexico. During this era a person named Quetzalcoatl returned to the east after there was no response to his teachings.

Regarding the phenomenon of the sun standing still, Ixtlilxochitl wrote: "... and in the year 8 Tochtli, which was 1,347 years after the second calamity, and 4,779 since the creation of the world, they have in their history that the sun stood (still) for a natural day without moving from one spot." (Hunter and Ferguson, *Ancient America and the Book of Mormon*, p. 298.)

Ixtlilxochitl was born about 1568 and studied at the College of Santa Cruz in Tlateloco. An interpreter in the court of justice of the Indians, he died in 1648 at the age of eighty. Historians have generally accepted the writings of Ixtlilxochitl as being authentic. Though his original manuscripts have been lost, various copies of these records are still in existence.

The Book of Mormon and the *Works of Ixtlilxochitl*, interestingly, seem to agree on certain dates assigned to important early historical events. They agree, for example, upon the approximate time of the crucifixion of Jesus.

WRITINGS BY NATIVE AUTHORS IN THEIR NATIVE LANGUAGE

Diego de Landa, a Franciscan bishop in Yucatan, in 1562 signed an order directing the burning of hundreds of Indian books; however, a few of them survived. In 1543, the Maya Indians wrote three books from their traditions and ancient documents. The Cakchiquels wrote *The Annals of the Cakchiquels* at Solola. The other two manuscripts, written by Quiche Maya Indians, are *Title of the Lords of Totonicapan*, written at Totonicapan, and the *Popol Vuh*, written at Chichicastenango. Francisco Ximinez discovered in the Santo Tomas Cathedral the manuscript from which the *Popol Vuh* was published. When the manuscript was published, it was named after a lost book that the sixteenth century Quiche author of the manuscript tells about. "The author of the manuscript indicates that he writes it because the Popol Vuh, or the original 'book of the people,' as Ximenez called it, is no longer to be seen." (Adrian Recinos, *Popol Vuh, The Sacred Book of the Ancient Quiche Maya*, p. 17.)

The *Popol Vuh* is a collection of traditions and histories written down soon after the Spanish conquest by one or more Quiche Indians. Both the Bible and the *Popol Vuh* contain the story of the sea parting miraculously to allow fugitive tribes to pass through; both tell of a confusion of tongues and a tower of Babel; and both relate how sacred law was handed down to priests on a mountaintop, the Maya god Tohil giving it to his priest, Chi-Pixab, just as Jehovah gave the law to Moses. The deluge story is also found in both books.

The original manuscript was written in the Quiche language in the characters of the Latin script. Father Ximenez, a parish priest of the village of Santo Tomas, Chichicastenango, in the highlands of Guatemala, translated the Quiche text into Spanish. It was first published in the Spanish language in 1857 and in French in 1861.

Title of the Lords of Totonicapan was written in the Quiche language in 1554 and was first published in French and Spanish in 1885. The writers wrote their account in the village of Totonicapan, Guatemala. Their small book claimed that the Quiche Maya were "descendants of Israel, of the same language and the same customs. . . . They were sons of Abraham and Jacob."

The Book of Mormon record, completed more than 1100 years earlier, indicates that the Nephites and Lamanites were descendants of Abraham and Jacob, and that their ancestor Lehi, a descendant of Israel through Joseph, had migrated from Jerusalem to America.

The Indian writings also record that the Lord gave the leader of their group a "present called Giron-Gagal" which guided them. (Hunter, *Great Civilizations and the Book of Mormon*, pp. 79-80.)

Now we will consider just a few of the topics mentioned by the Chroniclers that may have some relationship to the Book of Mormon.

1. *Agriculture.* Recinos has translated the writers of the *Popol Vuh* as saying that they ground their corn and wheat. (*Popol Vuh*, p. 92.) The Book of Mormon lists the following crops: corn (Mosiah 8:14), fruit (Mosiah 9:9), grain (1 Nephi 8:1), wheat (Mosiah 9:9), wine (Mosiah 11:5), all of which are also found in Sahagun's writings: corn (2:279), fruit (8:68), grain (11:279-89), wheat (10:71), wine (1:22). Of the agricultural products mentioned in the Book of Mormon, barley is the only one not mentioned in the *Florentine Codex*.

2. *Animals.* The following animals are mentioned in the Book of Mormon: chickens, dogs, fish, flocks, lions, oxen, serpents, sheep, wolves. They are all mentioned also in volume 11 of Sahagun's work. Animals mentioned in the Book of Mormon that are not mentioned in the *Florentine Codex* are the ass, bear, cureloms, cumoms, dragons, elephants, goats, horses, and swine.

3. *Banners.* Sahagun records: "In this month the Lord drew up a parade of all the warriors and of the young men who had never gone to war. These he gave arms and insignia, and they became soldiers; so from then on they could go to war." (Ibid., p. 20.) "Everywhere on mountain tops, blood

sacrifices were made and sacrificial banners were hung." (Ibid., p. 42.)

4. *Calendar.* Among the Indians, the first month of the year, called Atlcaualo, began upon the second day of February. This month and all the rest, totaling eighteen, have twenty days each. (Ibid., p. 1.) The calendar wheel that ran for fifty-two years was invented by Quetzalcoatl. It was based on four cycles of thirteen years each.

5. *Government.* The Aztecs had a custom that when a king was either killed or died, officials of the government would meet and elect a new king. They followed somewhat a patriarchal order of father to son, or father to brother, but this order could be interrupted by the election controlled by the authorities. (Duran, *The Aztecs*, p. 184.)

6. *Homes.* Sahagun lists thirty-four varieties of houses ranging from the stone house to the straw house—from the great structures to the dugouts; square and round houses, stone, wood, straw, and dirt houses, plain and painted houses. (*Historia General* 11:269-75.)

7. *Skin color.* "There they were then, in great number, the black men and the white men, men of many classes, men of many tongues. . . ." (Recinos, *Popol Vuh*, p. 172.) Ruth Underhill states that Indian complexions vary from dark to yellow and even white. (Underhill, *Red Man's America*, p. 1.) Sahagun wrote: "And [the Spaniards] seized and set apart the pretty women—those of light bodies, the fair [skinned] ones." (*Historia General* 12:118.)

8. *Social and moral beliefs.* "The good-hearted youth is obedient, happy, peaceful, careful, diligent. He obeys, works, lives in chastity and modesty."

"The bad youth goes about becoming crazed; he is desolate, mad; he goes about mocking, telling tales, being rude, repeating insults."

Definition of a harlot: "She goes about haughtily, shamelessly, head high, vain, filthy, given to pleasure. . . she perfumes herself, casts incense about her, uses rose water . . . she chews chicle . . . goes about disgracing the streets. . . ."

On curing a headache: "Inhale a herb named *ecuxo*, or inhale small tobacco. . . ."

On tooth care: ". . . eaten food is to be picked from the teeth; they are to be cleaned, brushed."

Concerning the Tolteca god: "They were very devout, only one was their god; they showed all attention to, they called upon, they prayed to one by the name of Quetzalcoatl." (Ibid., 10:169.)

9. *Tools.* Sahagun writes: "During the feast of Tlaxochimaco, they went forth into the forest [and] cut a tree of twenty-five fathoms height and brought it, dragging it into the courtyard of this God. There they pruned off all its branches and raised it upright, and it remained thus standing until the eve of the feast. Then they again laid it upon the earth with much caution and [using] many devices that it might not bump [the ground]. On the day before this feast, early in the morning, many carpenters came with their tools, and decorated it with many kinds of papers, they tied ropes and other cords to it and raised it up with much shouting and din, and they made it firm." (Ibid., 2:17.)

The ceremony in honor of a young man preparing to get married is recorded: "And at the beginning of the conversation they laid before him an ax for cutting lumber or firewood." (Ibid., 2:40.)

"They opened their breasts with a Txotxopxtli, which is an instrument with which the women weave, almost like a machete." (Ibid., 2:29.)

10. *Warfare.* Otomi Indians used shields against Cortez, in the battle that took place between the Mexicans and Spaniards. (Ibid., 12:27.) Obsidian-bladed swords are also mentioned. (Ibid., 12:117.) "They carried their children, their obsidian-bladed swords, [and] their devices, because they passed through the enemy's land. . . ." (Ibid., 9:17.)

The people carved and sculptured with a small metal blade in preparing molds for metal. Sahagun describes how molds were made for the forming of gold, silver, copper, and combinations of the same designs. (Ibid., 9:73-78.)

The Book of Mormon lists the following weapons, which are also found mentioned in the *Florentine Codex:* axe (Mormon 6:9; Sahagun, 2:40); bows and arrows (Mosiah 9:16; Sahagun, 2:25); club (Mosiah 9:16; Sahagun, 2:49); dart (Jarom 1:8; Sahagun, 2:109); sword (Alma 1:9; Sahagun, 9:17); shields (Alma 49:6; Sahagun, 9:17); javelin (Alma 62:36; Sahagun, vol. 12). The Book of Mormon mentions chariots, cimiters, and slings, which were not found among Sahagun's writings, while the Florentine Codex mentions obsidian knives and dart throwers, which are not mentioned in the Book of Mormon.

11. *Origin of the people in the New World.* Regarding the voyage to America recorded in *The Annals of the Cakchiquels*, we read: "Then it was said and commanded to our mothers: 'Go my sons, my daughters, these shall be your tasks, the labor with which we charge you.' Thus the Obsidian Stone spoke to them. 'Go to where you will see your mountains and your valleys; there on the other side of the sea are your mountains and your valleys. . . .'

"Then we arrived at the shore of the sea. There all the tribes and the warriors were reunited at the shore of the sea. And when they looked upon it their hearts were heavy.

"There is no way to cross it; we know of no one who has crossed the sea . . . who has a log on which we can cross, our brother? . . . Have pity on us, oh brother! who have come to gather here on the shore of the sea, unable to see our mountains and our valleys. . . .

"When we arrived at the gates of Tulan, we received a red stick which was our staff, and because of that we were given the name of Cakchiquels. . . . Thus we passed over the rows of sand, when it widened below the sea and on the surface of the sea. Immediately all were rejoiced when they saw the sands below the sea. Thereupon they held council. 'There is our hope, there on the first land we must be reunited,' they said; 'only there can we be organized now that we have arrived from Tulan.'

"They plunged forward then and passed over the sand; those who came at the rear entered the sea as we emerged from the waters on the other bank. . . ." (Recinos and Goetz, *The*

Annals of the Cakchiquels, p. 49.)

Ixtlilxochitl also taught that (1) the languages were changed and the people went to diverse parts of the world, and (2) seven companions and their wives came to this land. (These conclusions were made from the translation by Bateman and Kimball of Ixtlilxochitl's writings.)

Sahagun records that after the arrival of the group who "came over the water in boats in many divisions" they wandered, following the coastline, and then embarked and "carried off the writings, the books, the paintings; they carried away all the crafts, the casting of metals." The remaining people were lost without their writings. They buried their rulers in the pyramids and believed in a life after death. (Sahagun, *A History of Ancient America*, pp. 190-92.)

The account given in *The Annals of the Cakchiquels* concerning the legendary Tulan and the migration across the sea from the east is slightly different in the details given. The most pertinent information is digested in the following quotation:

"From the other side of the sea we came to the place called Tulan, where we were begotten and given birth by our mothers and our fathers, oh, our sons! We were four families who arrived at Tulan . . . and these four branches which began there were the tribes. From four places the people came to Tulan. In the east is one Tulan; another in Xibalbay; another in the west, from there we came ourselves, from the west; and another is where God is. Therefore, there were four Tulans, oh, our sons! . . . From the west we came to Tulan, from across the sea; and it was at Tulan where we arrived, to be engendered and brought forth by our mothers and our fathers. . . ." (Recinos and Goetz, *The Annals of the Cakchiquels*, pp. 44-45, 53.)

The *Anales de los Xahil* records:

"Then we arrived at the border of the sea. All of the warriors of the tribes gathered together at the seashore. Then the hearts of many were full of anguish.

"'It cannot be crossed. It has never been told that the sea has been crossed,' said all the warriors of the seven tribes. 'Who will tell us how we may cross the sea? Oh our younger brother, thou art our hope,' they all exclaimed. 'Yes, how shall we cross this?'

"'How shall we cross the sea, oh our younger brother?' they said. And we answered: 'We shall cross in the ships. . . .' Then we entered the ships of the Ah Nonovalco; then we traveled eastward and arrived there.'" (Hunter, *Great Civilizations of the Book of Mormon*, pp. 80, 87.)

RELIGIOUS BELIEFS AND TRADITIONS

The Chroniclers wrote about many religious beliefs of the ancient inhabitants of the American continents. Many of these traditions bear resemblance to teachings in the Book of Mormon, including the following:

1. *Jesus Christ*. The writings of Ixtlilxochitl relate some fascinating experiences that parallel events that took place at the time of the crucifixion. These are found in Milton R. Hunter and Thomas S. Ferguson, *Ancient America and the Book of Mormon:*

"Ixtlilxochitl [correlates] the ancient Mexican calendar with New Testament history, having learned the latter from the Catholic missionaries and soldiers in Mexico. The correlations and parallels between his account and *The Book of Mormon* on the events which occurred on the fourth day of the month in 34 A.D., 'when Christ our Lord suffered,' are very striking, to say the least. Ixtlilxochitl double checks his date, stating it was 166 years since the calendar was corrected and adjusted at the great council meeting. That meeting was held in 132 B.C. . . . Thus 166 years after 132 B.C. is the year 34 A.D. His other check, '270 years since the Ancient Ones had been destroyed,' also conforms. Ixtlilxochitl's Chronology indicates that the descendants of the settlers from the Great Tower met their fourth and final calamity in 236 B.C., and 270 years thereafter falls at 34 A.D." (P. 298.)

"The *Works of Ixtlilxochitl* make reference to a great destruction and desolation which took place among the inhabitants of ancient America, and then the significant statement appears that the destruction took place at the same time when Christ our Lord suffered. That statement is in complete accord with the account given in *The Book of Mormon*. Ixtlilxochitl also said: 'And, as it seems through the mentioned histories and annals, the aforementioned happened some years after the incarnation of Christ our Lord.' *The Book of Mormon*, on the other hand, tells in detail about the great 'destruction and desolation' which occurred on the western hemisphere and places the event exactly at the time of the crucifixion of Jesus Christ. Note that the datings of the event in the two records are identical with each other.

"As early as 600 B.C. the prophet Nephi looked down through the stream of time and saw the coming of Jesus Christ into mortality. He saw in vision the history of the ancient Americans following his day, and it was made known to him that exactly at the time that Jesus Christ was crucified in Palestine, a great destruction would take place on the American continent. One of the prime purposes of the destruction was to destroy the wicked people prior to the visitation that Christ would make among the more righteous people here on this continent.

"In 3 Nephi *The Book of Mormon* gives a very vivid and rather full account of this destruction, the record being made very soon after the destruction had occurred on this continent. . . .

"Another very significant point is made by both Ixtlilxochitl and the Nephite account—that Christ was crucified during the early part of the year. Ixtlilxochitl states, 'and they say it happened during the first days of the year'; and *The Book of Mormon* reported the event as occurring 'in the first month (and) on the fourth day of the month.'

"The Nephites changed their point of reckoning time when the signs of the birth of Christ were fulfilled in harmony with Samuel the Lamanite's predictions. From that time forward they dated from that point. . . .

"The Nephite record reports that the man of Galilee was thirty-three years and four days old when He was crucified; therefore, He was born in

THE CHRONICLERS 15

March or April, according to our calendar, and died during the first month of the Jewish (Nephite) year. Thus *The Book of Mormon* establishes the approximate time of the birthday of our Lord and Master and its testimony is confirmed by Ixtlilxochitl to the effect that Christ was crucified 'during the first days of the year.' . . .

". . . accurate historical data, recorded in *The Book of Mormon* at the time the events occurred, was handed down from age to age even from the time of Christ's crucifixion to the Spanish Conquest of Mexico.

"Both agree that the sun and the moon were darkened and that the earth trembled and rocks broke.

"Ixtlilxochitl says that many 'signs took place.' Signs of what? Everything in the two accounts indicates that Jesus Christ was the Messiah who, with his Father, is the God and Creator and Controller of our universe—and that he lives." (Pp. 192-94.)

2. *Anointing.* Sahagun writes: ". . . when a feast was celebrated . . . captives were slain; ceremonially bathed slaves were offered up. The merchants bathed them." (The footnote says bathed means to anoint.) (*Historia General* 2:1.)

3. *Baptism.* When a child was born the people consulted with the astrologers as to the good or ill fortune of the child, and if the sign in which he was born was propitious, he was baptized at once. If it was adverse, the people sought the most favorable house of that sign. After baptism, they banqueted the kinsmen and friends, giving food and drink to the guests and to children of the entire area. Baptism usually occurred at sunrise in the house of his father, with the midwife baptizing the baby, uttering many prayers, and performing much ceremony over the child. This same feast is also observed today in the baptism of children, with similar feasting, eating, and drinking.

Regarding baptism, Sahagun records: ". . . the water . . . is not only emblematic of the mutability and evanescence of early being, in that it sweeps away all things, but is also the *symbol of purification and cleansing:* it removes *filth, which is sin.* Thus speaks the midwife when four days after its birth she subjects the child to a ceremonious washing: My son, come unto thy mother, the Goddess of Water, Chalchiuhtlicue. May she cleanse of the dirt which thou hast of thy father and thy mother. . . . My son, come to Mother, thy Father, the Lady Chalchiuhtlicue, the Lord Chalchiuhtlstonac . . . *enter the water,* the blue (Matlalac), the yellow, (tozpalc), may it wash thee, may it cleanse thee perfectly, may it take from thee the evil which thou hast from the beginning of the world, which clings to thee from thy father, from thy mother." (Ibid., 1:8.)

Milton R. Hunter says: "Sahagun writes that when the holy bishop of Chiapas arrived at Campeche, in the year 1554, on his way to his diocese, in company with several Dominican friars, he not only saw what Montejo had written about the baptism of the Yucatecas, but also learned that all the natives of the country were baptized, no one being allowed to marry before the sacred ceremonies had been performed on him. It was the duty of the Maya to have their children baptized, for they believed that by this ablution they received a pure nature, were protected against evil spirits, and possible misfortunes. They held, however, that an unbaptized person, whether man or woman, could not lead a good life or do anything well." (Hunter, *Great Civilizations,* p. 195.)

4. *Belief in a Devil.* Sahagun observes: "A procuress is a demon. [The devil] truly dwells within her. In this picture you see two women, and the procuress with horns, a tail, feet like an animal, and yet a woman with the devil in her." (*Historia General* 10, illustration 111.)

5. *The creation.* All three chronicles have creation stories that closely parallel the Genesis account. *Popol Vuh* contains the most complete description, with an account of the creation of the earth, animals, and man. *The Annals of the Cakchiquels* contains a shorter version of man's creation. The original manuscript of the *Title of the Lords of Totonicapan* contained an account of the creation; however, it was not included in the English version. The translator made the following explanation:

"Translation of the first pages is omitted because they are on the creation of the world, of Adam, the Earthly Paradise in which Eve was deceived not by a serpent but by Lucifer himself, as an Angel of Light. It deals with the posterity of Adam, following in every respect the same order as in Genesis and the sacred books as far as the captivity of Babylonia. The manuscript assumes that the three great Quiche nations with which it particularly deals are descendants of the ten tribes of the Kingdom of Israel, whom Shalmaneser reduced to perpetual captivity and who finding themselves on the border of Assyria, resolved to immigrate." (Recinos and Boetz, *The Annals of the Cakchiquels,* p. 169.)

The Quiche also had a tradition wherein they called the gods who created the earth the Creator and Maker, the Mother and the Father of life, of all created things. Tepeu and Gucumatz were the names of these gods during the creation. The following are select quotations from the creation story found in the *Popol Vuh:*

"This is the account of how all was in suspense, all calm, in silence; all motionless, still, and the expanse of the sky was empty.

"This is the first account, the first narrative. There was neither man, nor animals, birds, fishes, crabs, trees, stones, caves, ravines, grasses nor forests; there was only the sky. . . .

"Then came the word. Tepeu and Gucumatz came together in darkness, in the night, and Tepeu and Gucumatz talked together. They talked then, discussing and deliberating; they agreed, they united their words and their thoughts.

"Then while they meditated, it became clear to them that when dawn would break, man must appear. Then they planned the creation, and the growth of the trees and the thickets and the birth of life and the creation of man. . . .

"Thus let it be done! Let the emptiness be filled! Let the water recede and make a void, let the earth appear and become solid; let it be done. Thus they spoke. Let there be light, let there be light, let there be dawn in the sky and on the earth! There shall be neither glory nor grandeur in our creation and formation until the human being is made, man is formed. So they spoke. . . ." (Recinos, *Popol Vuh*, pp. 73-74.)

6. *Degrees in heaven.* "And they understood that there were many divisions of the heavens; they said there were twelve divisions. There existed, there dwelt, the true god and his consort." (Ibid., 10:169.)

7. *Easter-type feast.* The fifth month was called Toxcatl. On the first day of this month the people celebrated a great feast in honor of the god Titlacavan and for Tezcatlipoca, whom they held to be god of the gods. In his honor, they slew a chosen youth who had no blemish upon his body, who was reared in luxury for a year, and who was trained in the playing of musical instruments, in singing, and in speaking. This feast, the most important of all the feasts, was like Easter; in fact, it fell a few days after Easter Sunday.

8. *Fasting.* "They fasted [some] forty days, others for twenty, in order to prevail over chance, in order to paint well and to weave textiles well." (Ibid., 2:35.)

9. *Immortality.* "And when the rulers died, they buried them there. . . . For so was it said: 'When we die, it is not true that we die; for still we live, we are resurrected.'" (Ibid.)

10. *Life after death.* The master of the sacrificed and flayed captives did penance for twenty days. The people neither bathed nor washed their heads until the skins of the dead captives were deposited in a special cave. They said that they did penance for the captives.

11. *Life beyond this world.* Speaking of their god Tezcatlipocathey, Sahagun wrote, "He was considered a true God, whose abode was everywhere in the land of the dead, on earth, and in heaven." (Ibid., 2:2.) Those who died in war, it was said, followed the sun; they went to heaven.

12. *Repentance.* To confess, the penitent went before the warden of Tlacolteutl (he who saw for her was a seer), and said unto him: "I wish to go to the master, our Lord, the Savior and protector of all, our Lord Tezcatlipoca, in secret." Upon his appointed day and time he came, with the seer preparing incense and flames, asking, "Master, our Lord, protector of all, also take away, pacify, the torment of this man." Then the seer addressed the person who came to confess, and the following phrases are parts of the speech directed to the penitent: "Overturn, pour forth thy vices, thy wrongdoing: [expose] thy evil odor, thy corruptness. And let our Lord, protector of all, have pity on thee who, stretching forth his arms to thee, embraceth thee and carrieth thee upon his back." The seer set a four-day fasting period. Also, the penitent had his choice of piercing his tongue or his ears with straws and maguey spines, because a blood offering was required. The act of penance is summed up thus: "Thus in the end he changed to a good life. It was said that if he were to sin again—so it was said—no longer might he gain mercy therefor." (Ibid., 1:8-11.)

13. *Sacrament.* "And when he had died, thereupon they broke up his body of amaranth seed dough. His heart was apportioned to Moctezuma.

"And as for the rest of his members, which were made, as it were, to be his bones, they were distributed and divided up among all. Two [parts] were given the Tlatelulca; and [with these] two, which were as the fundament, two more were offered to the old men of the tribal temples of the Tlatelulca. And as much was given to the Tenocha. And afterwards it was divided up among them, to each in his order, each year when they ate it. [Each] year [those of] two neighborhoods ate it, and also the old men of two tribal temples. And when they divided up among themselves his body [made of] amaranth seed dough, [it was broken up] exceeding small, very fine, as small as seeds. The youths ate it.

"And [of] this which they ate, it was said: 'The god is eaten,' and of those who ate it, it was said: 'They guard the god.'" (Ibid., 3:6.)

14. *Sacrifice.* "The third month they called Tocoztantli. On the first day of this month they observed a feast to the god of rain. . . . On this feast they offered the first fruits of the flowers which had bloomed earlier that year, on the pyramid named Yopico." (Ibid., 2:5.)

15. *Sin.* It is interesting to note that in the paganistic life of the Aztecs, sinning and repentance were part of the religious life. The Aztecs believed that sinning would bring sickness upon the individual. (Ibid., 13:13.) The sinner would come to the seer and confess the sin he had committed; then he was washed by special water. This was done to remove any corruption from the person. (Ibid., p. 8.) To be completely forgiven of a sin, one had to complete the following steps: (1) acknowledge the sin, (2) want to repent of the sin, (3) tell the sin to the seer, (4) fast, (5) pay for the sin with his own blood, and (6) never do it again. (Ibid., p. 10.)

THE CONQUERORS

Fascinating sights greeted Columbus, Cortez, Pizarro, and other Spanish explorers in the New World. For the most part they were treated with respect and curiosity. But as they became increasingly ruthless in their treatment of the natives, this hospitality turned into hostility, and the natives began to retaliate.

The letters, diaries, and records of the early Spanish explorers provide valuable details on the culture of the native Americans before it was infiltrated and influenced by customs and mores brought from the Old World. The early explorers were usually accompanied by a priest, a notary, and/or a treasurer, and it is from notes and journals kept by these persons as well as the explorers themselves that we learn about life in the pre-Columbian or pre-Spanish eras.

The coming of the explorers had been foretold centuries before the actual expeditions. In the Book of Mormon we read this vision of Nephi: "And I looked and beheld a man among the Gentiles, who was separated from the seed of my brethren by the many waters; and I beheld the Spirit of God, that it came down and wrought upon the man; and he went forth upon the many waters; even unto the seed of my brethren, who were in the promised land." (1 Nephi 13:12.)

What unusual sights greeted the early Spanish explorers? In the book *Narrative and Critical History of America* we read:

"Not even in the sweetest idealizing of romance is there a more fascinating picture than that . . . of those unsophisticated children of Nature, their gentleness, docility, and friendliness. They were not hideous or repulsive, as like Bushmen, Feejeans, or Hottentots; they presented no caricaturings of humanity, as giants or dwarfs, as Amazons or Esquimaux; their naked bodies were not mutilated, gashed, or painted; they uttered no yells or shrieks, with mad and threatening gestures. They were attractive in person, well formed, winning and gentle, and trustful; they were light and soft of skin, and their hospitality was spontaneous, generous, and genial. Tribes of more warlike and less gracious nature proved to exist on some of the islands, about the isthmus and the continental regions of the early invasion; but the first introduction and intercourse of the representatives of the parted continents set before the Europeans a race of their fellow-creatures with whom they might have lived and dealt in peace and love." (Winsor, ed., *Narrative and Critical History of America*, p. 27.)

So great was the impression made upon the early Spaniards by the Indians that Columbus recorded the following reaction:

"My messengers report that after a march of twelve miles they found a village with perhaps a thousand inhabitants. The natives, they say, received them with great ceremony, lodged them in the most beautiful houses, carried them around on their arms, kissed their hands and feet, and, in short, tried to make clear to them in every possible way that it was known the white men came from the gods. About fifty men and women asked my messengers to be allowed to travel back with them to the Heaven of the eternal gods.—Columbus, November 6th, 1492." (Honore, *In Quest of the White God*, p. 15.)

Of interest are descriptions of the Indians by the explorers. Ruth Underhill states: ". . . we now know that the Indian complexions vary from dark brown to yellow and even white." (Underhill, *Red Man's America*, p. 2.) "The people are thus naked, handsome, brown, well shaped in body; their heads, necks, arms, private parts, feet of men and women, are a little covered with feathers. The men also have many precious stones on their feet and breasts." (Winsor, *Narrative*, p. 244.)

Clavigero wrote: "There have been writers, who, building upon the tradition of the natives, and upon the discovery of bones, skulls, and entire skeletons of prodigious size, which have been dug up at different times in many parts of New Spain, have imagined that the first inhabitants of the country were giants. I, for my own

18 THE WORLD OF THE BOOK OF MORMON

part, have no doubt of their existence there, as well as in other parts of the New World: but we can neither form any conjectures as to the time in which they lived, although we have reason to believe they must be very ancient, nor can we be persuaded that there has ever been, as these writers imagined, a whole nation of giants, but only single individuals of the nations which we now know, or of some others more ancient and unknown." (Clavigero, *The History of Mexico*, pp. 111-12.)

NATIVE CUSTOMS

As the explorers became better acquainted with the inhabitants of the New World, they found many interesting customs, particularly with regard to laws, morality, and religion. The following description was recorded sometime between 1492 and 1504:

". . . all things are in common. And the men have as wives those who please them, be they mothers, sisters, or friends; therein make they no distinction. They also fight with each other, even those who are slain, and hang the flesh of them in the smoke. They become a hundred and fifty years of age, and have no government. One of the customs witnessed by the newcomers was human sacrifice." (Winsor, *Narrative*, p. 244.)

Lewis Spence reports that the theological advancement of the Nahua religion was greatly superior to that of the Greeks or Romans and on a level with that expressed by the Egyptians and Assyrians. (Spence, *Myths and Legends*, p. 54.)

After the natives became accustomed to Columbus and his men, some of them went running from house to house and to neighboring villages with loud cries of "Come! come to see the people from heaven." (Thacher, *Christopher Columbus* 2:22-23.)

According to Hyatt Verrill, laws were rigidly enforced among the Indians in South America. The laws were severe but just. Idleness was regarded as a crime, and so beneficial was this attribute that it was observed that throughout the entire Inca kingdom, the explorers never found a liar, a thief, nor an idle person. (*America's Ancient Civilization*, p. 228.)

AGRICULTURE AND ANIMALS

The explorers discovered many advances relating to agriculture and animals in the New World. Complicated irrigation systems had been built, leading the waters of mountain streams for hundreds of miles. Reservoirs, cement aqueducts, sluiceways, and plows also indicated a very advanced knowledge of methods of agriculture.

Thacher notes that the natives grew and used cotton. Several explorers, including De Soto, Alvarez, and Columbus, reported the use of honey. (See, for example, Winsor, *Narrative*, pp. 189, 244-47; Thacher, *Christopher Columbus*, vol. 2; Verrill, *America's Ancient Civilization*, p. 225. See also Alma 62:29.)

Elephants, and other large animals have been found in America. In 1560 the Italian cartographer Paulo de Furlani drew a map, which is preserved in the British Museum, depicting elephants in the region of the Mississippi Valley. (Winsor, *Narrative*, p. 438.) On the way to the New World, Columbus stopped at the Canary islands and observed: "Other Canarieans also inhabit the wild regions extending from Mount Atlas through the sands of Lybia, places covered with black dust and filled with serpents and elephants." (Thacher, *Christopher Columbus*, vol. 2.)

The mountains of Eoliman and Tochtlan, considerably distant from the capital and still more so from each other, have emitted fire and lava at different periods in our history. A few years ago an account was published in Italy concerning the mountains of Tochtland or Tuxtla, an account that was full of curious exaggerations in which there were descriptions of rivers, of fire, of frightful elephants, etc. (Clavigero, *The History of Mexico*, p. 19.)

As the Spanish invaded the New World, one of the phenomena observed by the natives was that of a man on a horse. When Pizarro reached Esmeraldas, his men attacked, and the Spaniards were saved when one of their soldiers fell from his horse in the course of battle. The Indians, who supposed that the horse and the rider were one creature, were so astonished at this sudden separation of the parts of the beast that they fled. (Verrill, *America's Ancient Civilizations*, pp. 195-206.)

METALLURGY AND PRECIOUS STONES

In the Book of Mormon we read of the use of iron and other metalwork.

The first treasures sent back to Spain included the following objects: a gold necklace composed of seven pieces with 185 small emeralds set in it, and 232 gems (like rubies) from which hung 27 small bells of gold and some pearls; two wheels, one of gold representing the sun, the other of silver bearing the image of the moon, 28 hands in circumference, and bearing various figures of animals; other devices beautifully worked in relief; a large mirror and several small ones of gold; and a number of coats, handkerchiefs, bedcovers, tapestries, and carpets of cotton stuffs. (Cortez, *Five Letters*, pp. 170-71.)

Columbus sent his men to obtain water, and on their return they reported the following: "The men who returned with the casks of water said they had seen a man whose nose was decorated with a piece of gold which had letters on it." (Landstrom, *Columbus*, p. 77.)

Pizarro and one of the natives became friendly with one another, and, according to Helps, they exchanged gifts. Pizarro's gift was an iron hatchet made by the Indians. (Helps, *The Life of Pizarro*, p. 123.)

The treasurer and the notary of Pizarro attested to the fact that at Cajamarca sixty Incan goldsmiths had to work steadily night and day for one month to reduce to bullion the gold and silver objects accumulated in the town. This was but a small portion of the gold and silver objects found in the temples, which totaled more precious metals than the world had ever known previous to the conquest. (Verrill, *America's Ancient Civilizations*, p. 230.)

As Pizarro and his men traveled through the villages of Peru, they rushed into one town and massacred the surprised and unresisting inhabitants, helping themselves to the gold and emeralds of the murdered Indians. Pizarro found an emerald the size of a pigeon's egg, and the soldiers helped themselves to many other huge stones. (Verrill, *America's Ancient Civilizations*, p. 221.) With respect to precious stones, there were (and still are) diamonds, amethysts, cateyes, turquoise, cornelians, and some green stones resembling emeralds. (Clavigero, *The History of Mexico*, p. 21.)

This engraving features the Arch of Labna in Mexico. It was done by a Mr. Catherwood, an artist who in 1839 accompanied John L. Stephens on his explorations of then-unknown areas in Mexico, Guatemala, and Honduras. Mr. Catherwood recorded their findings in numerous such engravings, the detail of which is so fine that modern archaeologists still refer to them to see how these ruins looked a hundred years ago.

BUILDINGS AND CITIES

The early explorers were astonished at some of the architectural wonders they found in the New World.

Cortez wrote, "There are forty towers at the least of all about construction and very lofty." (Cortez, *Five Letters*, p. 90.) He also stated that there were "forts larger and stronger and built better than the castles of Spaine" (p. 78) and "forts so big that within its [sic] lofty walls one could set a town of 50,000 inhabitants" (p. 90); the buildings "are not any finer in all of Spain" (p. 78). "The city of Cholula," he continued, "is situated on a plain with about twenty thousand houses within its walls and as many in the suburbs outside. . . . I counted more than four hundred pyramids." (Ibid., p. 78.)

Bernal Diaz reported: ". . . there were many high towers in the city where the idols stood." (Von Hagen, *The Ancient Sun Kingdoms of the Americas*, p. 144.) Factories for the manufacture of cloth, blankets, and other items were in evidence. (Verrill, *America's Ancient Civilizations*, pp. 278-79.)

When Pizarro reached Cuzco, the largest and finest city in the New World, he found a civilization that exceeded his wildest imagination. The massive wall surrounding the city was composed of enormous, beautifully cut stones fitted together without mortar and so engineered that a person could not force a knife blade between the joints. Magnificent houses, palaces, temples, and government buildings were everywhere. The plazas were filled with flowers and trees. Streets were laid out at nearly right angles and, though narrow, were well paved with cobblestones.

An immense statue carved from stone was found by Pizarro's men. The priests ordered that it be broken up. So huge was this piece of sculpture that it took thirty men three days to destroy it. (Verrill, *America's Ancient Civilizations*, p. 21.)

Sir Arthur Helps recorded that Pedro de Cleca, who visited Cuzco within the first twenty years after the Spanish conquest, remarked, "Cuzco was grand and stately. It must have been founded by a people of great intelligence." (Helps, *The Life of Pizarro*, p.

235.) Some archaeologists believe that the remains of the buildings seen today in this country are perhaps the most amazing works of man in America, if not in the entire world.

The Book of Mormon speaks of cities sinking into the sea. The following was recorded by Cortez: "We advanced four leagues to a little town lying on the shores of a great lake, half of it being indeed in the water." (Cortez, *Five Letters*, p. 65.)

BOATS

The Spanish visitors reported that the natives had many narrow canoes, each made of a single log. Some of the canoes, however, were large enough to accommodate as many as seventy to eighty men, each using an oar. (Thacher, *Christopher Columbus* 2:22-23.)

WARFARE

Renando Colon wrote: "The Indians on the Punta de Caxinas wore clothes like those in the canoe, in colored shirts and loin cloths. They also wore thick padded cotton corslets, which gave adequate protection against Indian arrows and even withstood several blows from our swords." (Landstrom, *Columbus*, p. 164.)

On the island of Bonacca the natives used axes made out of good copper. They had bells of the same metal, and crucibles to melt it. (Ibid., p. 162.) Also on Bonacca, Columbus discovered long wooden swords with grooves on each side, where the edges of the blade would have been, with sharp flints that cut like glass. Axes were used that were made out of copper. (Ibid.)

Poisoned arrows were the main weapon used in killing sixty-nine of Alonzo Alvarez's men at the harbor of Cartagena. (Winsor, *Narrative*, p. 191.)

According to the letters of Cortez, the natives owned shields and swords (translated "lances" in one source). (Cortez, *Five Letters*, p. 41.) Morris also translates Cortez as telling how the natives had erected forts with lofty walls, indicating that towers were a part of their architecture. (Ibid., p. 90.)

GEOGRAPHY OF THE BOOK OF MORMON

While knowing the exact landing place of the Lehi colony and the location of the ancient Cumorah and lands and cities described in the Book of Mormon can have little impact on personal salvation, it is a fascinating study to Latter-day Saints and of importance to LDS archaeologists.

It seems that no one in the history of the Church has been more enthusiastic about the external evidences of the Book of Mormon than Joseph Smith and other early leaders of the Church. Articles appeared often in the early newspapers on such topics as "Transatlantic Antiquities," "American Antiquities," and "Indian Antiquities." One example is found in the *Times and Seasons*, September 1, 1842:

"The following account of preparing and managing books is taken from Dr. John's Biblical Archaeology. Tablets, tables and plates are all of the same import, and the mode of fastening *leaves*, plates or tablets together at the back with *rings*, is the same way the Book of Mormon was connected. We may, at some future day, pursue this subject far enough to convince honest people, that the stone tablets of the Bible, and gold plates of the Book of Mormon, were constructed and carried alike."

John L. Stephens, a nineteenth century explorer, was sent by the United States government to explore unknown areas of southern Mexico, Guatemala, and Honduras. He took with him a Mr. Catherwood, an artist, to record his findings. After his first expedition he published volume 1 of *Incidents and Travels in Central America, Chiapas, and Yucatan*, which was met with great enthusiasm by the Church. After nine columns of extracts from Stephens' book were published, Joseph Smith made this comment: "The foregoing extract has been made to assist the Latter-day Saints in establishing the Book of Mormon as a revelation from God. It affords great joy to have the world assist us to so much proof, that even the most credulous cannot doubt." (*Times and Seasons* 3:914.)

The Prophet also stated concerning Stephens' book: "From an extract from 'Stephen's Incidents of Travel in Central America,' it will be seen that the proof of the Nephites and Lamanites dwelling on this continent, according to the account in the Book of Mormon, is developing itself in a more satisfactory way than the most sanguine believer in that revelation could have anticipated." (*Times and Seasons* 3:921.)

In 1843, John Taylor, who was editor of *Times and Seasons*, said concerning Stephens' work: "This is a work that ought to be in the hands of every Latter-day Saint, corroborating as it does the history of the Book of Mormon. No stronger circumstantial evidence of the authenticity of the latter book, can be given than that contained in Mr. Stephens' work." (*Times and Seasons* 4:346.)

Because the interest of Latter-day Saints in locating ancient sites can cause speculation and disagreement, President George Q. Cannon cautioned them that the "Book of Mormon is not a geographical primer. . . ." (*Instructor*, January 1, 1890.) Members of the Church do not base their testimonies on archaeological proof. External evidences are used as support and to interest the world in the truth of the Book of Mormon. When disagreements arise, we should keep in mind that "out of the studies of faithful Latter-day Saints may yet come a unity concerning Book of Mormon geography; or, the Lord may give a revelation that will end all differences of opinion." (John A. Widtsoe, foreword, in Ferguson, *Cumorah Where?*)

LEHI'S LANDING

The following quotation, thought by many to be a revelation to the Prophet Joseph Smith, appeared in print for the first time in *A Compendium of the Doctrine of the Gospel* by Franklin D. Richards and James A. Little (p. 289):

"*Lehi's Travels. Revelation to Joseph the Seer:* The course that Lehi and his company traveled from Jerusalem to the place of their destination: They traveled nearly a south-southeast direction until they came to the nineteenth degree of north latitude; then, nearly east of the Sea of Arabia, then sailed in a southeast direction, and landed on the continent of South America, in Chili [*sic*], thirty degrees south latitude."

B. H. Roberts gave similar background information with some cautions added:

"The only reason so far discovered for regarding the above as a revelation is that it is found on a loose sheet of paper in the hand writing of Frederick G. Williams, for some years second Counselor in the First Presidency of the Church in the Kirtland period of its history; and follows the body of the revelation contained in Doctrine and Covenants, Section vii., relating to John the beloved disciple, remaining on earth, until the glorious coming of Jesus to reign with his Saints. The hand-writing is certified to be that of Frederick G. Williams, by his son, Ezra G. Williams, of Ogden; and endorsed on the back of the sheet of paper containing the above passage and the revelation pertaining to John. The indorsement is dated April the 11th, 1864. The revelation pertaining to John has this introductory line: 'A Revelation Concerning John, the Beloved Disciple.' But there is no heading to the passage relating to the passage about Lehi's travels.

"The words 'Lehi's Travels,' and the words 'Revelation to Joseph the Seer,' are added by the publishers, justified as they supposed, doubtless, by the fact that the paragraph is in the hand writing of Frederick G. Williams, Counselor to the Prophet, and on the same page with the body of an undoubted revelation, which was published repeatedly as such in the life time of the Prophet, first in 1833, at Independence, Missouri, in the 'Book of Commandments,' and subsequently in every edition of the Doctrine and Covenants until now.

"But the one relating to Lehi's travels was never published in the life-time of the Prophet, and was published no where else until published in the Richards-Little's Compendium as noted above. Now, if no more evidence can be found to establish this passage in Richards and Little's Compendium as a 'revelation to Joseph, the Seer,' then the fact that it is found in the hand writing of Frederick G. Williams, and on the same sheet of paper with the body of the revelation about John, the beloved disciple, the evidence of its being a 'revelation to Joseph, the Seer,' rests on a very unsatisfactory basis." (Roberts, *New Witnesses for God* 3:501-2.)

A close examination reveals that through the addition of the title "Lehi's Travels," the accuracy of the original statement has been lost. Frederick G. Williams stated:

"The course that Lehi traveled from the city of Jerusalem to the place where he and his family took ship, they traveled nearly a south southeast direction until they came to the nineteenth degree of North latitude, then nearly east to the sea of Arabia then sailed in a south east direction and landed on the continent of South America in Chili [*sic*] thirty degrees south of lattitude [*sic*]." (Williams, *After One Hundred Years*, p. 103.)

There is no date and no explanation as to the source of the statement. However, three other items on the same piece of paper might help us find a date and/or the source: (1) a revelation about John the Beloved now found in Doctrine and Covenants, section 7; (2) the phrase "question asked in English and answered in Hebrew," followed by two lines of English and Hebrew, which could have been written during a number of Hebrew classes that Joseph and other brethren, including F. G. Williams, attended during the Kirtland period; (3) the phrase "Characters on the Book of Mormon" and the following characters and labels:

"The Book of Mormon"

"The interpretation of languages"

This part of the document may be the most helpful in establishing a date. During July 1837, about two years after Joseph Smith received the papyri from which the Book of Abraham was taken, he agreed to let five men try to translate the papyri with whatever spiritual or secular powers they could individually muster. Each of these men (W. W. Phelps, Frederick G. Williams, Warren Parrish, Oliver Cowdery, and Willard Richards) eventually formulated partial lists of an Egyptian alphabet and grammar. (Hugh Nibley, *BYU Studies*, Summer 1971, pp. 359-93.)

On one of the pages of the work done by Willard Richards are the same characters and explanation as those found on the aforementioned document by Williams, wherein we find the statement on Lehi's travels:

"The Book of Mormon"

"The interpretation of languages"

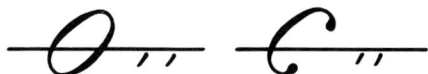

According to Dr. Hugh Nibley, these are the only sets of symbols he has seen with this particular interpretation. The exact correspondence of the characters and the interpretation suggests that Richards and Williams were collaborating in their work. The author therefore suggests a date of July 1837 for the document from which "Lehi's Travels" was taken, since that was the month the five men were working on the papyri translation.

It is interesting that Nancy Williams, author of *After One Hundred Years*, places the writing of "Lehi's Travels" chronologically between the dedication of the Kirtland Temple (March 27, 1836) and the birth of a son born to Emma and the Prophet July 20, 1836, whom they named Frederick G. Williams Smith. No explanation is given for the chronology. However, the following explanation was given for the event:

"Frederick had in his pocket a piece of paper which he carried to take notes on. On this he wrote in pencil: 'John the Beloved'—Then a space followed and a few lines written in another language. A large space followed and then at the bottom of the page he wrote the following revelation: [quotes statement on Lehi's travels].

"Returning home he transcribed the revelation in ink on another sheet of paper. Rebecca kept these papers with her other notes until her death. Their son, Ezra, loaned them to the Church Historian's Office in Salt Lake City in 1860 where they have lain these many years, known only to historians, to be brought to light and published for the first time." (Williams, *After One Hundred Years*, pp. 101-3.)

The question should be asked, From whom would Williams have gotten this idea on the direction of Lehi's travels? If it was not a revelation, not dictated by the Prophet, then we have the alternative that he himself wrote it, that he was dishonest, and that the Prophet knew nothing of the item. Do we have anything that would help us corroborate this statement?

The Book of Mormon does confirm the statement by Williams that Lehi's party journeyed along the Red Sea in nearly a south, southeast direction to the place Nahom, where Ishmael died, then nearly eastward until they came to the great sea. (1 Nephi 16:13; 17:1.)

Statements made during the Prophet's life on the subject of Lehi's travels also support Williams. The Prophet wrote in the *Times and Seasons*, September 15, 1842:

"When we read in the Book of Mormon that Jared and his brother came on to this continent from the confusion and scattering at the Tower, and lived here more than a thousand years, and covered the whole continent from sea to sea, with towns and cities; and that Lehi went down by the Red Sea to the great Southern Ocean, and crossed over to this land, and landed a little south of the Isthmus of Darien, and improved the country according to the word of the Lord, as a branch of the house of Israel, . . . we can not but think the Lord has a hand in bringing to pass his strange act, and proving the Book of Mormon true in the eyes of all the people." (*Teachings*, p. 267.)

After the death of the Prophet, his wife Emma had such high regard for Dr. John M. Bernhisel that she placed her deceased husband's revision of the Bible in his hands for three months and refused to allow Brigham Young or others to see it. Bernhisel copied the work and brought his copy with him to Utah in 1848. On the last page of what is now known as the Bernhisel manuscript, the following statement is found:

"The course that Lehi traveled from the city of Jerusalem to the place where he and his family took ship. They traveled nearly a south southeast direction until they came to the nineteenth degree of North Latitude then nearly East to the sea of Arabia then sailed in a south east direction and landed on the continent of South America in Chili thirty degrees south Lattitude."

This statement appears to be in Bernhisel's handwriting. It is not dated, but the portion of manuscript that precedes it is dated June 5, 1845. It is interesting that this statement is the same as that of Frederick G. Williams—word for word. Also note that the words Chile and latitude are misspelled in both quotations. The evidence suggests a common source for these two quotations; yet John Bernhisel was in New York until 1843. He met the Prophet six years after Williams wrote his statement (if we are correct in our analysis).

It seems apparent that the course that Lehi traveled had nothing to do with Joseph's revision of the Bible. Where did the revision come from? Brother Bernhisel must have realized its importance as he was copying it. It seems unlikely he would have added anything that was not of the greatest interest to him or that was of doubtful authorship. An explanation has been suggested by Dr. Robert Matthews, professor of religion at BYU. It is possible that when Bernhisel returned the manuscript to Emma Smith, she showed him a slip of paper with the quotation on it (Joseph's study must have been full of interesting papers and documents), and Bernhisel, like many others, accepted this quotation as revelation.

In a discourse delivered in the "Old Tabernacle" in Salt Lake City on December 27, 1868, Orson Pratt made the following comment on Lehi's route: "After the destruction of the Jaredites, the Lord brought two other colonies to people this land. One colony landed a few hundred miles north of the Isthmus on the western coast; the other landed on the coast of Chili, upwards of two thousand miles south of them. The latter were called the Nephites and Lamanites." (JD 12:342.)

On April 10, 1870, Elder Pratt said, regarding the Jaredite route: "One nation, or rather the colony which founded it, came from the Tower of Babel soon after the days of the Flood. They colonized what we call North America, landing on the western coast, a little south of the Gulf of California, in the south-western part of this north wing of our continent. They flourished some sixteen hundred years." (JD 13:129.)

On February 11, 1872, he was even more specific:

"By revelation from the Lord they [Lehi and his family] traveled southwest from the city of Jerusalem, and after reaching the Red Sea they continued along its eastern borders and afterwards bent their course eastward, arriving at the Indian Ocean. . . . [They were] guided by the Almighty across the great Indian Ocean. Passing among the islands, how far south of Japan I do not know, they came round our globe, crossing not only the Indian Ocean, but what we term the great Pacific Ocean, landing on the western coast of what is now called South America. As near as we can judge from the description of the country contained in this record the first landing place was in Chili, not far from where the city of Valparaiso now stands." (JD 14:325.)

The statement of the travels of Lehi was not included in the first edition of Richards and Little's *Compendium*, printed in England in 1857. In 1882, however, the book was reprinted in the United States and included the statement. It should be noted that Richards was a member of the Council of the Twelve at the time of the later printing, and he felt the statement was a revelation to the Prophet.

On November 1, 1959, at the Andes Mission headquarters in Lima, Peru, Elder Harold B. Lee of the Council of the Twelve offered the following insights on the subject:

". . . from the writings of the Prophet Joseph Smith, and of other inspired men, it seems all are in agreement that the followers of Lehi came to the western shores of South America. . . .

"I have recalled today that we are now very close to the center of some of the greatest Indian population in the world, and in all likelihood we may be near the place, in these two countries of Chili and Peru, where there has been a greater intermixture of Indian blood perhaps, than any other country on this continent. . . . I believe we are not far from the place where the history of the people of Lehi commenced in western America.

". . . As I look up and down the west coast of South America, I find very few seaports; and doesn't it seem likely to you that those who came here by ships directed by the Lord would be guided to a place where there was the most favorable landing? Where are the two most favorable seaports on the west coast? You know the answer to that question. Lima, Peru, and close by, Santiago, over on the west coast. . . ." (*Quarterly Historical Report for the Andes Mission*, November 1, 1959.)

THE HILL CUMORAH

There has been some disagreement about the location of ancient Cumorah. Here are some comments by Church authorities on this subject.

Concerning the record from which the Book of Mormon was translated, Brigham Young is reported to have said: "This book, which contained these things, was hid in the earth by Moroni, in a hill called by him, Cumorah, which hill is now in the state of New York, near the village of Palmyra, in Ontario County." (*Autobiography of Parley P. Pratt*, pp. 55-56.)

During the march of Zion's Camp in June 1834, the Prophet Joseph wrote that he "visited several of the mounds which had been thrown up by the ancient inhabitants of this country—Nephites, Lamanites, etc." He stated that he went up on a high mound, accompanied by some of the brethren. "On the top of the mound were stones which presented the appearance of three altars having been erected one above the other, according to the ancient order; and the remains of bones were strewn over the surface of the ground." Some of the brethren procured a shovel and hoe and began removing some of the earth, in the course of which they uncovered the skeleton of a man. The Prophet declared that the "person whose skeleton was before us was a white Lamanite, a large, thick-set man, and a man of God. His name was Zelph. He was a warrior and chieftain under the great prophet Onandagus, who was known from the Hill Cumorah, or eastern sea. . . ." (*History of the Church* 2:79.)

Lucy Mack Smith, the mother of the Prophet, records that Joseph referred to the hill near their Palmyra home as "Cumorah" immediately after his first visit there. (*History of Joseph Smith*, p. 100.)

David Whitmer is quoted as follows:

"When I was returning to Fayette with Joseph and Oliver, all of us riding in the wagon, Oliver and I on an old-fashioned, wooden spring seat, and Joseph behind us—when traveling along in a clear open space, a very pleasant, nice-looking, old man suddenly appeared by the side of the wagon, and saluted us with 'Good morning, it is very warm' at the same time wiping his face or forehead with his hand. We returned the salutation, and, by a sign from Joseph, I invited him to ride, if he was going our way. But he said very pleasantly, 'No, I am going to Cumorah.' This name was something new to me. I did not know what Cumorah meant. We all gazed at him and at each other, and as I looked around inquiringly at Joseph, the old man instantly disappeared, so that I did not see him again." (As quoted in Ferguson, *Cumorah Where?*, p. 7.)

Orson Pratt made the following statements:

"The Hill Cumorah is situated in western New York. . . .

"It . . . is distinguished as the great battlefield on which, and near which, two powerful nations were concentrated with all their forces, men, women and children, and fought till hundreds of thousands on both sides were hewn down, and left to molder upon the ground. Both armies were Israelites; both had become awfully corrupt, having apostatized from God: the Nephites, as a nation, become extinct; the Lamanites alone were left....

"The Hill Cumorah is remarkable also as being the hill on which and around which, a still more ancient nation perished, called Jaredites.... Millions fought millions, until the Hill Ramah, and the land round about, was soaked with blood, and their carcasses left in countless numbers unburied, to molder back to mother earth." (Lundwall, *Masterful Discourses and Writings of Orson Pratt*, pp. 390-94.)

And finally, President Joseph Fielding Smith wrote: "Locale of Cumorah, Ramah and Ripliancum: This modernistic theory of necessity, in order to be consistent, must place the waters of Ripliancum and the Hill Cumorah someplace within the restricted territory of Central America, *notwithstanding the teachings of the Church to the contrary for upwards of 100 years.* Because of this *theory* some members of the Church have become confused and greatly disturbed in their faith in the *Book of Mormon.* It is for this reason that evidence is here presented to show that it is not only possible that these places could be located as the Church has held during the past century, but that in very deed *such is the case.*" (*Doctrines of Salvation* 3:233. Italics in original.)

ANCIENT SITES IN NORTH AMERICA

Numerous other places in North America have been identified by modern-day prophets as having significance in ancient times. For example, when the site was selected for the St. George Temple in St. George, Utah, President Brigham Young "explained that the Temple must be built at that place, because the Nephites had previously dedicated that very site for the erection of a Temple, but had been unable to bring their hopes to a full fruition." (McGavin, *Mormonism and Masonry*, p. 156.) He also identified St. George as the site where the Gadianton robbers were found. (Lundwall, *Temples of the Most High*, p. 86.)

On April 25, 1877, President Young, accompanied by Warren S. Snow, went to the place where the Manti Temple was to be built and declared: "Here is the spot where the Prophet Moroni stood and dedicated this piece of land for a Temple site, and that is the reason why the location is made here, and we can't move it from this spot; and if you and I are the only persons that come here at high noon today, we will dedicate this ground." (Whitney, *Life of Heber C. Kimball*, p. 477.)

An ancient site identified by the Prophet Joseph was "Tower Hill," which he said was north of Far West, Missouri. The Prophet wrote: "He [Wight] lives at the foot of Tower Hill (a name I gave the place in consequence of the remains of an old Nephite altar or tower that stood there)...." (*History of the Church* 3:34-35.)

The ancient city of Manti was also identified by the Prophet as Zion's Camp passed through Huntsville, Randolph County, Missouri. (Jenson, *Historical Record*, Book 1, p. 601.)

CENTRAL AMERICAN SITES

Central America has been identified in modern times as the location for many significant events of Book of Mormon times. The Prophet wrote:

"Central America, or Guatemala, is situated north the Isthmus of Darion and once embraced several hundred miles of territory from north to south.... The city of Zarahemla stood upon this land as will be seen from the following words in the book of Alma.

"It is certainly a good thing for the excellency and veracity of the divine authenticity of the Book of Mormon, that the ruins of Zarahemla have been found where the Nephites left them.... We are not going to declare positively that the ruins of Quirigua are those of Zarahemla, but when the land and the stones, and the books tell the story so plain, we are of opinion, that it would require more proof than the Jews could bring to prove the disciples stole the body of Jesus from the tomb, to prove that the ruins of the city in question, are not one of those referred to in the Book of Mormon." (*Times and Seasons* 3:927.)

It is important to note that Joseph accepted the responsibility for this statement when he said: "This paper commences my editorial career, I alone stand responsible for it, and shall do so for all papers having my signature henceforward." (*Times and Seasons* 3:710.)

"Let us turn our subject," the Prophet wrote, "to the Book of Mormon, where these wonderful ruins of Palenque are among the mighty works of the Nephites:—and the mystery is solved.... They lived about the narrow neck of land, which now embraces Central America, with all the cities that can be found. Read the destruction of cities at the crucifixion of Christ, pages 459-490." (*Times and Seasons* 3:914-15.)

After comparing researches in Mexico by a Baron Humbolt with chapter 1 of the book of Ether, the Prophet declared:

"Again, those nations, or families, embodied themselves together and traveled *they knew not where,* but at length arrived in the country of Aztalan, or the lake country of America. The Book of Mormon says, that the brother of Jared cried unto the Lord, that he would give them another land; the Lord heard him, and told him to go to a certain place, 'and there I will meet thee and go before thee into a land which is choice above all the land of the earth.' This further speaks of the land of America. The coincidence is so striking that further comment is unnecessary." (*Times and Seasons* 3:820.)

Orson Pratt, in his discourse in the Salt Lake Tabernacle April 10, 1870, made the following statements:

"[God] brought [Lehi and his family] from Jerusalem first down to the Red Sea. They travelled along the eastern borders of the Red Sea for many days, and then bore off in an eastern direction which brought them to the Arabian Gulf. There they were commanded of the Lord to build a vessel. They went aboard of this vessel and were brought by the special providence of God across the great Indian and Pacific Oceans, and landed on the western coast of South America.... They wended their way into the northern part of South America. About four hundred years after this the two colonies amalgamated in the northern part of South America and they became one nation. . . .

"About forty-five years before Christ a very large colony of five thousand four hundred men, with wives and children, united themselves together in the northern part of South America, and came forth by land into North America, and travelled an exceedingly great distance until they came to large bodies of water and many rivers, very probably in the great Mississippi Valley. In the next ten years numerous other colonies came forth and spread themselves on the northern portion of the continent and became exceedingly numerous. . . .

"Five years after the discovery of this remarkable memento of the ancient Israelites on the American continent, and thirty-five years after the Book of Mormon was in print, several other mounds in the same vicinity of Newark [Ohio] were opened, in several of which Hebrew characters were found. Among them was this beautiful expression, buried with one of their ancient dead, 'May the Lord have mercy on me a Nephite.' It was translated a little different—Nephel." (JD 13:129-31.)

In a speech on December 27, 1868, Elder Pratt stated:

"They [the Jaredites] landed to the south of this, just below the Gulf of California, on our western coast. They inhabited North America, and spread forth on this Continent, and in the course of some sixteen hundred years' residence here, they became a mighty and powerful nation. . . . The Lord warned them by a dream to depart from the land of Moran, and led them forth in an easterly direction beyond the hill Cumorah, down into the eastern countries upon the sea shore. . . . But after they were destroyed, the Omerites, who dwelt in the New England States, returned again and dwelt in the land of their fathers on the western coast.

". . . Their greatest and last struggles were in the State of New York, near where the plates from which the Book of Mormon was translated were found. . . . Coriantumr, King of a certain portion of the Jaredites, after the destruction of his nation, wandered, solitary and alone, down towards the Isthmus of Darien, and there he became acquainted with a colony of people brought from the land of Jerusalem, called the people of Zarahemla. . . .

"A little over one century before Christ the Nephites united with the Zarahemlaites in the northern portions of South America, and were called Nephites and became a powerful nation. The country was called the land Bountiful, and included within the land of Zarahemla. . . . Nephi and the righteous separated themselves from the Lamanites and traveled eighteen hundred miles north until they came to the head waters of what we term the Amazon river. There Nephi located his little colony in the country supposed to be Ecuador, a very high region, many large and elevated mountains being in that region.

". . . the Nephites fled again some twenty days' journey to the northward and united themselves with the people of Zarahemla. . . . numerous hosts of the Jaredites. . . . once spread over all the face of North America." (JD 12: 341-43.)

On February 11, 1872, Elder Pratt again talked about the ancient inhabitants of North America:

"[The faithful Nephites], under the guidance of prophets and revelators, came still further northward, emigrating from the head waters of what we now term the river Amazon, upon the western coast, or not far from the western coast, until they came on the waters of the river which we call the Magdalena. On this river, not a great distance from the mouth thereof, in what is now termed the United States of Columbia [sic], they built their great capital city. They also discovered another nation that already possessed that country called the people of Zarahemla. They also were a branch of Israel who came out from the city of Jerusalem five hundred and eighty-nine years before the coming of Christ. . . .

"The Nephites and the people of Zarahemla united together and formed a great and powerful nation, occupying the lands south of the Isthmus for many hundreds of miles, and also from the Pacific on the west to the Atlantic on the east, spreading all through the country. The Lamanites about this time also occupied South America, the middle or southern portion of it, and were exceedingly numerous. . . .

"About fifty-four years before Christ, five thousand four hundred men, with their wives and children, left the northern portion of South America, passed through the Isthmus, came into this north country, the north wing of the continent, and began to settle up North America. . . . [The] Nephite nation about this time commenced the art of shipbuilding. They built many ships, launching them forth into the western ocean. The place of the building of these ships was near the Isthmus of Darien. Scores of thousands entered these ships year after year, and passed along on the western coast northward, and began to settle the western coast on the north wing of the continent. . . . In process of time they spread forth on the right and on the left, and the whole face of the North American continent was covered by cities, towns and villages and population. . . .

". . . twelve Nephites who were called by the personal ministry of Jesus, were commanded to go forth and preach the Gospel on all the face of the North and South American continent. . . .

"Here let me say again; according to the Book of Mormon, many of those great islands that are found in the Indian Ocean, also in the great Pacific Sea, have been planted with colonies of Israelites. Do they not resemble each other? Go to the Sandwich Islands, to the South Sea Islands, to Japan—go to the various islands of the Pacific Ocean; and you find a general resemblance in the characters and countenances of the people. Who are they? According to the Book of Mormon, Israelites were scattered forth from time to time, and colonies planted on these islands of the ocean." (JD 14:325-30, 333.)

In his discourse in the Salt Lake Tabernacle on November 27, 1870, Elder Pratt talked about the restoration and made the following statement concerning the appearance of Jesus Christ to the Nephites:

"On what part of this continent did Jesus appear? He appeared in what is now termed the northern part of South America, where they had a temple built, at which place the people were gathered together, some twenty-five hundred in number, marvelling and wondering at the great earthquake that had taken place on this land, which had destroyed so many cities, &c., and the great darkness that had overshadowed the land, which was a sign given them by prophecy concerning the crucifixion of Christ." (JD 14:298.)

Another controversy to which Elder Pratt addressed himself was one concerning Yucatan in Central America. An article was published in the mid-1800s concerning Yucatan in which the writer evidently wrote that an ancient civilization in Yucatan had left no history. Elder Pratt responded in the *Millennial Star* (10:346-57):

Old engraving of Hill Cumorah in Palmyra, New York. It was from this hill that Joseph Smith took the gold plates containing the history now known as the Book of Mormon. Many sources cite the Hill Cumorah as the final battleground between the Nephites and the Lamanites, where the Nephites as a nation became extinct.

"The first great nation that anciently inhabited Yucatan, passed away about 2,400 years ago; but their prophets left a *history*, an abridgement of which has been translated into the English language, called the 'Book of Ether'. ... The last great nation that inhabited that country and passed away, have also *left their history*, which was discovered, translated, and published in the English language nearly 20 years ago by Mr. Joseph Smith. ... The Book of Mormon says that in the 367th year after Christ, 'the Lamanites'—the forefather of the American Indians—'took possession of the city of Desolation,'—which was in Central America, near to or in Yucatan—'and this because their number did exceed the number of the Nephites,' the Nephites being the nation who inhabited the cities of Yucatan, and the Lamanites 'did also march forward against the city of Teancum.' In the 384th year, the occupants of Yucatan and Central America, having been driven from their great and magnificent cities, were pursued by the Lamanites to the hill Cumorah in the interior of the state of New York, where the whole nation perished in battle."

In 1879 Elder Pratt divided the Book of Mormon into chapters and verses with references, and added geographical references that are consistent with the above views. These references did not appear in the Book of Mormon until 1920.

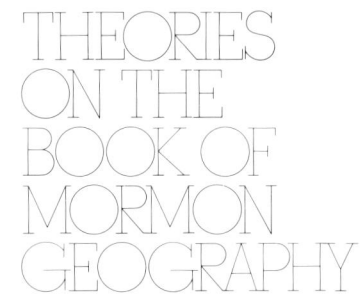

THEORIES ON THE BOOK OF MORMON GEOGRAPHY

The writers of the Book of Mormon indicate there were five general areas of "lands" in the Americas. While we do not know the specific locations of these lands, the Book of Mormon does give some clues as to their relative positions to each other.

When Lehi's colony landed, they established the first of the five lands in the New World and called it the land of their first inheritance. They called the New World itself the promised land. (1 Nephi 18:23.)

The land of Nephi was settled approximately twenty years after Lehi and his followers first landed. When Lehi died and the rivalry between his sons intensified, Nephi, Lehi's righteous son who listened to the promptings of the Lord, led his family and followers from the land of the first inheritance and traveled to the north "for the space of many days." (2 Nephi 5:5-7.) They settled in a place that the people called the land of Nephi. (2 Nephi 5:8.)

The Nephites remained there for approximately 350 years. Then, because the people were becoming wicked, the Lord raised up another prophet, who led the faithful ones northward once again. After a difficult journey they discovered a group of people who were also from Jerusalem but were not descendants of Lehi. These people were called the people of Zarahemla, and their land was the land of Zarahemla. (Omni 13-14.) Most of the movement in the Book of Mormon was between the land of Nephi on the south and the land of Zarahemla on the north. (Alma 22:28-29.) Just north of Zarahemla was the land of Bountiful. (Alma 22:29.)

The land of Desolation was a great distance to the north of Zarahemla and Bountiful. This land, which was strewn with the bones of men and animals, had been the country of the Jaredites, who had destroyed themselves in civil war. Because of the barrenness of the land, the Nephites called it Desolation. (Alma 22:30.)

Some of the major theories concerning the positions of these Book of Mormon lands follow. The maps depict the relative positions of the lands described in each theory. It is important to note that The Church of Jesus Christ of Latter-day Saints does not take an official position on the geography of the Book of Mormon sites.

SOUTH AMERICAN THEORY

CENTRAL AMERICAN CIVILIZATIONS: "The student should be aware of the fact that certain of the Book of Mormon peoples could have migrated from South America and settled in colonies in Central America and Mexico. Such migrations could have taken place during the time of Hagoth and at other times." (Birrell, *The Book of Mormon Study Guide*, p. 563.)

NARROW NECK OF LAND: "The narrowest section of the Andean chain is to be found in the district of Ecuador. In southern Ecuador is to be found, likewise, some of the most impassable country on the west coast of South America." (Ibid., p. 568.)

LAND OF FIRST INHERITANCE: "The reader will note that the prevailing winds along the west coast of South America, the Peruvian (Humbolt) current, and two important Andean passes—all contact the southern coast of Peru in the vicinity of Arequipa (or near Arica, Chile). Much in the way of interesting archaeology is to be found in this triangular area bounded by Arequipa (Peru), Arica (Chile), and La Paz (Bolivia), and its adjacent areas. Could this land be the land of the 'First Inheritance' of the ancient Nephite and Lamanite peoples in the Book of Mormon?" (Ibid., p. 568.)

TEHUANTEPEC THEORY

LAND NORTHWARD: "In Mormon's summary of early events in the history of his nation, he reports on the discovery of this region of lakes and streams where many earlier inhabitants from Babel had previously lived for over 2,000 years. This is Olmec country—early Pre-Classic territory, to use the archaeological terms, or Jaredite country, to use a Book of Mormon term. The geography and archaeology of the Valley of Mexico meet all the requirements of the documentary sources. There are three regions of many waters in Mexico, north of Tehuantepec: (1) the Alvarado area southwest of the city of Vera Cruz; (2) the Tampico area; (3) the Valley of Mexico. Since the region was inland (Ether 9:3), the first two are eliminated, leaving the Valley of Mexico as the likely choice. Ixtlilxochitl (the sixteenth-century Mexican historian) refers to the central New World homeland of the people from the Great Tower as 'these northern lands.' The Book of Mormon refers to it as 'the land northward.'" (Ferguson, *One Fold and One Shepherd*, p. 314.)

NARROW NECK: "In [Ferguson's] personal construction of the geography of the Book of Mormon, the city built at the narrow neck of land, 'by the place where the sea divides the land,' could be the archaeological site known today as La Venta, on the Gulf of Mexico side of the Isthmus of Tehuantepec—Mexico's narrow neck of land." (Ibid., p. 252.)

NARROW PASS: "At the Isthmus of Tehuantepec, adjacent to ancient Huehuc-Tlopallan (ancient Bountiful-land), is a narrow pass meeting all the requirements of the pass referred to by the Nephite historians. It is on the Gulf of Mexico side of Tehuantepec. One of the writers studied and photographed it from a Cub airplane in 1948. It runs by the sea for about seventy miles in a general north-westerly-southeasterly direction. The seashore pass is between the gulf on one hand and the high Tuxtla Mountains on the other. The pass is but a few yards wide in some places. The dense vegetation that covers the mountains extends to the narrow beach which constitutes the pass." (Ibid., p. 183.)

LIMITED TEHUANTEPEC THEORY

ZARAHEMLA: ". . . this 'limited Tehuantepec' theory . . . is in agreement with a statement of Joseph Smith—i.e., the asserted translator of the Book of Mormon from ancient records—that the city of Zarahemla, which was in the 'land southward,' was located in Central America. It should also be noted that this restriction of the Book of Mormon area to the central part of the New World does not rule out the possibility that the Book of Mormon peoples, before the end of the account, established settlements also in parts of North and South America outside this area." (Jakeman, *Discovering the Past*, p. 83.)

GENERAL: "But the seas bounding the 'Tehuantepec' area of central and southern Mexico and northern Central America fully meet the requirements of the account's internal geography as to the position of *its* seas (i.e., in this view the Gulf of Mexico and Caribbean Sea constitute the general 'east sea' and the Pacific Ocean, of course, the general 'west sea,' with the Bay of Campeche or southernmost part of the Gulf of Mexico the local 'sea south' which seem to have bounded the region of the 'small neck of land'). This area also meets all the other major requirements of the physical geography of the Book of Mormon, such as that of general forestation, wet tropical or subtropical climate, abundance of 'all manner of wild animals . . . of the forest' (Alma 22:31; Ether 10:19), and rich mineral deposits (gold, silver, and other ores frequently mentioned), in addition to the regional topographic and hydrographic features previously dealt with, such as the mountainous highland region in the southern part of the land-southward division, the important river Sidon flowing northward from this southern highland through the center of the lower northern part of the 'land southward,' and the region of lakes in the northern part of the 'land northward.' This 'Tehuantepec' area is therefore now accepted by nearly all students of the geography of the Book of Mormon as the area of that account, at least on the basis of agreements in physical geography." (Ibid., p. 84.)

YUCATAN THEORY

NARROW NECK OF LAND: The face of the Yucatan Peninsula is much too wide to be considered a narrow neck of land; therefore, it is proposed that at the time of the Nephite occupation of those lands, there were arms of the

NORTH AMERICA

SOUTH AMERICA

COMPARATIVE CHART OF GEOGRAPHICAL THEORIES

Equator

Area shown on map is 5,000 ft. (or higher) above sea level

------- indicates present coast line

Land of Nephi

Land of First Inheritance

Narrow Neck of Land

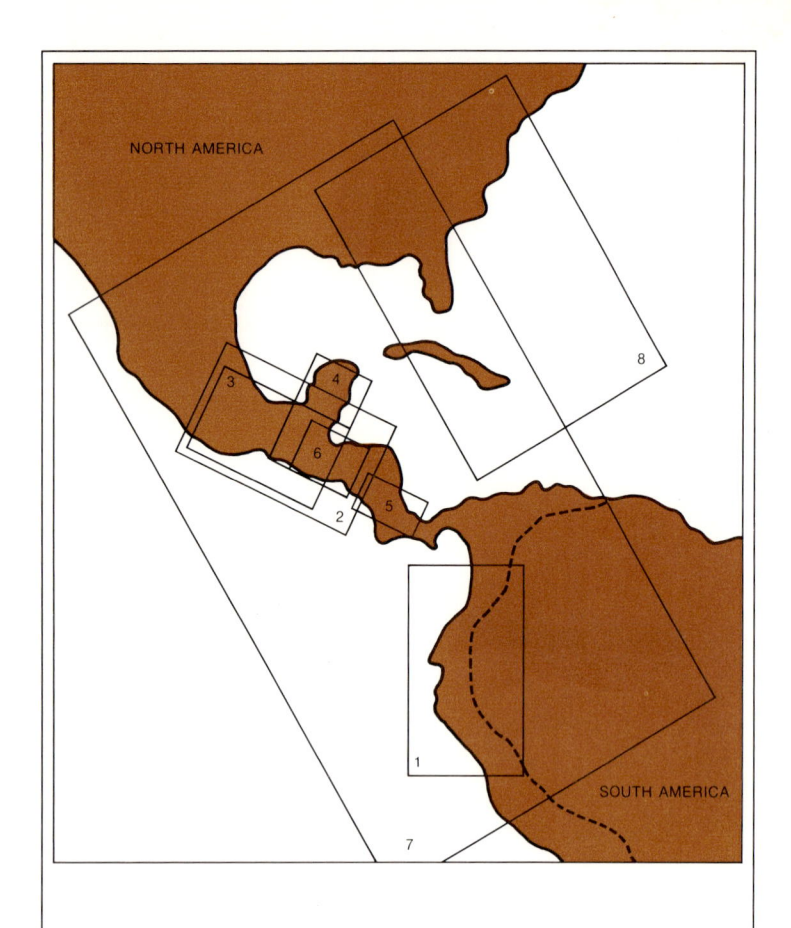

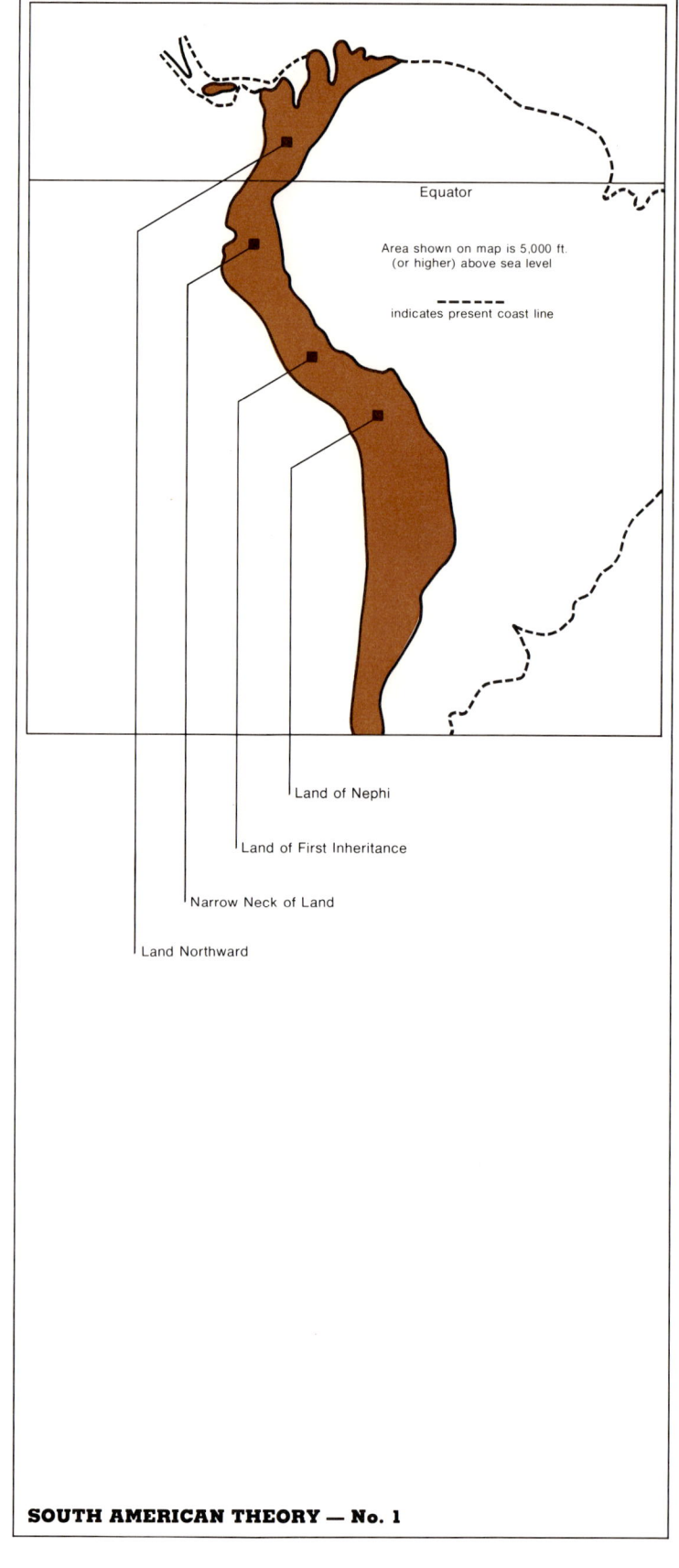

Land Northward

SOUTH AMERICAN THEORY — No. 1

THE WORLD OF THE BOOK OF MORMON

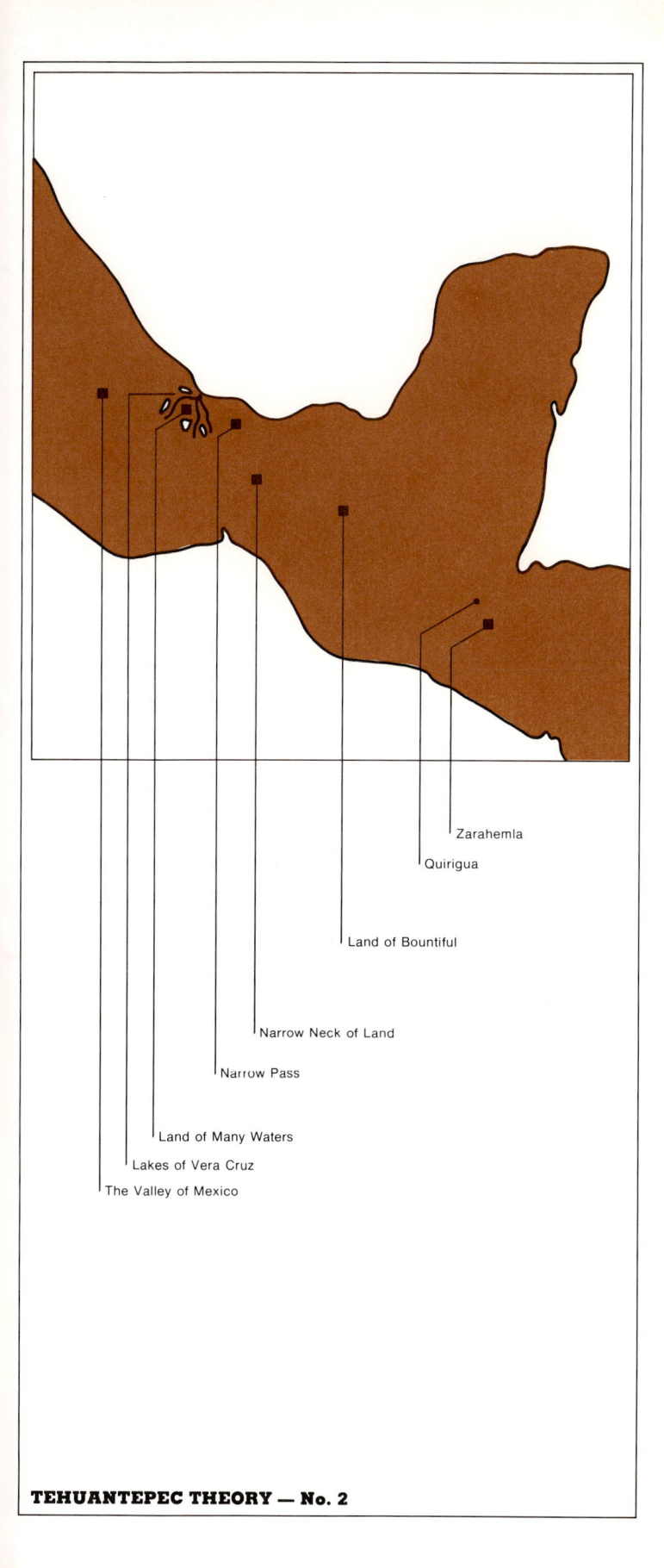

TEHUANTEPEC THEORY — No. 2

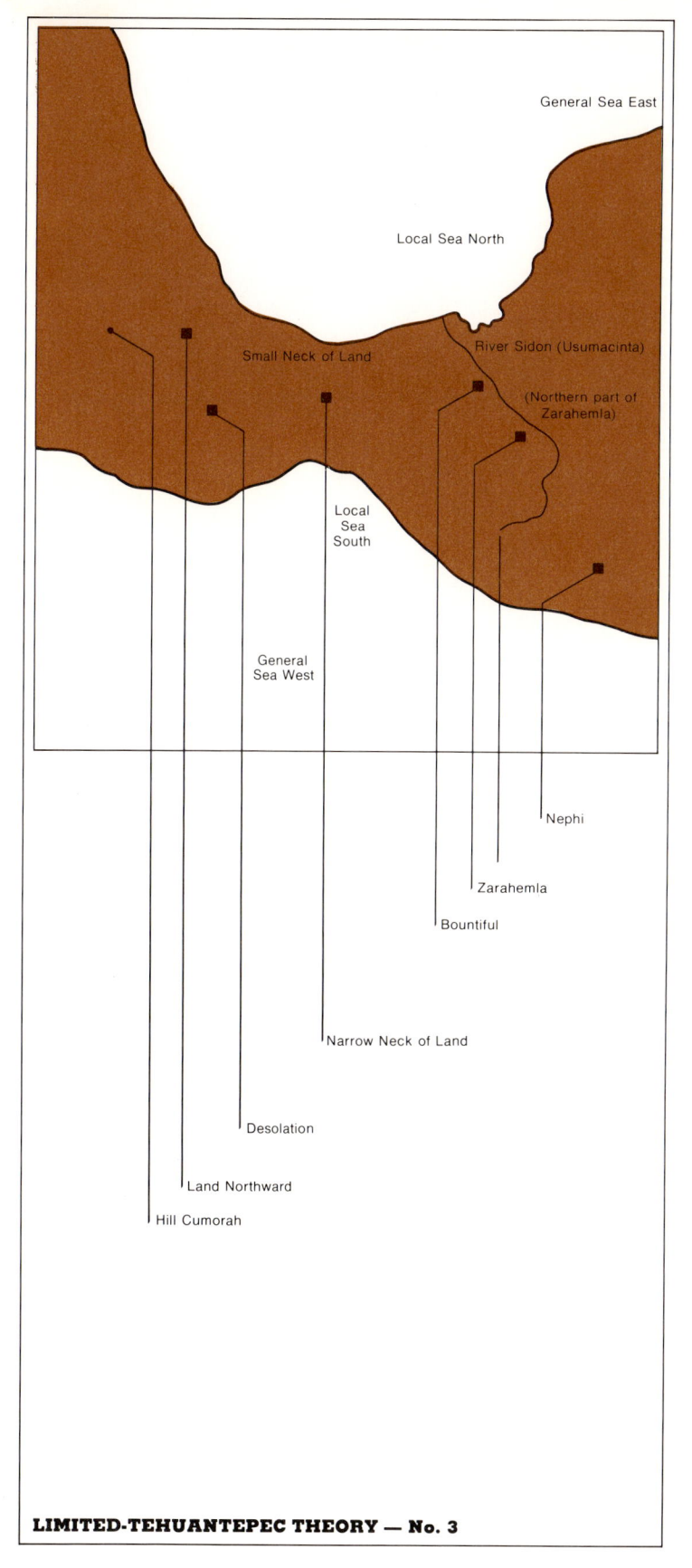

- Zarahemla
- Quirigua
- Land of Bountiful
- Narrow Neck of Land
- Narrow Pass
- Land of Many Waters
- Lakes of Vera Cruz
- The Valley of Mexico

LIMITED-TEHUANTEPEC THEORY — No. 3

- General Sea East
- Local Sea North
- Small Neck of Land
- River Sidon (Usumacinta)
- (Northern part of Zarahemla)
- Local Sea South
- General Sea West
- Nephi
- Zarahemla
- Bountiful
- Narrow Neck of Land
- Desolation
- Land Northward
- Hill Cumorah

THEORIES ON THE BOOK OF MORMON GEOGRAPHY 31

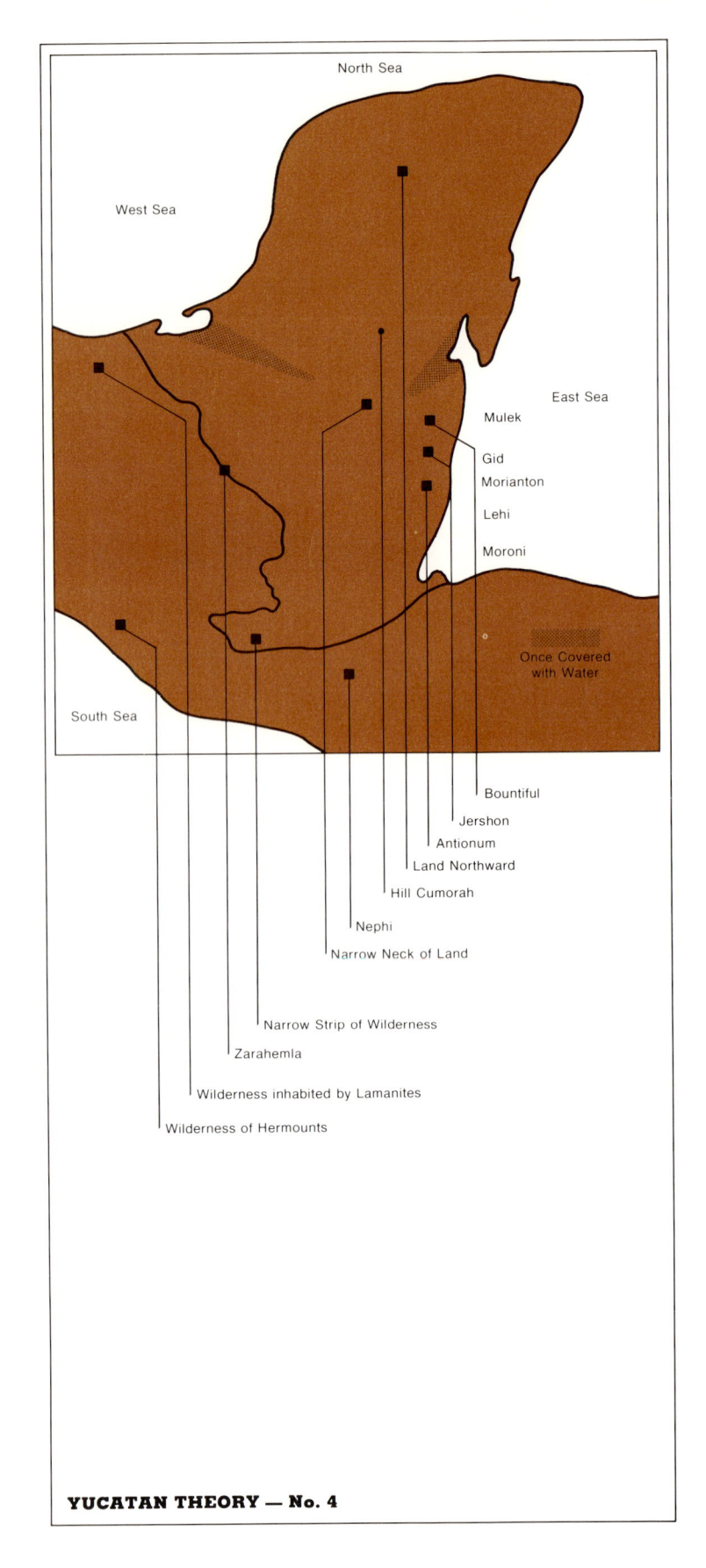

YUCATAN THEORY — No. 4

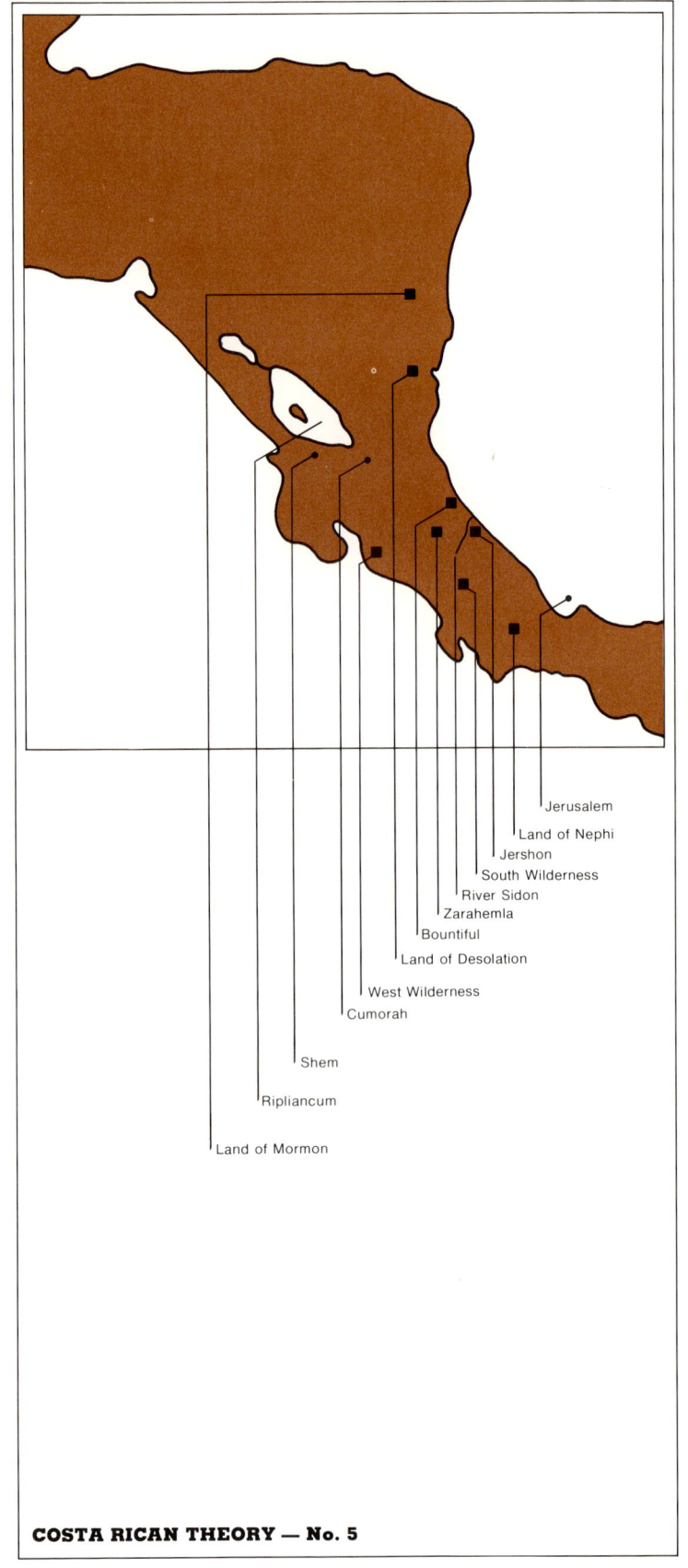

Map labels:
- North Sea
- West Sea
- East Sea
- South Sea
- Mulek
- Gid
- Morianton
- Lehi
- Moroni
- Once Covered with Water
- Bountiful
- Jershon
- Antionum
- Land Northward
- Hill Cumorah
- Nephi
- Narrow Neck of Land
- Narrow Strip of Wilderness
- Zarahemla
- Wilderness inhabited by Lamanites
- Wilderness of Hermounts

COSTA RICAN THEORY — No. 5

Map labels:
- Jerusalem
- Land of Nephi
- Jershon
- South Wilderness
- River Sidon
- Zarahemla
- Bountiful
- Land of Desolation
- West Wilderness
- Cumorah
- Shem
- Ripliancum
- Land of Mormon

32 THE WORLD OF THE BOOK OF MORMON

sea that reached inland, one from the Laguna de Terminos on the west and the other from the Chetumal Bay, probably following the Hondo River. Both of these areas are less than fifty feet above sea level. The proposal is that during and after the Nephite occupation the heavy rains washed the topsoil off the farmlands and then later abandoned lands into these two rivers, and they gradually filled with silt until today the Chetumal Bay and the Laguna de Terminos are only small inlets and not long arms of the sea, as they were before the Peten region of Guatemala or the Land Bountiful.

COSTA RICAN THEORY

EXPLANATION OF MAP: "The narrow strip of wilderness is a high, abrupt, narrow range of mountains extending from the head of the river Sidon to the sea. It was called the south, also the east wilderness. (Alma 50:7, 9-11.) I call it the mysterious wilderness. It is a continuation of the west wilderness. The two of them make the boundary line between the lands of Nephi and Zarahemla. (Alma 22:27.) The land Bountiful is the north and northwest part of Zarahemla. The west wilderness along the panhandle of the land of Nephi was sometimes called Bountiful. (Alma 22:31-33.) The land of Zarahemla included all the land between Nephi and the land Desolation. The name Bountiful disappears after the coming of the Savior. The small square of Bountiful, on the east sea, is the land of Jershon, which was given to the converted Lamanites and Zoramites." (Alma 27: 22; 35:1-6.) (Stout, *Harmony in Book of Mormon Geography,* p. 14.)

"The Narrow Pass was in the land of Bountiful near the land of Desolation. (Alma 52:9). There seem to be two of them, one on the west and the one on the east. (Alma 50:34, Mormon 3:5.) Joining Bountiful on the north is the land of Desolation. (Alma 22:31-33.)" (Ibid., p. 14.)

CONCLUSION: The author seems to base his conclusions on the internal description of the geography of the Book of Mormon lands and correlates them with present-day maps. External evidences such as archaeology are not used to any great degree to support his claims.

SOUTHERN YUCATAN THEORY

NARROW NECK OF LAND: "The narrow neck of land separated the Nephites and the Lamanites. On the north it was 'a day and a half's journey for a Nephite on the line Bountiful and the land Desolation' (Alma 22:32) and on the south it was 'a day's journey for a Nephite' (Helaman 4:7) on the line of fortification on the south border of the land of Bountiful. Hence the neck of land was probably 210 miles on the north and 140 miles wide on the south. The journey could have been made by horses and/or chariots pony express style on a road running the width of the neck of land. The narrow neck of land was probably located immediately south of the Yucatan Peninsula and during Book of Mormon times was lower and therefore narrower. Sea terraces and reefs above the present day sea level and the building up of the Pacific coastal plain in Guatemala support this claim." (Keith Christensen, unpublished paper.)

NARROW PASS: "A narrow pass (Alma 52:9) transversed the narrow neck of land diagonally and led into the land northward from the east sea on the south to the west sea on the north. (Alma 50:34.) The elevations of the mountains in this region would make it difficult to go through without a passage and furthermore the narrow neck of land had to be sufficiently rugged to make a pass meaningful. A natural pass does run the length of this area from the east side to the west side." (Ibid., p. 22.)

RIVER SIDON: "The Ulua River of Guatemala that runs northward through Mexico fits the description given of the River Sidon in the Book of Mormon." (Ibid., p. 23.)

JERUSALEM: "A small town in El Salvador called Jerusalé closely resembles the Book of Mormon town of Jerusalem that was destroyed at the time of Christ's crucifixion by being sunk into the sea. Geological Survey Bulletin No. 1034, describing the area, states that several of the lakes have been formed in part by the collapse of the earth." (Ibid., p. 23.)

NEW YORK—PANAMA THEORY

JAREDITES: "The Jaredites, on their journey to the land of promise from the Tower of Babel, probably traveled 'eastward across the central part of Asia' to the Pacific where they built barges. The eastward flowing ocean currents north of the equator carried them to the shores of Mexico or Central America. 'The Jaredite people lived on the North American continent approximately 1800 years while South America was designated as a hunting ground during that time. (Ether 10:19.) Their extinction resulted from a series of great battles fought in New York near the waters of Ripliancum 'which Orson Pratt has suggested is Lake Ontario.'" (Dixon, *Just One Cumorah,* pp. 18-29.)

LAND OF NEPHI: The Land of Nephi included Bolivia, Peru, Ecuador, and the northern half of Chile based on the above revelation of their landing point and the internal account of their travels. The center of civilization was probably located near the region of Lake Titicaca. The ruins of Tiahuanco near this lake are some of the oldest and most extensive in South America, estimated to be 2,500 years old. (Ibid., pp. 44-46.)

LAND OF ZARAHEMLA: The Land of Zarahemla was in South America (Alma 22:32), which would put it north of the Land of Nephi (Alma 50:7-11) in northern Colombia near Panama. (Dixon, *op. cit.,* p. 59). The ruins of an ancient city located 600 miles up the Magdalene River near a prominent hill about 1,000 feet high on the east side of the river fit Alma's description of the ancient city of Zarahemla. (Ibid., p. 65.)

NARROW NECK OF LAND: The Isthmus of Panama is the narrow neck of land. "There is no other spot on the Western Hemisphere that fits the description." (Ibid., p. 62.)

LAND BOUNTIFUL: "The Land Bountiful was north of Zarahemla (Helaman 5:14-16) and was the region most densely populated in all Book of Mormon history. Its southernmost boundary was the line of fortification of Moronihah (Helaman 4:6-11), which was near the narrowest point of the Isthmus. From here, Bountiful extended north and westward to the

Thousands of arrowheads like the above have been found in North and South America, silent testimonies to the existence of large groups of people who warred with one another many ages ago.

Isthmus of Tehuantepec over a land of sunken cities and much higher terrain. The terrain has been vastly changed because of the cataclysmic destruction at the time of the crucifixion of Christ. Some archaeologists say that there are several cities buried in the waters between the Peninsula of Yucatan and the Canal Zone and that some can be seen by plane when the weather is calm and the water quiet and smooth." (Ibid., pp. 73-74.)

LAND OF DESOLATION: "The land of Desolation begins at about the Isthmus of Tehuantepec and reached up into parts of the United States, based upon the remains of cement buildings, canals to convey water or irrigate, and the scarcity of timber in that area which was once used extensively by the Jaredites." (Ibid., p. 78.)

HILL CUMORAH: "The Hill Cumorah was and is located in New York. The early Church leaders supported this claim; no president of the Church has stated otherwise. New York is 'a land of many waters, rivers and fountains.' (Mormon 6:4.) Remains of fortified hills, numerous bones, bushels of stone axes and flint arrowheads have been found in western New York." (Ibid., pp. 136-39.)

INTERNAL GEOGRAPHY

NEPHITE LANDS: The principal Nephite lands were in what is now Central America, according to Joseph Smith. "They [Nephites] lived about the Narrow Neck of Land, which now embraces Central America. . . ." (*Times & Seasons*, vol. 3, p. 915.) Hence the "land southward" was north of what is now the Isthmus of Panama. (Hammond, *Geography of the Book of Mormon*, p. 4.)

NARROW NECK OF LAND: "Bountiful is this narrow neck of land being about 45 miles east and west on its north line, if we assume that a Nephite's ordinary day's journey was 30 miles." (Ibid., p. 6.)

RIVER SIDON: The Usumacinta River, with headwaters in Guatemala, flows northerly through Southern Mexico and empties into the Gulf of Mexico. It could be a modification of the River Sidon because of its general course and length. (Ibid., p. 12.)

ZARAHEMLA: It seems that the city of Zarahemla was within Guatemala, Honduras, or Yucatan because all of those countries are within the tropics and subject to "fevers, which at some seasons of the year were very frequent in the land." (Alma 46:40.) (Ibid., p. 36.)

DESTRUCTION: "The geography of what is now Central America must have been greatly changed by that 'great and terrible destruction of the land' (3 Nephi 3:5-23), as well as other parts of North and South America. The River Sidon and the 'narrow neck of land' appear to have remained as they were before this great event." (Hammond, *op. cit.*, p. 62.)

HILL CUMORAH: The New York Hill Cumorah is not the Hill Cumorah of the Nephites. It is simply the hill where Moroni hid the plates and the Urim and Thummim which he later gave to Joseph Smith. (Ibid., p. 89.) "No amount of juggling of the Book of Mormon text can place the hill Ramah-Cumorah in what is now New York state. It was somewhere in what is now Central America." (Ibid., p. 90.) The distance to New York is too great; there are other lands of many waters in North America; the Zelph incident as correctly quoted in the 1904 edition of the *Documentary History of the Church* has nothing to do with the Nephites or the Hill Cumorah; and the New York theory "disrupts and confuses the entire concept of the Book of Mormon geography." (Ibid., p. 72.)

PRE-COLUMBIAN CULTURES AND RUINS

Some travelers are startled to see the magnificent grandeur of the ruins of ancient America and to find that they compare favorably with the great cultures of ancient Rome and Greece. As the author has viewed the ancient structures in Central and South America over the past two decades, he has been awed at the engineering and artistic accomplishments of the pre-Columbian Americans.

The beginning of human life on the American continents has been given various dates. Archaeologists call the time period that would include the first inhabitants (3000 B.C. and earlier) the Archaic period.

The pre-Classic period, which dates from 2000 to 300 B.C., is divided into early, middle, and late periods. The early farmers of this period developed numerous food crops. Although few animals were domesticated, the farmers developed methods of irrigating their crops and produced a large variety of products, including maize.

The Classic period (A.D. 300 to 900) includes civilizations that enjoyed an aesthetic, architectural, and intellectual flowering. A series of mysterious disturbances brought the Classic period to an end.

The post-Classic period (A.D. 900 to 1520), which began in an atmosphere of confusion and lasted until the Spanish conquest, includes cultures that developed following the end of the Classic period. The people were attempting to build a new society over the breakdown of an old order by regrouping and forming new, militaristic states.

One of the major focal points of the ancient civilizations of the American Indian is in the present-day countries of Mexico, Guatemala, Honduras, and El Salvador. A modern term for this area is Mesoamerica. The other major center includes the narrow coastal region and the highlands of the middle Andes, covering most of Peru, part of Ecuador, and Bolivia. While the Andean cities were built apparently to be lived in and to give shelter, many of the structures of Mesoamerica were ceremonial centers. The soil on which the Central American native lived was more fertile than that of coastal Peru; the climate was milder; and the forests were rich in game.

The Incan empire developed within the central highlands of Peru, with Cuzco as the capital city. A well-balanced social order characterized this civilization, as well as an influential nobility and a strong religion. A network of roads kept communications open to all surrounding cities in a surprisingly efficient manner.

This study will treat both areas, starting with the ruins of Mesoamerica. Our discussion will begin with six major Mesoamerican cultures: Aztec, Mayan, Mixtec, Olmec, Toltec, and Zapotec.

AZTEC

Beneath the present-day metropolis of Mexico City are the ruins of Tenochtitlan, the ancient capital of the Aztecs. This great society began about A.D. 1300 and grew rapidly, encompassing the surrounding tribes and the neighboring cities. Young men were trained as warriors in special military colleges, resulting in the Aztecs' becoming a mighty force.

The Aztecs, who were not a closely united society as were the Incas of Peru, preferred to exist as independent tribes with no central government. The entire culture was based on a deeply theocratic philosophy. The people worshiped a number of gods and even practiced ritualistic human sacrifice. This sacrificial ceremony involved the removal of the victim's heart, because the Aztecs believed the gods needed hearts and blood to live on.

The Aztecs used cut stone blocks, volcanic rocks, and unbaked clay in constructing their buildings. Their craftsmanship is seen in ornate stone carvings, decorative buildings, iconographic signs and statues. Tenochtitlan was built upon a lake. As the city expanded, the lake was filled in with a network of canals connecting the var-

EARLY AMERICAN CIVILIZATIONS

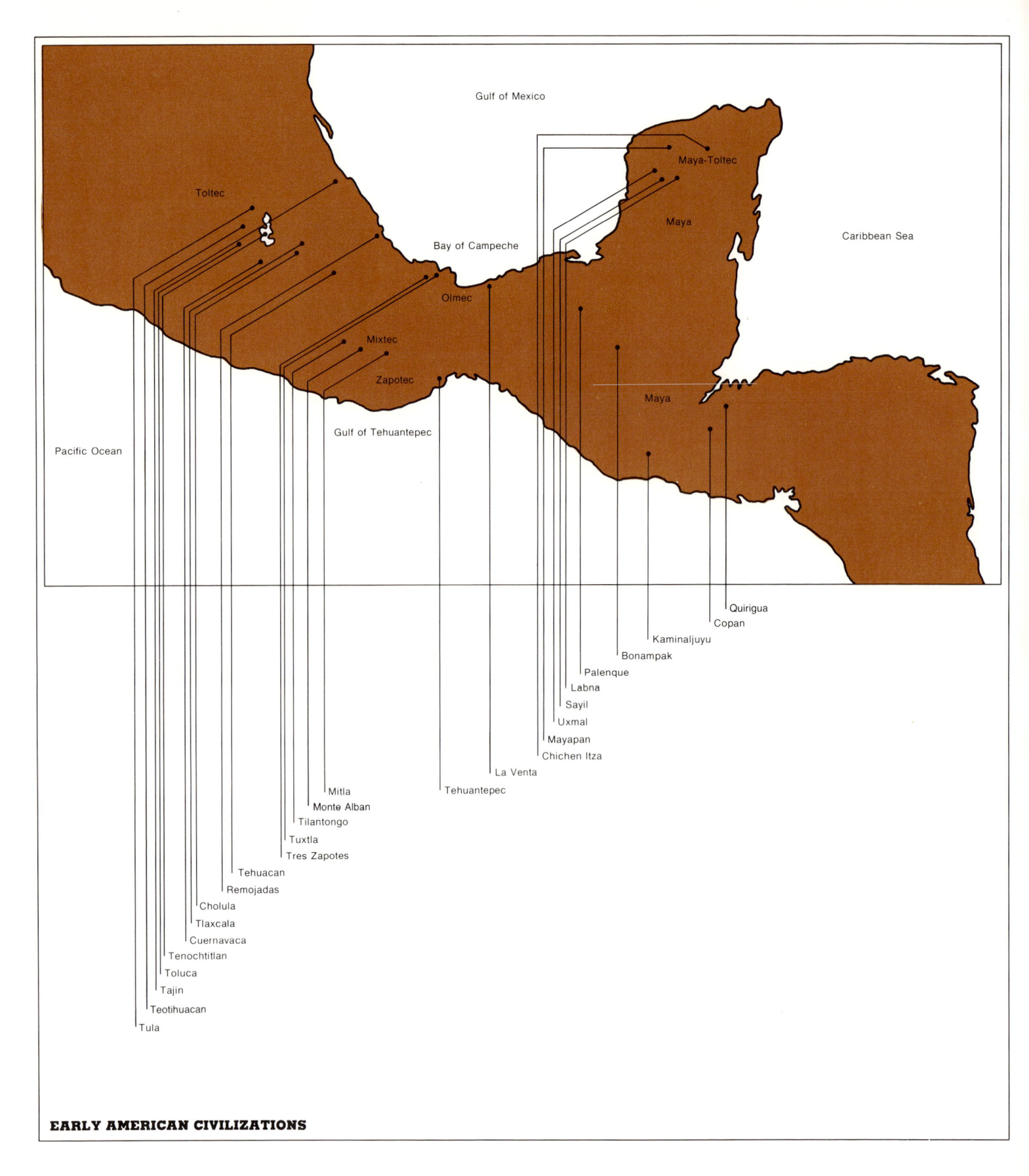

36 THE WORLD OF THE BOOK OF MORMON

ious parts of the city. The great pyramid, topped by two temples, was the main building.

The Aztecs excelled not only in crafts, but also in the arts and sciences; fine examples of jewelry, jade carvings, pottery, paintings, murals, and statuary have been found. They created a complex system of writing with drawings and conventional signs representing ideas or motion. Today only numbers, dates, and names of months and gods can be translated from these ancient hieroglyphs.

Probably the most noted of the Aztec achievements is their calendar. Begun in 1427 and finished in 1479, it is an immense monument to ancient Aztec art, astronomy, and mathematics. On the outer edge of this huge carved disc—12 feet in diameter—are eight equidistant holes into which pegs were inserted so the stone could be used as a sun dial.

MAYA

The Mayan civilization is considered by some to be the most enlightened and influential culture in all Mesoamerica. Indeed, the achievements of the Mayas in astronomy, mathematics, and hieroglyphic writings would certainly testify to their supremacy.

The Mayas were thought to have originated first in the Guatemalan highlands around 600 B.C. or earlier. They then moved to Peten, where Tikal, the largest and perhaps oldest city, was established. From there the culture expanded into Palenque, then southeast to Copan, and into the southwest. They finally settled in the Yucatan Peninsula, where they established centers at Uxmal, Chichen Itza, Calakmul, and Coba.

Scholars believe the Mayan decline began long before the Spaniards arrived. The Mayan calendar at the time of Columbus commenced on August 11, 3113 B.C. The historical significance of this date is not known. One by one, keepers of the records died, and through generations of war and struggle with the white man, many valuable histories were destroyed. The translation of the existing writings and histories (in the form of hieroglyphs and pictoglyphs) is imperfect.

From what we have learned through studying their ancient centers, the Mayan people appear to have had a strong sense of community, clean habits, and deep religious feelings. Mayan buildings were erected around courts and plazas, which became religious, governmental, educational, and trading centers. The more important leaders lived in this central area, while the common people lived on the outskirts.

Masonry plastered with pulverized limestone and finished with a facing of carefully worked stone was the primary building technique used. This building method bore two distinguishing characteristics unique to Central America: the corbeled arch and the false facade at roof level.

Religion appears to have been the motivating influence in the Mayas' lives. The nature and doctrine of their graded priesthood system has been the subject of some speculation. In certain aspects their religion was polytheistic, with most of the gods representing agricultural ideologies. The *Sacred Book of the Quiche Maya* seems to reveal, however, that the gods were symbols and that one main god, Itzamna, was the Lord of the heavens. According to this ancient book, written in Mayan with Spanish characters, there is every indication of a monotheistic belief and knowledge of baptism, immortality, and the basics of good versus evil. Ceremonies practiced by the Mayas included fasting, prayers, exorcism, abstinence, and sacrifices.

The Mayas elaborated, with great success, on the inventions and ideas of previous Middle American cultures. For example, their writing does not appear to be based on an alphabet, but rather on the use of glyphs representing ideas, words, and numbers. Their numbering system involved placing one figure above another rather than side by side. Some deduce that the Mayas developed a combination of ideographic and phonetic writing.

Mayan artisans created beautiful stone mosaics, carvings in jade, paintings, codices (pictorial records), and objects made of gold and copper. The farmers practiced an efficient method

An outstanding testimony of the high degree of civilization among the Aztecs is their calendar. This calendar stone from Mexico is covered with intricately carved symbols designating seasons and divisions of time.

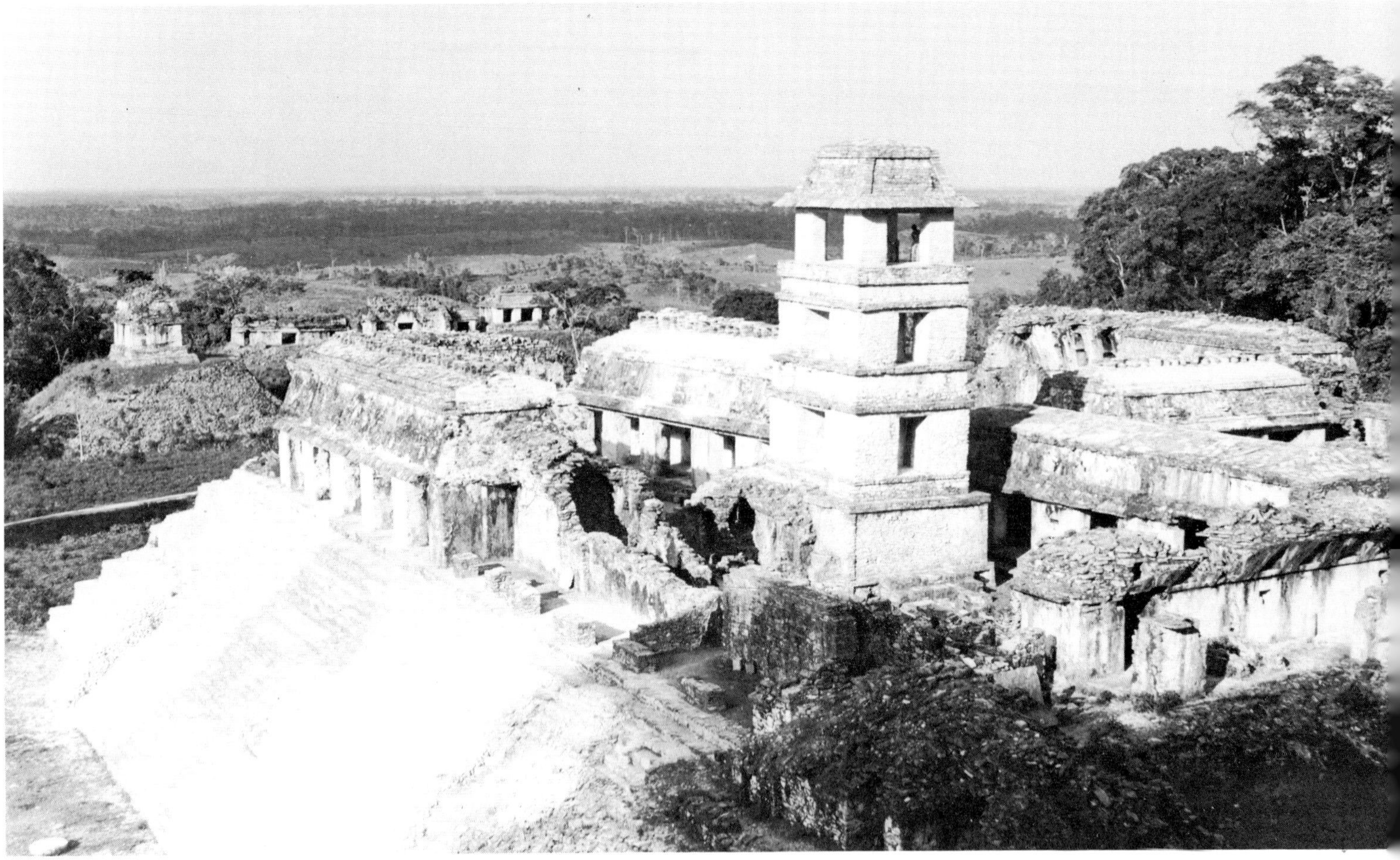

Ruins of Palenque, Mexico, thought by some scholars to have been the cradle of Mayan civilization. Pictured here is the ancient palace, actually a complex of buildings resting on a platform 3 feet high, 300 feet long, and 240 feet wide. The four-story tower is thought to have served as both an astronomical observatory and a watchtower.

of planting that entailed the burning of plant overgrowth and then planting seeds. After two years of use the field lay fallow and the farmer repeated the process on another plot. Though corn was the principal crop, the Mayas also harvested beans, squash, cassava, tomatoes, chayote, bread nut, and sweet potato. The people seasoned their food with spices, vanilla, and chili peppers.

The class system of the Mayas was composed of slaves, lords, and royalty. A thief was made a slave to the person from whom he had stolen until he had paid for his theft. Captives of war were enslaved. A person could, however, be redeemed from slavery at birth. Slaves built the houses of the rich and tended their fields.

The dress of the Mayas was simple: the men wore a wrapped loincloth and the women wore long sacklike dresses. The rich decorated their garments. Mayan men did not have mustaches or beards. Mothers used hot cloths on the faces of their young sons and plucked any growing hair. Many a newborn baby had his head tied between two flat boards to elongate the head, and a child often had his ears, nose, and lips pierced.

MIXTEC

Mixtec means "dweller in the land of the clouds." The people of this culture came from Oaxaca in about the ninth century A.D., their culture commencing about one hundred years before this date. They were largely responsible for the rise of the city Cholula, then spread out over Middle America, south to Guatemala, and north to the Mississippi River. They took over the ruins of Monte Alban and Mitla, which eventually became the culture's religious and political center. The kingdom was subdivided into chiefdoms, each ruled loosely by a hereditary chief. There were two social classes, one comprised of nobles, priests, and merchants and the other of craftsmen and peasants.

The Mixtecs favored craftsmanship over artistry, evidenced in their beautiful ceramics (bichrome pottery—vermillion, black, or dark maroon on white), engraving, polychrome pottery, jars, tripods, zoomorphic vessels (eagles and jaguars), and metalwork. Jewelry was produced by the respousse method, and the people wore pictoral plaques, nose ornaments, rings, and necklaces. The Mixtecs, superior as goldsmiths, produced earrings and other jewelry of remarkable beauty.

Their sculpture is limited, but some seated male and female figures in green stone have been found, representing the funerary position. The temples and pyramids were simple in design, but highly decorated with such elements as stone mosaics in relief on painted backgrounds. The Mixtec religion included a host of gods, one for every occasion.

The Mixtecs loved war and through their conquests made extensive use of the conquered peoples' resources. They were advanced in calendrics, astronomy, and writing. Some of what we know of the Mixtecs is recorded on codices, carefully painted pictures that tell of their history, religion, and everyday life.

OLMEC

Flourishing from approximately 1200 B.C. to 400 B.C., the Olmec culture is often referred to as the mother culture of Middle America. Also known as the La Venta development, the Olmecs lived near the southern portion of Mexico, near Vera Cruz and Tabasco. Dating from the middle pre-Classic period, this culture is one of the earliest (if not the earliest) to develop in southeastern Mexico. Perhaps one of its most extraordinary developments was excellent religious art, which suggests that the religion centered around a jaguar and ceremonies of the priests.

The Olmecs were the first people to build large, planned religious centers that included pyramids and stepped platforms as temples and altars. The temple sites often included sacrificial altars, stelae of various sizes, colossal stone carvings, and sculptured panels, walls, and temple mounds. An interesting comparison can be made between the hieroglyphs and calendrical systems of the Olmecs of La Venta and those of the early Mayan cultures.

The Olmecs' impressive art is considered the most exquisite in Middle America. The people were masters in carving and left an excellent collection of sculptured art in round terracotta figurines and jade statuettes, as well as decorated pottery and masks.

Probably the most fascinating Olmec relics are massive stone heads more than five feet high, carved in hard basalt stone. Many of the basalt heads appear to be wearing helmets. These heads, weighing up to twenty tons, are a source of mystery, since no one knows how the Olmecs transported such large stones to their present site. The source of the stone is not in the immediate area.

TOLTEC

One of the cultures greatly influenced by the Mayas was the Toltec civilization. About A.D. 900 the Toltecs conquered the Mayas and became another forerunner of the high cultures from the Valley of Mexico.

They were a wealthy people, masters of art, medicine, calendrics, engineering, and carving, and lovers of sports, as evidenced by their ball courts and massive caryatids. Although wealthy, the people seemed to be more interested in a well-balanced everyday existence than an excessive, luxurious life.

The Toltecs were the builders of the classic pyramid El Castillo, or Temple, of the god Kukulcan in Chichen Itza. The pyramid's terraces recede in size as they move upward, forming a seventy-five-foot building. A variety of roofs were constructed on the Toltec buildings, among them beam and mortar, thatched, and Mayan corbel vaulting.

Evidences of Toltec artistry can still be found on the walls of pyramids in the capital city, Tula, where archaeologists have unearthed magnificent frescoes of jaguars and vultures feed-

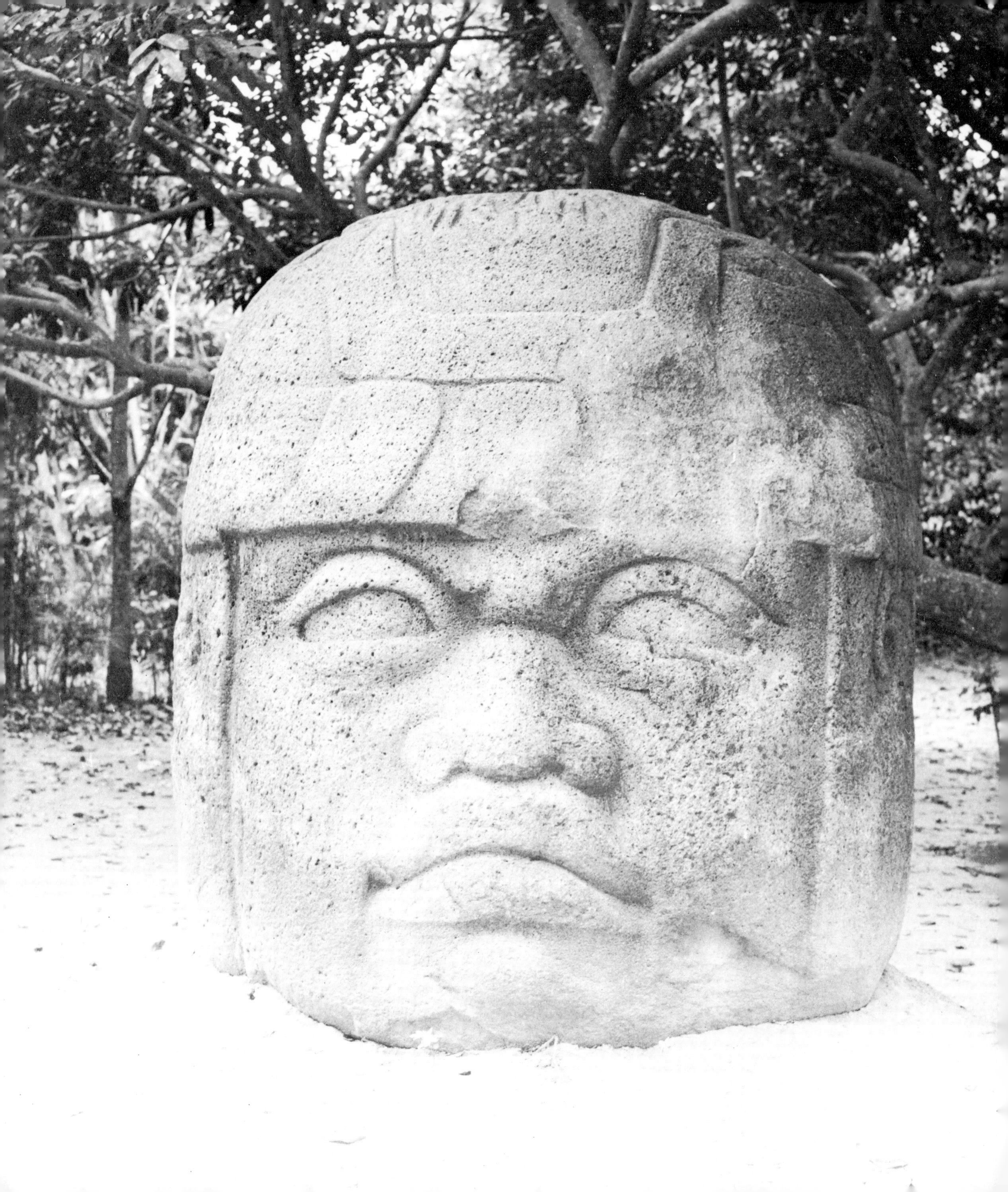

ing on human hearts. The cities had sunken plazas and courts, walls of carved serpents, and altars decorated with skull motifs and images of the plumed serpent Quetzalcoatl.

The Mayan influence is evident in the religion of the Toltecs. Mayan priests helped in the design of the temples, and the Toltecs abstracted Mayan art, imagery, ceremony, writing, and disease cures. The high priest of Yucatan was supported by gifts from the people, and in turn he appointed other priests from the lords' sons.

The Toltecs were a warlike race who had a catalytic effect upon their neighbors, both in culture and in politics. The Toltec laws were strict and just; nevertheless, civil strife was the peoples' downfall. Because of internal decay, they were forced south by their enemies to the central part of Mexico.

ZAPOTEC

High in the valleys of Oaxaca, Ejutla, Tlacolula, and Zimatlan are the great cities of Monte Alban and Mitla, where the mighty Zapotec culture began during the second century B.C. The power and influence of this culture eventually spread from the Gulf of Mexico to the shores of the Pacific Ocean.

The mountains, a primary influence on the lives of the people, forced them to remain peaceful and remote, but apparently were no hindrance to the building of huge pyramidlike temples where priests carried out religious ceremonies. The Zapotecs were marvelous engineers, scraping and leveling hills and building huge stone monuments, circular pillars, wide and numerous steps, and impressive bas-relief figures.

They were also skilled in arts and crafts, as evidenced by the many sizes, shapes, and colors in their pottery, as well as in unusual funerary urns. These terra cotta urns, elaborately decorated, were molded in the shape of human figures bearing lifelike facial expressions. Tomb walls were covered with carved relief panels and elaborate frescoes. Feathers and ornaments were commonly used.

Opposite: One of the huge stone heads carved in basalt by the Olmecs, the oldest known culture in Central America. Many of these heads are over five feet high, and they weigh up to twenty tons. *Below:* A Zapotec deity on a clay urn. The Zapotecs were skilled in crafts and created pottery in many different sizes, shapes, and colors.

ANCIENT CIVILIZATIONS IN MEXICO

Mexico is a land rich in history. The Aztecs and Mayas once dwelt there, as did many other ancient cultures. According to legend, the Aztec Indians entered the Valley of Mexico in the 1320s and were told they must establish a city where they saw an eagle perched on a cactus, clutching a snake in its talons. When an eagle fitting this description was found, it was in the middle of a lake. This did not deter the Aztecs from building up the earth out of the water and making a city called Tenochtitlan (now Mexico City). When the Spanish conquerors came in the 1500s, they found a beautiful city with sixty thousand homes and over three hundred thousand people.

The crumbled remains of ancient pyramids and temples are mute evidence of the days when the Aztec, Mayan, and other civilizations flourished in Mexico. Spanish-style cathedrals and other public structures are reminiscent of the days when the Spaniards conquered this country and introduced a more modern civilization. Most Mexicans have both Spanish and Indian ancestors.

CHICHEN ITZA

Seventy miles east of Merida, Yucatan, in the extreme eastern part of Mexico, is the large pre-Columbian city of Chichen Itza. Combining the Mayan and Toltec styles, this complex of buildings indicates the existence of at least two great periods of development. Some researchers believe it was inhabited as early as the fifth century A.D., but we know it was inhabited once in the late Classic period, from A.D. 650 to A.D. 900, and also once during the later Toltec period. Many of the structures built during the early period were altered for use by later inhabitants, while other dwellings were erected over the older structures.

The temple and other buildings appear to have been placed randomly. Archaeological workers have found among these buildings a sacred well called a cenote from which many articles have been extracted, including sacrificial offerings. Sometimes these sacrifices were human; jewelry, pottery, and other valuable possessions were also used.

The Castillo, or temple, of Kukulcan is perhaps the best known and most photographed pre-Columbian temple in Central America or Mexico. Located near the center of the complex, this ziggurat temple has four stairways with 91 steps on each side leading to the top of the pyramid. The theory that the steps represent the days of the year seems plausible, since adding the top step to the side steps brings the total number of steps to 365.

At the top of the temple is a small building believed to have been used for religious purposes. The entrance to this edifice is divided by two columns, each representing a serpent's head facing down. An effigy of a reclining figure, or a chacmol, was found at the bottom of the main stairway. In one room inside the temple is a red painted jaguar with the spots represented by jade discs. The present temple of Kuculcan was built over another temple that has been uncovered through tunneled excavation. Both structures are still somewhat intact.

Another building situated amid the random complex is the Caracol, a dome-shaped tower that may have been used for astronomical purposes. An interior spiral staircase, called a snail-shell stairway, appears to have been built in a series of succeeding periods. The doors and windows were constructed so that the equinoxes and solstices could be readily observed.

The people of Chichen Itza appear to have been great fans of a popular ancient Mexican ball game. The ball court is probably the largest yet discovered, measuring 272 feet long and 199 feet wide, with walls 27 feet high. Scholars have decided that the game was played by knocking a rubber ball through two donutlike stone rings placed midway on the upper part of the two walls of the court. The participants were apparently involved in a ritualistic religious

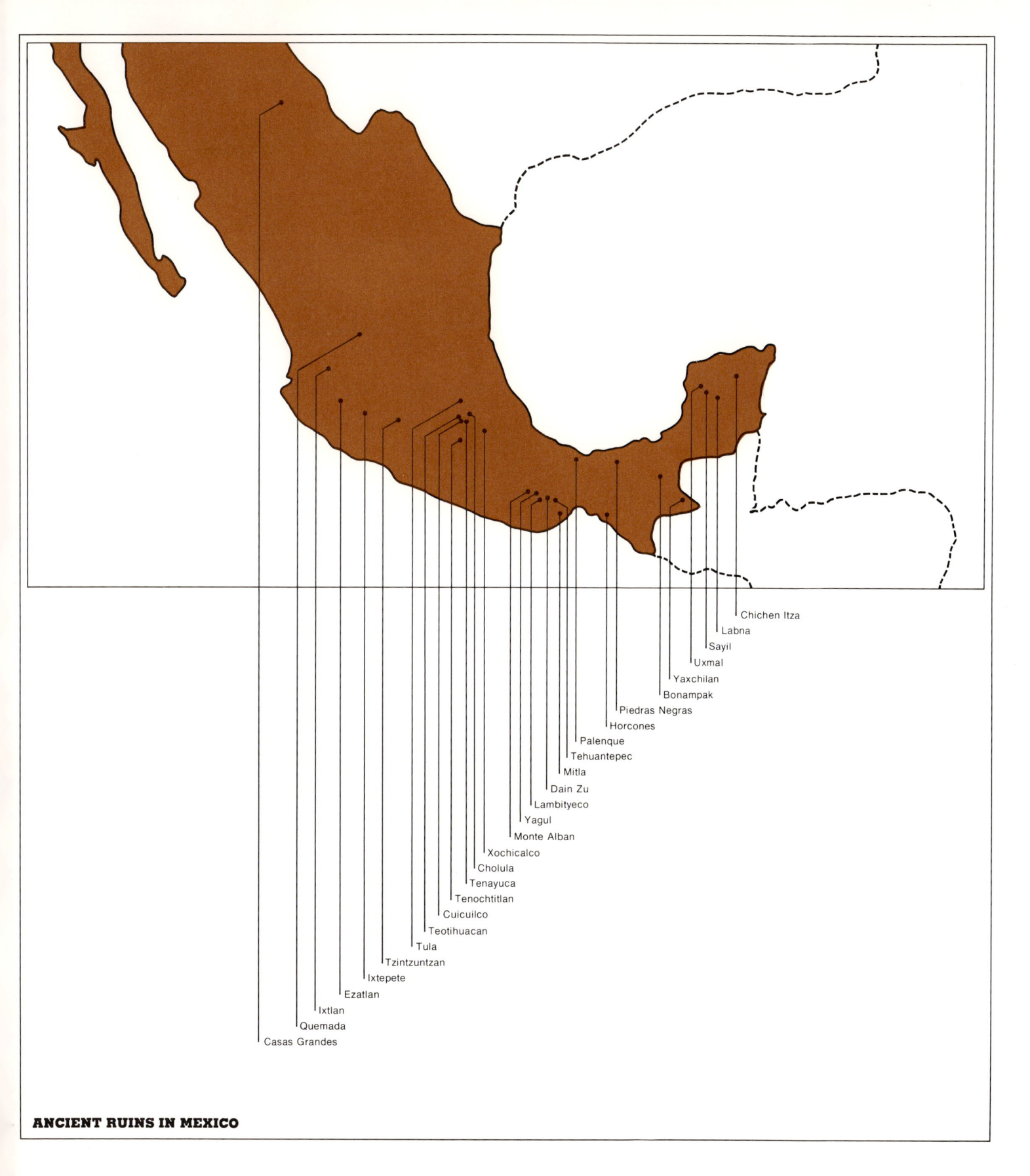

Chichen Itza
Labna
Sayil
Uxmal
Yaxchilan
Bonampak
Piedras Negras
Horcones
Palenque
Tehuantepec
Mitla
Dain Zu
Lambityeco
Yagul
Monte Alban
Xochicalco
Cholula
Tenayuca
Tenochtitlan
Cuicuilco
Teotihuacan
Tula
Tzintzuntzan
Ixtepete
Ezatlan
Ixtlan
Quemada
Casas Grandes

ANCIENT RUINS IN MEXICO

ANCIENT CIVILIZATIONS IN MEXICO 43

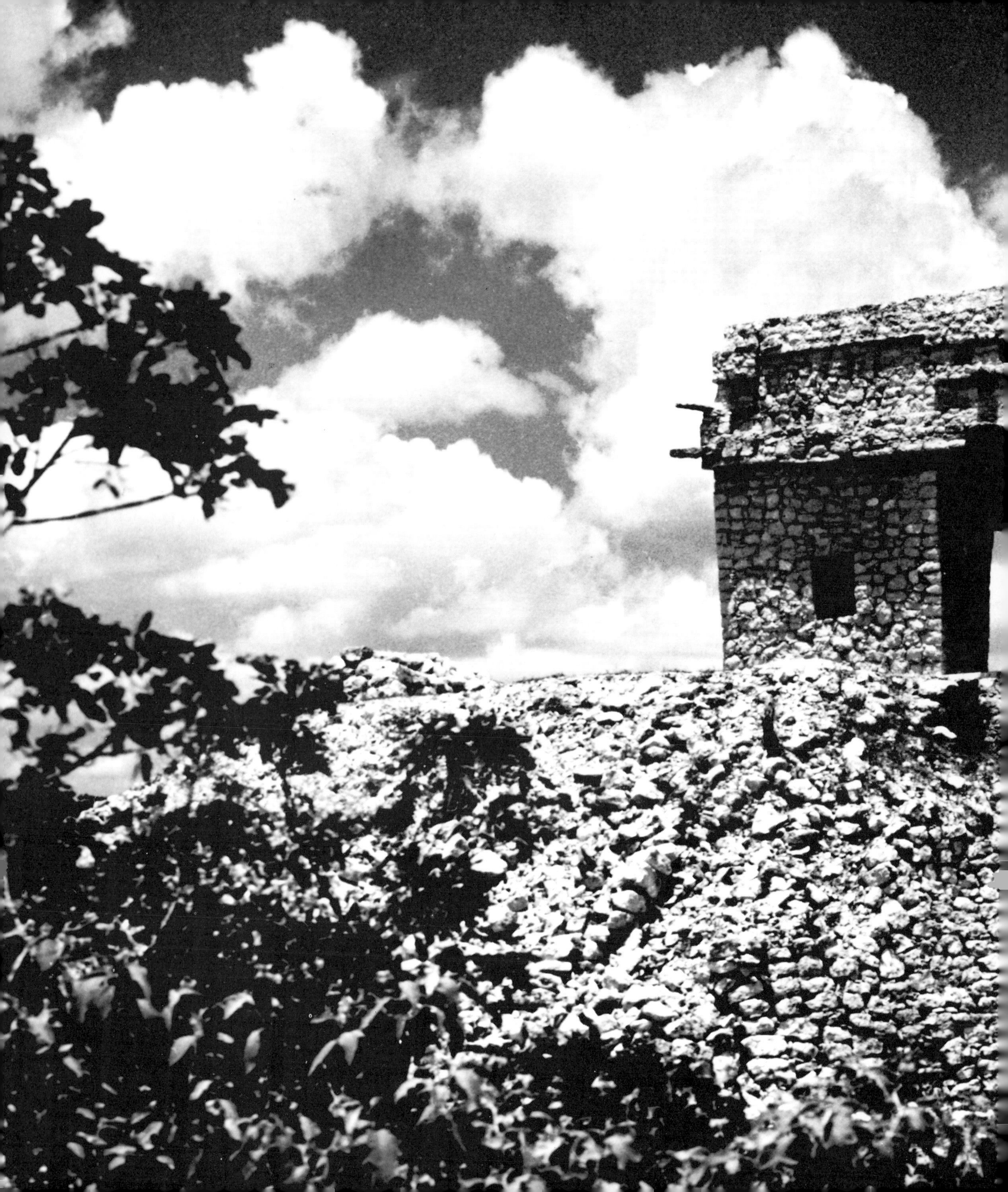

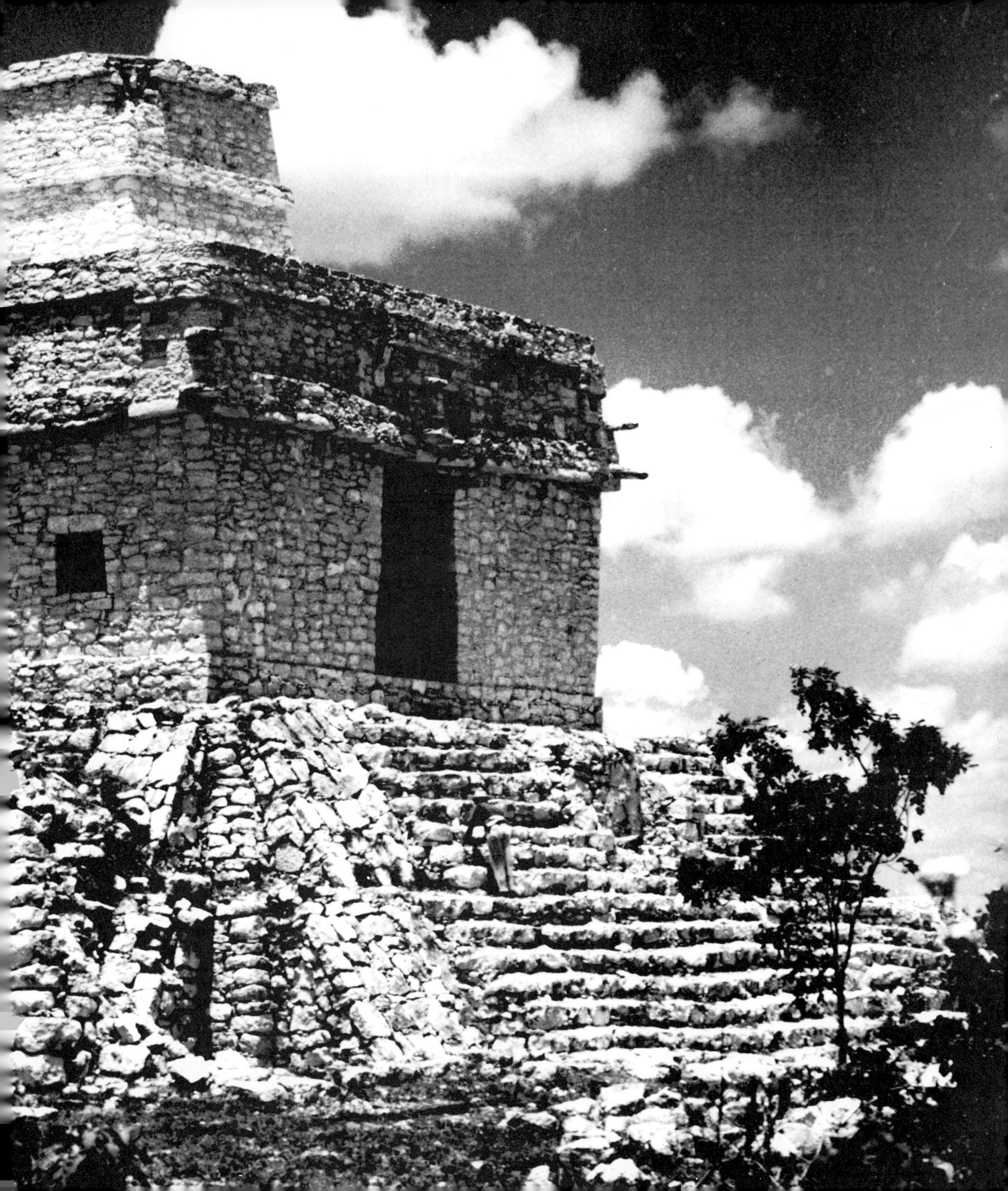

ceremony, for some legends and sculptured artifacts reveal decapitated players. At either end is a small temple, with extensive bas-reliefs of Toltec life in the buildings to the north.

The Mayan and Toltec civilizations that once used these structures left abruptly and mysteriously; however, their contributions are numerous, and the study of their civilization is fascinating.

CHOLULA

Near Puebla, Mexico, is the pyramid with the largest base in the world. The 187-foot-high pyramid of Cholula, though not as tall as the pyramid of Cheops (King of Egypt) or the Pyramid of the Sun in Mexico City, is almost twice as long as either with a base of 44 acres. The early Spanish destroyed most of the ancient structure when they used the materials to build Puebla.

Through excavations, archaeologists have discovered that the pyramid was constructed perhaps seven times, one layer over the other, with the earliest erected around 2000 B.C. A Catholic church has been built atop the pyramid. Cholula is noted for its intricate system of passages, one of which was the burial section, apart from the main structure.

West of Cholula is the beautiful extinct volcano Popocatepetl, which covered much of the surrounding countryside with lava. The pyramid of Cholula is indeed a magnificent sight and is perhaps best described by the term given to it by people of the region: *Tlachi-hualtepetl*, which means "Man-made Mountains."

CUICUILCO

A high standard of culture existed in the pre-Classic era in the southern end of the Valley of Mexico, centered at Cuicuilco, a city supported by agriculture, pottery making, and weaving. It is here that some of the first monuments on the American continent were erected.

The oldest is the pyramid of Cuicuilco, a giant oval made of earth and stone. Near the time of the birth of

Preceding pages: Dzibilchaltun, one of the largest Mayan cities yet excavated, covers over twenty square miles. It was evidently a major trade center and may have been populated as early as 2000 B.C. *Above:* The temple of Kukulcan, in Chichen Itza, has on each of its four sides 91 steps leading to the top of the pyramid, where sits a small building believed to have been used for religious purposes. Since the total number of steps after adding the top one equals 365, it is theorized that they represent the days of the year.

46 THE WORLD OF THE BOOK OF MORMON

Christ, this monument was built near the outskirts of what is now Mexico City. The pyramid is a truncated cone, 80 feet high and 389 feet in diameter, with the top four sections connected by a ramp and stairway. Uncut stones were placed one on top of the other without mortar. The building was initially composed of only two sections, with others added later. Today it bears only a general resemblance to its original form. It has been impossible for archaeologists to authenticate it exactly, since it was in such a crumbled condition when discovered. Around the central buildings were other structures of smaller dimensions. These are the first ceremonial complexes found among the later pre-Columbian monumental cities. Also unearthed in the temple were the remains of a square, thatch-roof altar attesting to ancient religious practices here.

Sometime before the Christian era, the city of Cuicuilco was destroyed by volcano. The lava of Zitle, although from a small volcano, not only covered this entire city but also a vast region to the south and west of the Valley of Mexico (known today as the Pedregal, or "Stony Ground"). The only remains from this catastrophe are found at nearby Copilco. Imprints of men and dogs indicate that the victims were probably caught by surprise.

DZIBILCHALTUN

In 1956 E. Wyllys Andrews began excavating the ruins of what may have been the largest Mayan city. North of the city of Merida, Yucatan, lie the ruins of the great city Dzibilchaltun, covering more than twenty square miles. Archaeologists have been able to determine that the earliest habitation of this city may have been about 2000 B.C., and that the city was continually inhabited until the Spanish conquest.

Dzibilchaltun was the center of a populous urban area and a main trade center for the entire region—perhaps even for cities of other empires. Discarded and broken pottery from several periods in Mayan civilization have been found in the bottom of a large well (cenote) at the center of the city. The pottery resembles that of Oxhintok and Tzakol. Plazas and patios were also found in the ruins, with decorative motifs and murals of stucco adorning the walls. Tulane University and the National Geographic Society are presently excavating this site.

EL TAJIN

In Veracruz is one of the best known temples in Mexico, the Temple of Niches, located just a few kilometers from the Gulf of Mexico. Found among the ruins of El Tajin, the temple represents one of a compact group of temples, buildings, and palaces that reveal cultural influences from Teotihuacan, Maya, and Oaxaca.

The temple, which is about 36 meters wide on each side and 25 meters high, is constructed in a ziggurat fashion. Each story has an extended panel and a projecting cornice, with decorated panel and niches, or indentations. It is interesting there are 365 niches. Scholars have concluded that they were once painted red with blue frames and were used exclusively as decoration.

Also in El Tajin are other buildings called Lesser Tajin, decorated with friezes, panels, and facades. Stone carvings abound. Another unusual building is the building of the Columns, adorned with Greek crosses.

The people who inhabited El Tajin were apparently interested in sports, for several ball courts have been discovered. The walls of these courts are covered with sculptured figures, depicting various ritual scenes of an ancient religious game. They also participated in a ceremonial game called *voladores*, or "flying dancers." In this game five participants climbed to the top of a tall pole. Four of the men attached themselves to long ropes and gradually unwound themselves from the top, simulating birds in flight as they descended. The fifth person remained on top of the pole, playing a musical instrument and dancing.

KABAH

The builders of Kabah, located south of Uxmal on the Yucatan Peninsula, made extensive use of columns with capitals, decorated lintels, and groups of columns. The buildings rise on a series of artificial platforms. An archway west of the main building complex is the beginning of a highway leading to Uxmal.

One of the most famous of the buildings in Kabah is the Codz-pop, which, although in ruins, is an example of a type of architecture very different from the styles found in most Mayan cities. The Codz-pop has rooms on different levels as if it were designed with two stories. The builders must have become dissatisfied, however, because an enormous roof comb was erected where the second story was to be. The facade was decorated with masks of the ancient rain god, Chac, referred to as the hook-nosed rain god. There were originally 270 masks.

LA VENTA

Another of the oldest known communities in Mexico or Central America is the Olmec culture. Coming from San Lorenzo around 1160 B.C., the Olmecs settled in 880 B.C. at La Venta, where their cities became a great religious ceremonial center. Here the people of surrounding areas gathered to worship the plumed serpent Quetzalcoatl through (it is believed) infant sacrifice and burnt offerings. The cross was carved into stone walls five centuries before the birth of Christ.

The greatest monuments of the Olmecs are found at La Venta. Large basalt heads, some measuring ten feet in height, are believed to be depictions of Olmec lords. Their function remains a mystery, as do the engineering methods that transported these massive stones from the far-off Tuxtla Mountains to the barren land of La Venta.

Many rectangular stones found here seem to be trimmed in a twisted rope design, a motif used by the Phoenicians. The altars also include carvings of people with beards and upturned noses. Mosaics are plentiful and seem to have been made with asphalt paving into which serpentine chips were set. Talismans of jade found at La Venta were more highly prized by the people than either gold or silver. All of the ancient artifacts of La Venta have now been moved to Villahermosa, where they may be viewed in a small park.

LABNA

Near Uxmal is another ancient ruin, the city of Labna. Most noted for the great palace, Labna is built entirely in the Puuc style. Although in a poor state of preservation, the great palace is still obviously the most important building in the city. A long stone highway leads from the palace to a group of buildings, including the temple of Mirador.

Entering the temple, the visitor sees that the front part is divided into three rooms with a sanctuary behind the center room. An important feature of this temple is the enormous roof comb, which is more than four meters high and gives a lofty appearance. Unlike the combs of Palenque, this one is not placed on the transverse axis of the building. Rather, it is aligned with the facade so the facade seems to be prolongated from the front of the building and to consist of a single wall. The facade of this building, simpler than the ones at Palenque, features large standing figures on pedestals. Few of these figures remain standing today.

MITLA

The ruins of Mitla lie about twenty-five miles southeast of Monte Alban in the eastern valley of Oaxaca. These ancient ruins are unique in that instead of large temple pyramids, they consist of several lower, sprawling buildings with flat roofs and courtyards. Possibly the most interesting aspect of this architecture is the angular mosaic of stones set in rhythmic repetition of geometric designs put together with no mortar and with patterns and joints blending flawlessly. It has been estimated that 130,000 individually cut stones were made anciently to produce these beautiful mosaic patterns.

Mitla was a mixture of Zapotec and Mixteca-Puebla cultures. It is believed that the Zapotec culture of Monte Alban moved and settled here. In the Zapotec language Mitla is called *Yoo-Paa* or "Place of the Dead." The people at Mitla believed in afterlife and maintained their tombs with great care. An ancient tomb was found beneath a pyramid floor in the form of a large cross. These ancient Americans were familiar with hieroglyphic writing, astronomy, mathematics, calendrics, and realistic art.

A beautiful mosaic wall at Mitla, constructed without cement.

MONTE ALBAN

Probably the richest archaeological find in all the Americas is the ancient metropolis of Monte Alban. Discovered in 1930 by Alfonso Caso, this city is situated atop a 1300-foot hill overlooking Oaxaca, Mexico. Although Monte Alban was built approximately eight hundred years before Christ, it still stands, a fabulous example of ancient glory. Monte Alban means literally "Sacred Mountain."

Monte Alban was inhabited constantly, by one culture after another, including the Olmec, Maya, Zapotec, Mixtec, and Aztec peoples. There are evidences of an observatory, a ball court, staircases, pyramids, temples, and burial vaults. Because of its desirable location, Monte Alban also appears to have been an excellent site for a military center, though no weapons have yet been found.

Monte Alban apparently had brilliant engineers, for the entire hill was scraped and leveled to provide ground for a magnificent complex of religious temples and buildings. The most impressive temple is north of the quadrangle. It has crumbling circular pillars and wide, majestic steps covered with white stucco leading to the summit. This stairway reveals three separate periods of construction and is believed to be the widest of all temple entrances in the Americas.

In one of the buildings to the west of the quadrangle was the tomb of a very important personage. The treasures of this tomb are now on display at the Museum of Anthropology in Mexico City. Still another beautiful edifice is the Templo de los Danzantes, or "Temple of the Dancers." Numerous bas-relief figures carved on large stone slabs and thought to resemble dancers have been found here.

Many exquisite artifacts have been found in this ancient city, including magnificent gold work in the style of the Mixtecs, jade and obsidian jewelry, bracelets of gold and silver, a golden diadem, and a lovely translucent vessel fashioned of onyx.

Some scholars believe that writing in the New World began at Monte Alban. Indeed, the numerous artifacts and articles of writing found there would seem to indicate great intellectual advancements. Some date glyphs have been deciphered, but most of the hieroglyphs cannot be discerned.

PALENQUE

East of Villahermosa, Mexico, lie the ruins of Palenque, a Spanish word meaning "Palisade," or "Place of War." A modern road leads to the center of a complex of ornate buildings marked by recent diggings. The Ostolum River, flowing through the center of these ruins, supplied water for the ancient community. An artificial bed in the river indicates that it might have been used for bathing, swimming, or even religious rites.

One of the many interesting buildings is the ancient palace. Actually a complex of buildings, the palace rests upon a platform 3 feet high, 300 feet long, and 240 feet wide. A four-story tower rising from this structure supports a series of stairs that climb the entire height. Scholars conclude that this tower was used both as an astronomical observatory and as a watchtower.

The Temple of Inscriptions, an impressive pyramid near the palace, appears to be a tomb of an ancient and honored leader. On the surface of this tomb is engraved the Tree of Life, an Old World insignia, in the shape of a cross. Sculptured figures and hieroglyphs cover much of the inner and outer walls of these buildings and date Palenque before the time of Christ. Some scholars believe this ruin could have been the cradle of the Mayan civilization.

The Museum of Anthropology in Mexico City displays three tablets originally found in the Temple of the Cross at Palenque. Both sides of the panel have long rows of hieroglyphs.

Palenque had a ball court used both for playing ball and for religious rites, with opposing teams representing opposing deities. The priests could interpret the winning or losing of sides as prophecies as to whether the world would have drought, famine, or good fortune. The art and relief carvings in Palenque are jewels of ancient American art. The proportions are nearly perfect, with an Oriental influence predominating.

TENAYUCA

One of the few known ruins dating from the period before the fall of Tula, but prior to the triumph of Tenochtitlan, is the great Temple of Tenayuca. Located on the outskirts of Mexico City, this building is part of the deceptively designated Chichimec period (A.D. 1200-1400). Its builders copied the old architecture of Tula, as the Aztecs were to do later. A characteristic feature is the Coatepantli, or "Wall of Serpents"; here, however, instead of running around the entire pyramid, this chain of realistic reptiles encompasses only three sides.

The temple was constructed very economically; instead of the pyramid serving as a base to support a single temple, it now holds two, each with its own stairway and low balustrade. The Aztecs later used this idea in the construction of the temple at Tenochtitlan. There the god of war and the god of rain were honored on one pyramid. Like most temples in Mesoamerica, Tenayuca was covered with stucco and painted in vivid colors.

TENOCHTITLAN

This most famous of the Aztec cities was founded on the western shores of Lake Texcoco around A.D. 1300. Tenochtitlan, now buried beneath Mexico City, became the capital of the powerful Aztec nation. In 1519 the Spaniards, led by Hernando Cortez, invaded the city and found a rich, flourishing culture. The conquistadores strode along wide streets, viewing mansions built of a red porous stone, nearly all with roof gardens full of luxuriant plants. They also saw the lower classes of Indians living in huts built of mud and rushes.

The city was divided into twenty calpullis, or "clans," with each calpullis governed by the group of families within its borders. Each section had its own schools, priests, and temples. Children were taught farming, arts and crafts, warfare, history, citizenship, and religious practices. Special schools trained boys who wished to join the priesthood and girls who wanted to be priestesses.

TEOTIHUACAN

About thirty miles northeast of present-day Mexico City is the ancient city of Teotihuacan. The Aztecs who arrived there after the city was in its prime called it "the place where the gods reside." This pre-Columbian city covers about eight square miles and appears to have been begun in 300 B.C., reaching a peak about A.D. 1000. At one time Teotihuacan had a population of over one hundred thousand.

Craftsmen, painters, sculptors, masons, and artisans contributed their talents toward making Teotihuacan a truly magnificent city. The people also devised their own calendrical system. Concourses, plazas, smaller temples, palaces, public buildings, and many residential units were found throughout the area. Some walls are plastered; on others are murals. Cement streets cover underground drain conduits.

The largest structure is the Pyramid of the Sun, rising 210 feet from a square base more than 738 feet long on each side. Covering an area of 544,644 square feet, with a volume of 3.25 million cubic feet, it is larger in volume than the Pyramid of Cheops in Egypt, and contains about one million tons of sun-dried mud bricks.

The second most prominent building is the Temple of the Moon, a ceremonial center that served as the hub of the city. In front of the temple are several symmetrical buildings, similar in height and size. Teotihuacan appears to have been the religious center for the entire Valley of Mexico.

The central figure of deity here was a bearded god called Quetzalcoatl, who fought against evil. A temple dedicated to Quetzalcoatl has been partially restored, and the motif of the serpent is used extensively.

Along the Avenue of the Dead is the Temple of Agriculture, on the walls of which are many murals depicting people engaged in various types of agricultural pursuits.

TULA

In Hidalgo, 60 miles northwest of Mexico City, is the city of Tula, which belonged to the Toltecs and flourished around A.D. 900. Tula was obviously a beautiful city during the Toltec period, but was changed by the conquering Aztecs when many of the buildings were demolished and others carried off to form parts of other cities.

The Nahuatl name *Tula* refers to the god of the planet Venus, the morning and evening star, which is associated with the figure of the god Quetzalcoatl. A gigantic temple once existed in Tula, but nothing remains today except the base pyramid and enormous carved columns that supported the roof. These columns, 17 feet high, represent warriors, each holding in his right hand an *atlatl*, or "spear thrower," and in his left hand a bundle of darts.

Much of the sculpture is representative of humans, but there are also many animals, including the coyote, eagle, ocelot, and jaguar. The Tula Chac-Mool, a stone statue of a prone figure, is also found in Chichen Itza.

TZINTZUNTZAN

Tzintzuntzan is a small but lovely ruin on a hill overlooking the city of San Pablo in the state of Michoacan, on the shores of Lake Patzcuaro. Pottery unearthed in Tzintzuntzan indicates that this was the home of the Tarascan

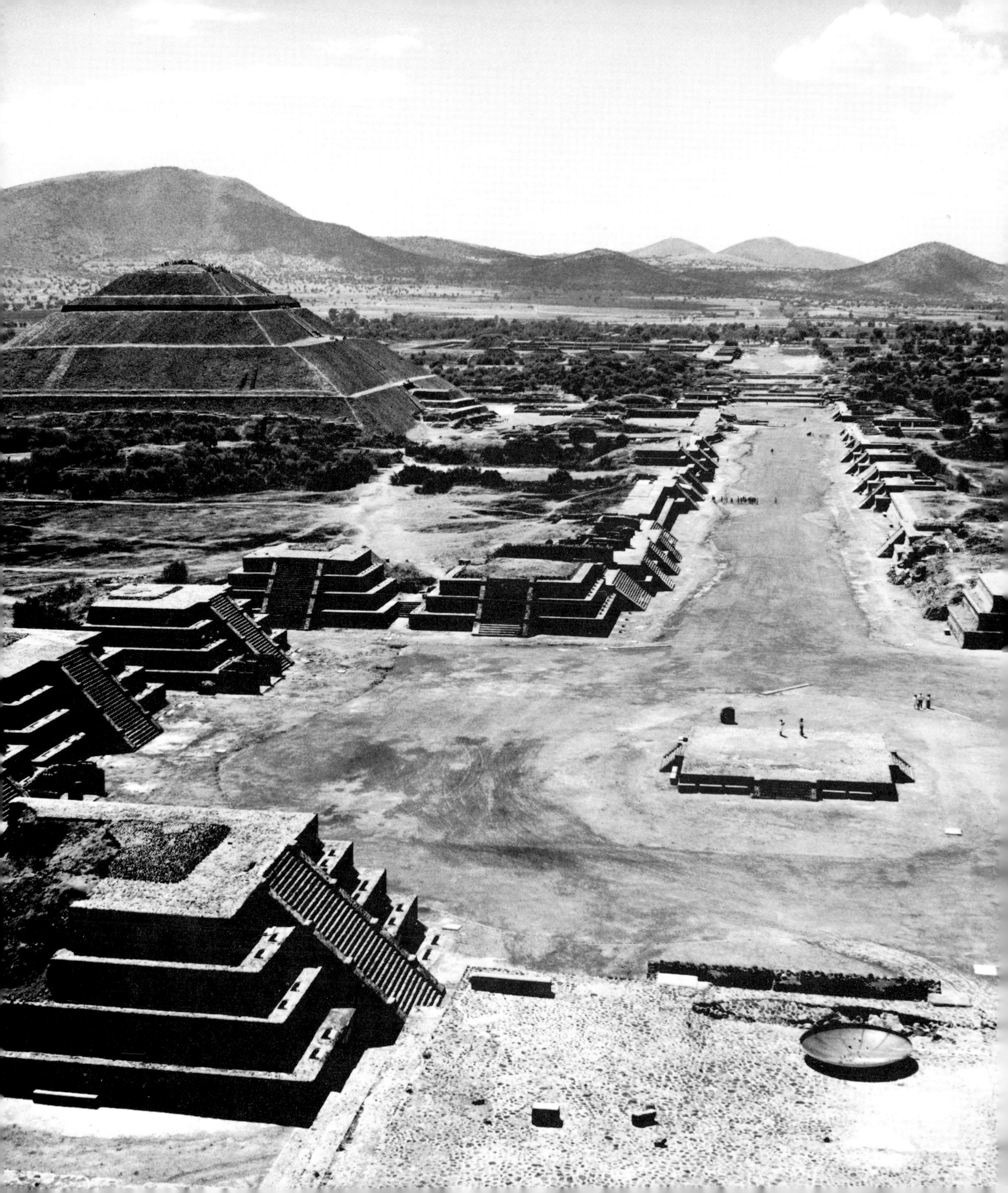

Opposite: The Avenue of the Dead in Teotihuacan, Mexico, so called for the numerous tombs along the road. This picture was taken from atop the Temple of the Moon. *Above:* The ruins of Xochicalco, thought to have been built in the eighth or ninth century A.D.

culture around A.D. 500-700. The Tarascans were able to withstand the aggressions of the Aztec Empire, and consequently are thought to have been very powerful. They expanded from this area and took possession of most of the state of Michoacan, as well as Jalisco and Colima.

The largest building of the ruin is a terraced structure about 1400 feet long by 900 feet wide, with 325-foot wide steps leading to the top of the terrace. In a chieftain's tomb at the foot of the stairs were ornaments, copper and gilt half-moons, funeral offerings, bells, filigree work, obsidian, and hard stone artifacts. People who had been sacrificed to the gods were buried near the king.

These people were superb metallurgists and were among the first in Mexico to develop techniques of casting, gilding, soldering, alloying, and smelting, using both gold and silver.

UXMAL

The archaeological city of Uxmal, thrice built, is considered one of the most successful architectural triumphs of the Mayan civilization. Buildings have been found there from the Classic Mayan period, the Mayan-Toltec period, and the Decadence period.

A good example of the corbelled arch is found in the group of buildings known as the Nunnery, which is ornamented with masks of the rain god. Stones cut into a beautiful mosaic pattern decorate its four-sided patio. The Nunnery has a cloistered effect, with many individual rooms. At one time a statue of a jaguar stood in the center of the large courtyard. The god Chac is also represented in the front of the building. The tallest building in the Nunnery is the Temple of the Magician, which has rounded sides and three terraced areas, and is topped by a temple for worship. The Pyramid of the Magician is shaped somewhat elliptically at the base, with other temples on the top.

The beautiful Governor's Palace, 600 feet long by 500 feet wide and 40 feet high, is also terraced. The stone carvings on the facade of the upper portion of the building are superb. Another section of the building features stepped terraces 400 feet long, 90 feet wide, and 23 feet high. The third section is 320 feet long, 40 feet wide, and 26 feet high. Roofed, vaulted hallways connect the three sections.

A few feet northwest of the Governor's Palace is the House of Turtles, so called because of the turtles carved in the lintels of the cornice. The architecture of this building is classically

Greek. Ancient interpretations of the rain god are everywhere. Inhabitants used cisterns to catch rainwater for drinking and culinary purposes.

XOCHICALCO

During the eighteenth century, Mexican archaeologists uncovered the site of Xochicalco, near Taxco. The city is thought to have been built about the eighth or ninth century A.D. Quetzalcoatl seems to have been the god of these people, judging by the many monuments to him. For example, Xochicalco, one of the first pyramids uncovered, is remarkable not for its size, but for the low reliefs that originally covered the entire structure. Among these is Quetzalcoatl, represented with a skillfully carved head from which a forked tongue protrudes, followed by an undulating body, and terminating in tall feathers. The serpent is depicted with an eyebrow and a beard, as it is throughout Mesoamerica.

One of the spaces formed by the reptile's curves has hieroglyphs with the sign of fire. The other space is even more important, for it reveals a seated figure holding one hand over the breast and wearing an enormous headdress of plumes. The posture, the design, and the general aspect of this individual recall—even if only remotely—a Mayan priest.

Unlike the ancient city of Teotihuacan, Xochicalco was easy to defend. On the uppermost level of the remains is a fortress. Again we find a ball court among the ruins. This court, much larger than the one at Monte Alban, is similar to the court at Tula. Both are 69 meters long with the field shaped like a capital letter *I*. In the center is the familiar stone ring. The platforms behind the walls, where the remains of small buildings can still be seen, are not identical; on the northern side the natural rock has been utilized, and to the south the platform begins on a lower level and follows the slant of the hill. Slopes, porticos, and staircases compensate for this difference.

YAGUL

In the valley of Oaxaca on a raised platform area lie the ruins of the city of Yagul, which has military designs and functions rather than the religious motifs found in most ancient Mesoamerican ruins. The location was ideal for protection, and the inhabitants enjoyed a panoramic view of the beautiful valley below. The city was actually built on various levels of the hill and evidences of once-spectacular buildings still exist today.

The largest building is the Palace of Six Patios, so named because most of its thirty rooms were designed around patios. The entire unit had but one entrance leading into a long hallway, dividing the palace into two unequal parts. The two best-constructed patios are in the east wing, with the remaining four in the west wing. At one time, portions of the exterior walls were apparently covered by stone mosaics such as those found at Mitla, but most of these are gone now. Some mosaics have been preserved, but scholars believe the stone was used to build part of the modern town of Tlacolula, its neighbor. Many of the walls are still covered by the original red plaster.

On a lower level is another large unit containing an assembly hall, or *sala del consejo*. This is a large room similar to the one at the entrance of the main palace at Mitla but without the monolithic columns. Other civic buildings include the ball court and additional courts surrounded by large rooms. Only a tall pyramid, now in very bad condition, suggests that a temple once existed here.

XLAPAK

In the jungles of the Yucatan Peninsula, from the ruins of Kabah to Labna, portions of other ruins can be seen. Xlapak is one of the ancient Puuc cities only partially excavated, but a beautiful corner of the palace, with three superimposed masks of the god of rain, can be seen. Short columns separate the decorated area above from the plain area below. In the center the masks assume a geometric form, while to their left can be seen the beginning of a *xicolcoliuhqui*, a fret that in a multitude of variations represents a stylized serpent and was used in all Mesoamerica from the end of the pre-Classic period.

The ruins at Xlapak suggest the romantic drawings from the middle of the nineteenth century in which wild plants are shown growing in profusion over intricately carved stones, slowly destroying the masonry until finally it falls to the ground.

SAYIL

The construction and habitation of Sayil, the second of the three Puuc palaces described in this book, began sometime around A.D. 800. Many mounds are apparent but three buildings remain to testify of the people—the Mirador, the ball court, and the palace. Though poorly preserved, the Sayil palace still reveals the great skill of the workmen.

The palace has three stories in stepped formation, the upper stories being supported by a solid fill set back from the floor below. They are connected in front by a great stairway of three flights, allowing access to terraces on each level. The lower facade, rather plain, has adornments of stucco or rows of little columns above the level of the doors. The middle story, by far the most elaborate, has a series of little columns on the mouldings, between the doors, and on the frieze. At the corners the characteristic masks may be seen, while in the middle of each section a carved panel shows a god descending—a frequent figure in Mesoamerica—flanked by two serpents in outline. The third story above each of the seven doors (five at the front and one on each side) has a human figure in stucco placed on a pedestal.

The whole structure is characterized by rich ornamentation contrasted with extensive plain surfaces. Not without justification do various scholars consider the palace to be one of the great triumphs of Mayan art.

We do not know who built or inhabited this seventy-room structure. The city, like Labna and Kabah, seems to have been abandoned before the arrival of Toltec influence in the tenth century A.D. There were no dated inscriptions here (or at least none have been found), but in neighboring Puuc cities all the latest dates are around the middle of the ninth century except that of Uxmal, which gives the year 909.

PRE-COLUMBIAN RUINS IN GUATEMALA

The history of Guatemala begins long before the sixteenth century conquest by the Spanish. The remarkable civilization of the Mayas produced cities, pyramids, and stone monuments that still stand today as mute evidence of the advancement of their civilization. The Spanish, guided by Pedro de Alvarado, came south from Mexico in the early sixteenth century and began to establish themselves throughout the country. They chose the ancient city of Antigua as their capital. The Spaniards freely married with the natives, and their descendants constitute most of the population of the settled areas of today.

Guatemala's conquest was definitely sealed with the death of Tecunuman, the chief of the Quiche's army. He fought against the Spanish conqueror Pedro de Alvarado during the *Battalla del Pinar* at Xelaju on February 20, 1524. With much difficulty the Spanish conquerors defeated other Indian towns until they subjugated the entire country. The city of Santiago de los Caballeros de Guatemala was established in Tecpan in July 1524, and was moved to the Almolonga Valley in November 1527. This valley was flooded in 1543 in the aftermath of an eruption of Volcan de Agua, a water-filled volcano. In March 1543 the city was moved once again, this time to the Panchoy Valley; it was destroyed by the Santa Marta earthquakes of 1773. In 1775 the capital city was established in the Ermita Valley, where it become, over the years, the modern Guatemala City.

TIKAL

The ruins of the ancient Mayan city of Tikal lie in the Peten jungle of northern Guatemala. Some scholars conclude that a pre-Classic period commenced at Tikal circa 600 B.C., a Classic period at A.D. 250, and a later Classic period at A.D. 550. The last period included the collapse of the Tikal community around A.D. 900. The peak of the culture seems to have been near A.D. 700. In the northern part of the main plaza of the city are the remains of as many as a hundred buildings, with some built over several earlier structures, one atop the other, the earliest dating to 600 B.C.

Modern studies of Tikal commenced with the work of Sylvanus G. Morley, his main concern being Mayan writing. It is now believed that the permanent records were kept in folded books. Three such Mayan codices have survived.

In 1848 Colonel Modesto Mendez, guided by stories of a fabled city, led an expedition to the site. In 1956 the University Museum of the University of Pennsylvania inaugurated an eleven-year program of study and excavation of Tikal. Today's visitors may enjoy six square miles of restored ruins amid the 222 square miles of the Tikal National Park.

The original buildings were erected at the center of the city, where there is now a museum housing many of the excavated artifacts. The more than 3,000 structures in Tikal include temples, palaces, shrines, sacrificial altars, ceremonial platforms, residences, ball courts, terraces, causeways, baths, and stone monuments.

Over 100,000 tools, ceremonial objects, personal ornaments, and other items have been found. More than a million potsherds have been collected in Tikal. Without exception, the existing structures have been built over previous construction, sometimes over two or more underlying structures.

The most magnificent building in Tikal is the Temple of the Giant Jaguar, designated as Temple I. Built around A.D. 700, this limestone edifice has nine sloping terraces and three rooms set behind each other in random fashion. The color scheme appears to have been cream, red, and perhaps green and blue. Another, older temple has been designated as Temple II. Both temple chambers were spanned by high corbelled vaults and beautifully carved wooden lintels. Temple I is more solidly constructed than Temple II. Both appear to have

ANCIENT RUINS IN GUATEMALA

54 THE WORLD OF THE BOOK OF MORMON

been used for religious ceremonies and astronomical pursuits of the church. Near the ruins are large carved monoliths, or stelae, as well as sacrificial altars. The inscriptions on these stelae were not meant to be permanent because many of the carved stones were purposely destroyed by the Classic Mayas, who defaced the features of the individuals depicted.

ZACULEU

On a plateau in the Guatemalan highlands in the shadow of the Cuchumatanes mountains is the ancient city of Zaculeu, or "White Earth." This ruin lies close to the modern city of Huehuetenango and was built sometime in the early post-Classic period. Scholars have determined that some Mayans were still living there at the time of the Spanish conquest.

Between February 1946 and April 1949 the job of restoration was undertaken by the United Fruit Company and the Guatemalan government's Institute of Anthropology and History. Their efforts represent the most complete restoration of any ancient ruin in Guatemala.

When excavated, the area revealed the foundations of long-removed altars, architecturally plain and lacking the ornate trimmings of Tikal. Zaculeu was also found to be a burial ground, its graves housing not only the dead, but also such treasures as beads, jade jewelry, bowls, jars, effigy penants, figurines of all sizes and shapes, and pottery.

The city is completely surrounded by rivers, streams, trenches, and moats, its main type of defense. Many buildings at Zaculeu have three doorways and three rooms, believed by some to represent the members of the deity.

Zaculeu's ceremonial importance is characterized by forty-three structures arranged in courts, or plazas. The largest temple was built in terrace fashion, with rough masonry walls covered with plaster. Several sets of stairs lead to the top of the temple.

Zaculeu also has a ball court. The main portions of the buildings surrounding the court are raised platforms with stairs, allowing spectators to reach their seats easily.

KAMINALJUYU

Kaminaljuyu means "hills of the dead people." The tombs of this ancient civilization are beautiful and valuable. The date of this civilization, on the outskirts of Guatemala City, has been estimated at approximately 2000 B.C., and evidence indicates that many groups lived here, with each successive culture building over the previous one. More than two hundred mounds have been discovered.

A single stairway leads to each cultured stage, with a temple at the top of the platform. Excavations allow the visitor to walk through narrow passageways to view by candlelight some of the interior structures erected in previous periods. The absence of stone sculpture is noticeable. The temple platforms appear to have been built to enclose the ruler's tomb, with successive burials placed over the older ones. The bodies, including one skeleton measuring about 7 feet in length, were surrounded by jade, pearls, and mica. The ceramic and jade date from 2000 B.C. to 1500 B.C., perhaps the oldest known in Central America.

The people of Kaminaljuyu were apparently skilled craftsmen who displayed their talents in ceramics, jade, wood carvings, stone mosaics, and pottery. Also gifted writers, they compiled almanacs and codices and decorated them with pictures of their religious lore. No Quetzalcoatl is among their many gods, but the people had a number of rain gods and other gods to which they offered human sacrifice by removal of the heart from the living.

QUIRIGUA

From a reference in the *Times and Seasons* (3:927) we learn that Joseph Smith speculated that the ruins of Quirigua in Guatemala may have been the ancient city of Zarahemla spoken of in the Book of Mormon.

Quirigua, one of the most interesting and accessible of all Mayan sites, is just two miles from the north shore of the Motague River, thirty miles south of Copan, Honduras. The ruins as well as the statues compare with the ruins of Copan. It may well be that these two sites were part of a large complex.

Quirigua is famous for its glyph-covered stelae and many sculptured altars. Perhaps the finest glyphs ever carved on stone are found at Quirigua. Examples of dancing figures, which are rare in Mayan reliefs, are found there. The largest block of stone quarried by the Maya was Stela E, which measures 35 feet long, 5 feet wide, and 4 feet 2 inches thick and weighs 65 tons.

Two stelae from Tikal, Guatemala. These large sculptured stones appear to have conveyed messages of some sort, though as yet no satisfactory interpretation of the glyphs covering them has been made.

PRE-COLUMBIAN RUINS IN GUATEMALA 55

ANCIENT RUINS IN HONDURAS

On his fourth and last voyage, Columbus discovered the Central American mainland on August 14, 1502, at what is now known as Cape Honduras. It was he who gave the land its name. He chose the Spanish word *Honduras* to describe the deep waters found offshore.

When the Spanish explored the area, they found it inhabited by various Indian tribes, none of which were highly civilized, although in earlier times the great Mayan empire had included the extreme western portion of the present nation. Columbus's discovery of the land was followed by numerous Spanish conquests headed by such men as Juan Diaz de Solis, Cristobal de Olid, Francisco de las Casas, and Hernando Cortez.

The great wave of emancipation that swept over Latin America early in the nineteenth century found an echo in Central America. On September 15, 1821, the independence of the province comprising the captaincy general of Guatemala was declared in Guatemala City.

The country's cultural heritage includes the remains of one of the greatest centers of pre-Columbian civilization in America—that of the Mayan city of Copan, which rose and mysteriously declined some seven centuries before Columbus set foot on Cape Honduras. It is the civilization of the Old World, implanted by the Spanish colonizers of Honduras, that forms the foundation of the present-day culture, however.

COPAN

The "lost city" of Copan has been explored, excavated, and studied by some of the world's leading archaeologists since its discovery in 1839 by John Lloyd Stephens. Southernmost of the Mayan cities, Copan lies at an altitude of 2,000 feet above sea level, on the edge of the Copan River. The Mayas have been called the Greeks of the

An elaborate statue, perhaps honoring an early leader, from the Plaza of Stelae at Copan, Honduras.

New World because of their architectural achievements, stone construction, painting, sculpture, astronomy, and other arts and sciences. Scientists have said that the Mayan counting system and calendar, among the great scientific achievements of antiquity, were superior to those of Europe when America was discovered. The Mayas also developed one of the first written languages in America—a system of hieroglyphics—and barkcloth paper.

Copan was a seat of learning. It is often referred to as the "college of architecture" because of the many styles of architecture found there.

Most of the monuments in Copan were built during a twenty-year period, and each building is dated. This ancient city is also the home of many burial tombs and markers carved with Mayan hieroglyphics. According to a Mayan glyph, Copan was founded in A.D. 176.

The spectacular Acropolis, the main structure, covers about seventy-five acres and is composed of five adjoining plazas. Within this complex of pyramids, terraces, and temples are the most complete inscriptions in Mayan hieroglyphics. Scientists believe the calculations determining the exact length of intervals between eclipses were made here. Such calculations of the heavenly bodies regulated the peoples' lives.

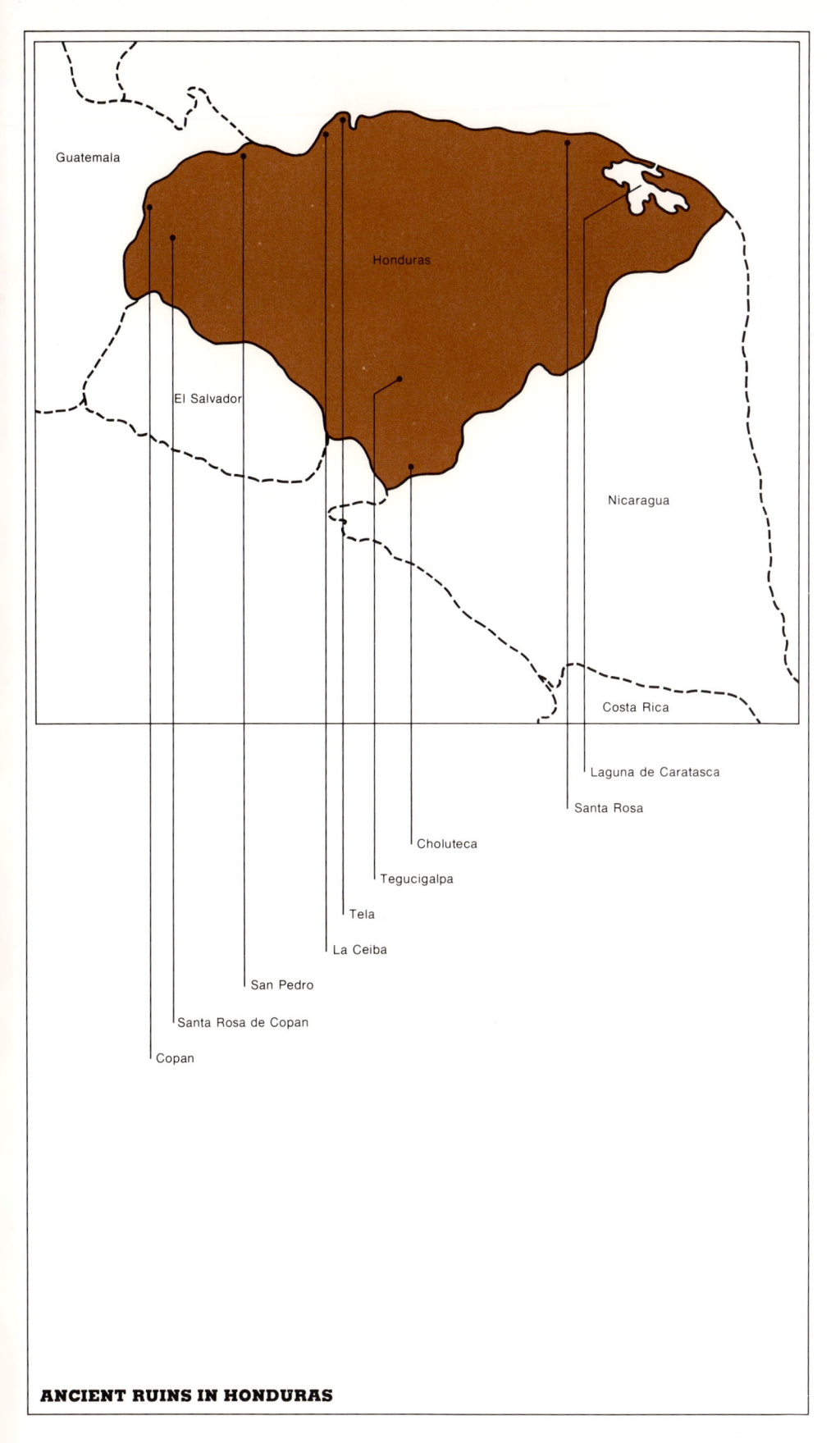

The people were exceptional sculptors, as evidenced by the elaborately carved altars and monoliths. Here also is a superb hieroglyphic stairway, 33 feet wide, 62 steps long, and decorated with 1500 to 2000 individual glyphs.

Erosion from the river has exposed a vertical face of the Acropolis 118 feet high and nearly 1,000 feet long. Even earlier plaza floor levels and drains can be distinguished in the remarkable structure.

ANCIENT RUINS IN HONDURAS

ANCIENT CULTURES AND RUINS IN PERU

Some of the most exciting archaeological findings of ancient cultures in the Americas have been made in Peru.

The Peruvian empire reached its climax in the Classic era, approximately 300 B.C. to A.D. 500, a period that produced an advanced intelligent culture. However, many mysteries still surround the crumbled ruins of the ancient cities.

The Incas, centered at Cuzco, started to expand and conquer neighboring tribes between A.D. 1100 and 1200, when the Incan empire was founded. In 1522 a Spanish explorer, Pascual de Andagoya, was the first white man to enter Peru. In 1531-33 forces led by Francisco Pizarro and Diego de Almagro conquered most of Peru. Pizarro's conquest destroyed the social and economic structure of the Incan empire and changed the population distribution. The people were forced to regroup into villages where they could be supervised. Titles to property were abolished. Deities were forgotten. The lowest class drifted about, becoming servants or serfs.

Many of the Incas were enslaved by the conquerors. In 1542 the Spanish passed a law that granted freedom to them, but because the Spanish settlers refused to recognize the law, their status remained unchanged. This situation led to revolts against the conquerors, including a widespread one in 1780 led by Tupca Amaru. Unsuccessful, he was apprehended and executed in 1781.

Lima, Peru, was founded by the Spaniards in 1535 and became the headquarters of their South American territories. In 1820 General Jose de San Martin of Argentina started a liberation movement in Peru; however, only a small group of Peruvians aided him. The next year he claimed Peru as an independent nation, even though most of the country was owned by the Spanish. The Venezuelan revolutionary leader Simon Bolivar invaded Peru in 1822 and claimed victory over the Spanish on December 9, 1824.

The Chancay, Chavin, Chimu, Mochi (or Mochica), Nasca, and Incan were perhaps the most outstanding civilizations and cultures in South America. In addition, other pre-Columbian ruins uncovered by archaeologists include Cajamarquilla, Chan Chan, Sacsahuaman, Ollantaytambo, Kenko, Machu Picchu, Pachacamac, Paracas, Cuzco, Pisac, and Tiahuanco. Here are some of the most important findings at these sites.

CHANCAY

The most striking—though crude—pottery on the central coast of Peru was produced by the Chancays, who emerged about A.D. 1300. This culture was centered in the ancient city of Cajamarquilla. The artistry of their pottery was not sophisticated; rather, it was dependent on unusual shapes and varieties, such as an egg-shaped jar with a flaring collar and a pair of small loop handles. Brown on white was the predominant color scheme.

The ancient artists of this culture were also noted for their superb skill in weaving. Embroideries and lace reveal their mastery of this art as well as their extraordinary use of color. The Chancays developed skillful techniques in combining gold and copper alloys. Clay panpipes have been found, as well as graves covered with poles or rough stone vaults.

CHAVIN

The Chavin culture commenced around 900 B.C. along the northern coastal areas of Peru. There is some speculation as to exactly how much area this culture encompassed. Some believe it extended as far north as Ecuador and as far south as Chile and Argentina, with religion and art as the main uniting forces. The primary religious motifs of these peoples were the jaguar, the serpent, the bird of prey, and the alligator. Because of the similarity of this art with those of the cultures of Mexico, Yale archaeologist Michael Coe suggests that a maritime trade network existed between the Pacific coast of Middle America, Ecuador, and Peru.

The largest of the cultural centers is believed to have been Chavin Huantar, a city 140 miles north of Lima in the small Mosna Valley, 10,000 feet higher than Lima. The majority of the people apparently lived on the outskirts of the center, using many ramps, stairways, and underground passageways to reach the main site. Religion was advanced, and the temples were well-planned, with numerous rooms, platforms, and steps. The common man's home was probably a one-room, rectangular structure with a thatched roof. Tombs that have been found indicate that these people believed in an afterlife, since food and drink were interred with the body. Skull deformation was a common practice, as was multiple burial. No one knows why some of the bones have been covered with a red powder pigment.

These people enjoyed arts and crafts. Chavin pottery was excellent in its day, simply shaped with thick rims and stirrup spouts. Tapestry and embroidery have been found among the Chavin ruins, as well as a lacelike gauze, but not with all the later techniques found elsewhere. Cotton was used for weaving. Many techniques of metallurgy were used, with gold as the predominent metal, as well as some silver and copper.

CHIMU

Near Trujillo one can still see the ruins of the ancient city of Chan Chan, which covers over eight square miles and boasts many beautiful arabesque designs and architecture. The later Chimu culture was contemporary with the Incan, but produced no outstanding ceramic art. Nearly all the pottery was black, made from molds, with stirrup pottery predominating. Some unusual double-spouted vessels have been found. These pots may have been used for whistles, for when liquid is poured out one spout, the air coming into the other spout causes the pot to whistle.

MOCHI OR MOCHICA

During the later pre-Classic period of Peru (300 B.C.-A.D. 500), a high-level culture called the Mochi or Mochica flourished. The Mochi lived on the northern coast of Peru at the same time as the Nascas and the Paracas lived on the southern coast. These ancient Americans were builders, as evidenced by their enormous temples. One of the most outstanding of these is their Temple of the Sun, which is estimated to have been built with 130 million adobe bricks.

An agricultural people, the Mochi built canals and developed a system of irrigation. The sport of hunting animals was restricted to the upper class. Men shooting birds and hunting with blow guns were depicted on pottery jars.

The people were divided into classes. The wealthiest dressed in fine linens, feathers, and jewelry; the middle class dressed in simple cloth shirts with breechclouts. Most of the men wore ear or nose jewelry. The warring class dressed in skirts, metal armor, and helmets. Prisoners (the lowest class) were depicted naked with ropes around their necks. They were eventually sacrificed to the gods.

The Mochi practiced metallurgy with great skill, using alloys of gold, silver, and copper. The culture is most noted, however, for its naturalistic ceramics. Pottery, in a variety of shapes and sizes, is impressive. So expressive are the head jars that they could easily be portraits. Some figures are even shown wearing modern-looking poncholike shirts. Geometrical painting was popular, especially in red and black. The painted pottery depicts people suffering from diseases and amputations of limbs, and medicine men working their cures.

NASCA

A relatively new discovery was made by Max Uhle in 1901. One hundred miles southeast of Paracas he found the remains of the Nasca culture, which dated from 200 B.C. to A.D. 600, possibly coming from the older Paracas culture. These people built no large structures or cities; rather, they preferred to live in small villages. The Nascas are most noted for their beautiful polychrome pottery. They also wove beautiful textiles, using over 190 tints. Metallurgy was limited to gold pounded into thin sheets, cut into various shapes, and decorated with designs.

The Nascas practiced an interesting custom that some have attributed to their religion. They made designs, including the outlines of animals, that can be seen only from an airplane. These huge designs were possibly made to please celestial deities. Some are thought to point toward solstitial or equinoctial points, and therefore were of astronomical importance.

INCA

Among the best-known cultures in South and Central America is the Incan civilization, which some archaeologists have estimated began in about A.D. 1000. The empire, linked by progressive mountain and coastal highways, included Peru and much of Ecuador, Chile, and Bolivia. The Incas are estimated to have numbered over 16 million people at one time. They organized an efficient government, had excellent communications systems, and were accomplished agriculturalists. The land was divided according to the needs of the family, with each married couple assigned half an acre, each boy child half an acre, and each girl child one-fourth acre.

A warring people, the Incas developed such weapons as slings, spear throwers, and bolos (three stone balls joined by cords). Some groups also used the bow and arrow. The Incan soldier protected himself with square or round shields, helmets, and cloth tunics stuffed with cotton.

The Incas were proficient artists and craftsmen in gold and silver, and their supply of these precious metals was so abundant that their plates and utensils were often gold that was painted over, presumably to relieve the monotony of the golden color. Much of the gold and silver work was destroyed when the Spanish conquerors forced the people to melt their treasures down for shipment to Spain. What we see today in public and private museums, therefore, is merely a pittance compared to the treasures found by the Spaniards who conquered the area.

CAJAMARQUILLA

A short distance up the river from Lima is the Rimac Valley of Peru, where explorers have found ruins of

ANCIENT RUINS IN PERU

- Iquitos
- Pisac
- Ollantaytambo
- Lake Titicaca
- Urubamba River
- Juliaca
- Tacna
- Puno
- Arequipa
- Puruchuco
- Kenko
- Puuc Pucara
- Sacsahuaman
- Tambo Machay
- Nazca
- Cuzco
- Ayacucho
- Machu Picchu
- Huancayo
- Tarapoto
- Cajamarquilla
- Paracas
- Pisco
- Pachacamac
- Chavin de Huantar
- Callao
- Lima
- Chan Chan
- Trujillo
- Ascope
- Chiclanvo

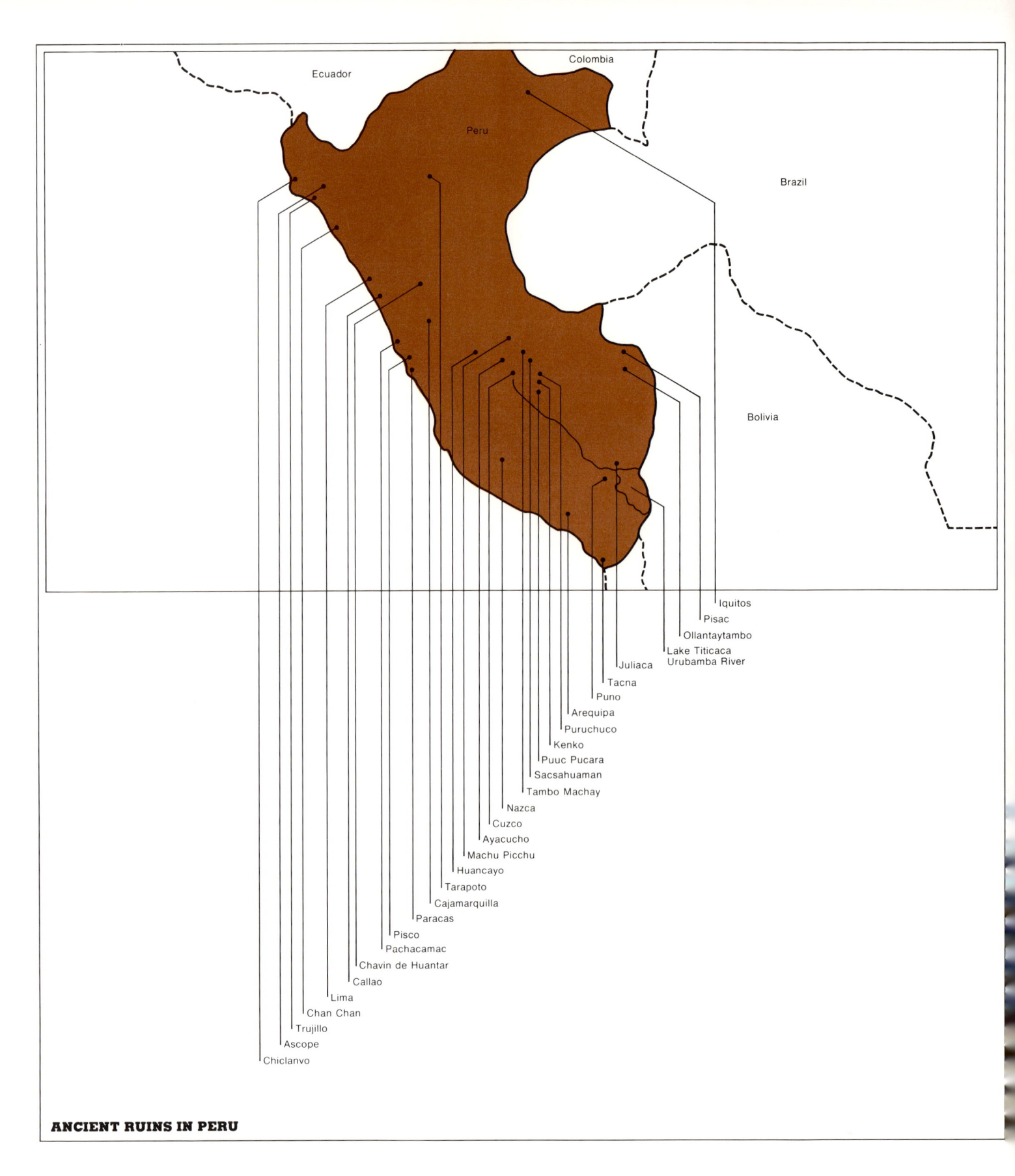

60 THE WORLD OF THE BOOK OF MORMON

an urban metropolis called Cajamarquilla. This city, in the state of Cuismancu, reached its height around A.D. 1300. The actual construction of the center is similar to that of Chan Chan. Large, congested areas of houses, streets, and temples crowd the site, mud bricks being the main building material used. Unlike Chan Chan, however, Cajamarquilla is not large, and the walls in the city are not high.

One of the most interesting parts of the ruined city is the plaza where the people stored their food. Several holes, nearly twenty feet deep, enlarge as the cavity goes into the earth, somewhat like a bottle. With a rope ladder, a native could lower himself into this bottlelike cavity and store food in the cool cellars.

CHAN CHAN
The Chimu capital of Chan Chan is the largest pre-Columbian city of the New World. Covering about ten square miles, this ancient city is systematically laid out with walls surrounding the whole, and other walls dividing it into sections. The long, straight, well-planned streets meet at right angles. Some of the roads were used to guard the vast water systems and reservoirs. Open land was used for cisterns, canals, vegetable gardens, and cemeteries.

SACSAHUAMAN
Above the Cuzco valley is the great fortress of Sacsahuaman, the largest Incan building. The fortress walls, made of limestone, stretched for over 1800 feet. Three terrace walls reached a total height of about 60 feet. The largest of the stones found in the lowest wall is 27 feet high, 14 feet broad, and 12 feet thick, and weighs an estimated two hundred tons. The massive blocks in the fortress and other surrounding buildings are fitted together with such precision that no mortar was necessary. Transportation of these mammoth blocks required supreme engineering ability, and it is believed that a labor force of thirty thousand was needed to put the stones into place. Ropes, animals, simple machinery, levers, rollers, and perhaps even the pulley and windlass were used.

OLLANTAYTAMBO
The plans of streets and squares reveal the Incan origin of the fort of Ollantaytambo, which, according to Incan legend, was a refuge of General Ollantay. The megalithic fortress was composed of a series of trenches and defenses, passages and lookouts. It also gave temporary asylum to Inca Manco, when he rebelled against the Spanish conquerors.

KENKO
Six kilometers from Cuzco, Kenko is made of rocks carved in the shape of chairs, forming a huge circle. In the middle stands a single gigantic stone. It is believed that this was the sanctuary or altar for a mysterious cult. Concealed subterranean passages would seem to confirm the belief that secret ceremonies were held at Kenko.

MACHU PICCHU
A great find was made in July 1911 by Hiram A. Bingham, who discovered the renowned ruins of Machu Picchu high in the Andes at 8,875 feet. Scholars have dated this amazing ruin

The fortress of Sacsahuaman, the largest Incan structure. The limestone walls, 1800 feet long, were constructed so precisely that no mortar was needed to fit the stones together. It is estimated that a labor force of 30,000 was required to build this stronghold.

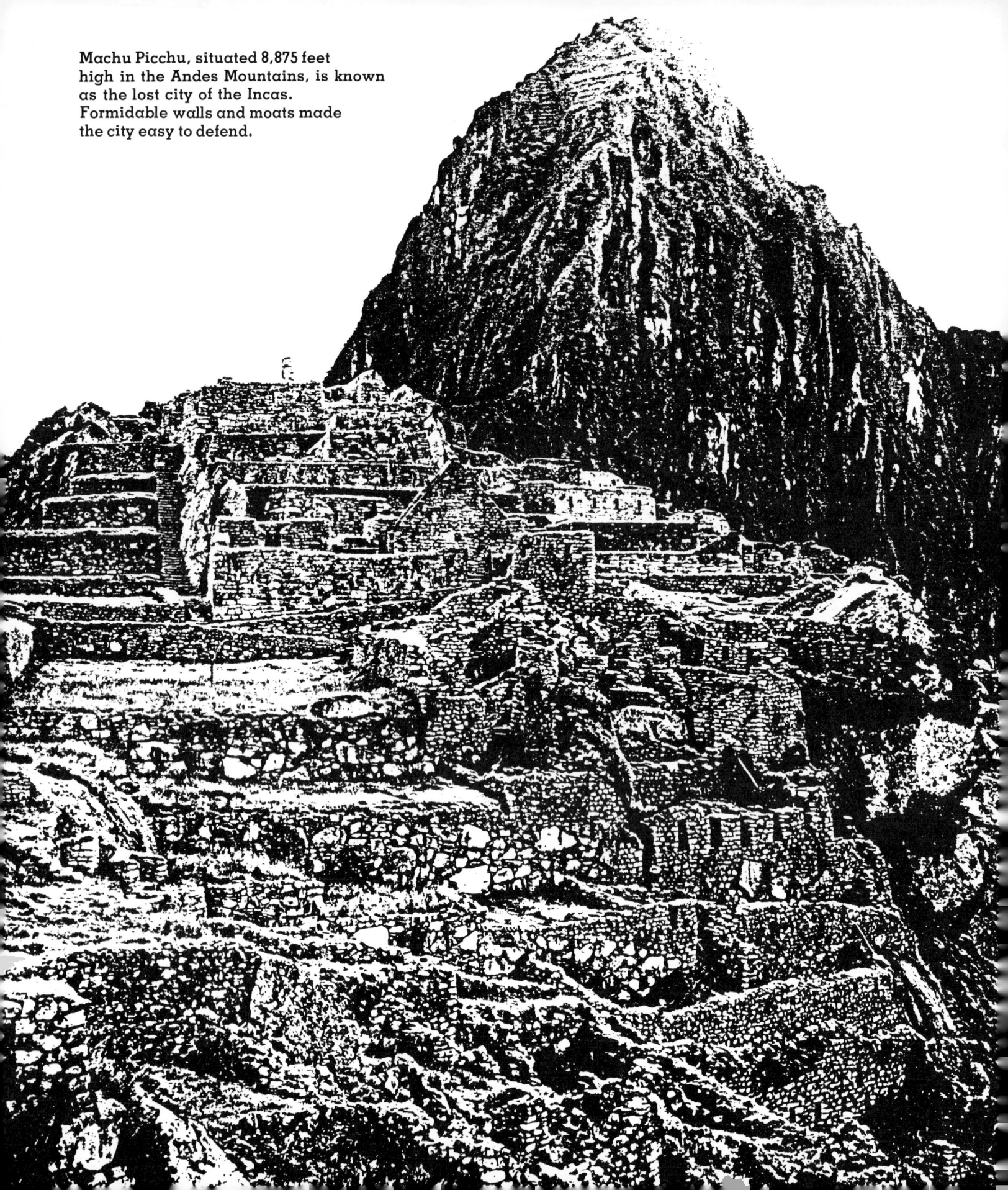

Machu Picchu, situated 8,875 feet high in the Andes Mountains, is known as the lost city of the Incas. Formidable walls and moats made the city easy to defend.

somewhere in the late tenth or eleventh century A.D. Known as the lost city of the Incas, Machu Picchu is protected by mountains and formidable walls and moats. Situated some seventy miles northwest of Cuzco on the Urubamba River, it is difficult to reach.

Much of the masonry is rock walls, with bricks cut so precisely that cement was unnecessary. This is similar to the stone-masonry found in Cuzco and Sacsahuaman. One two-storied building, with many trapezoidal doors and niches, has been excavated. The city has palaces, temples, towers, fountains, baths, and residential districts. The many terraces are connected by approximately 3,000 steps, or 109 flights. Since ancient times, terraces have been used to grow crops.

PACHACAMAC

The first scientific archaeological work in Peru was initiated at Pachacamac under the direction of Dr. Max Uhle. This temple and its city are located in the Lurin Valley, near Lima, overlooking the Pacific Ocean. The ruin is believed to have been a pilgrimage center where the pre-Inca creator-god Pachacamac (and later the Inca Viracocha) was worshiped. At the Temple of the Sun, northeast of the restored Temple of the Moon, beautiful trapezoidal doors have been carefully restored. Interlocking designs of fish in white, yellow, red, and black still remain on the stucco walls. A large reservoir, aqueducts, and other indications of sophisticated ancient water systems suggest that irrigation was understood and practiced during pre-Columbian times.

PARACAS

The Paracas peninsula, eleven miles south of the port of Pisco, is devoid of vegetation. Yet the culture that existed there from approximately 200 B.C. to A.D. 500 produced some of the most exquisite textiles in the world. Netting, knotting, twining, knitting, plaiting, brocading, weft-patterns, embroidery, and painted cloth were made, sometimes using as many at 397 threads per inch.

The bodies of the Paracas were buried in bottle-shaped chambers at a depth of twenty feet. Group burials were prevalent and have provided archaeologists with ample insight into certain practices of these people. Many skulls were artificially deformed and a large portion were trephined. The tree of life—an Old World symbol—is found here. This gigantic carving on a hillside facing the sea remains in spite of the constantly moving sands blowing over it for centuries. The people who live here today still call it the tree of life.

CUZCO

One researcher has concluded that Cuzco, the ancient capital of the Incas, is the oldest continuously inhabited city in the Americas. Believed to have been founded in the eleventh century, it was the center of a powerful nation that encompassed Peru, Ecuador, Bolivia, and parts of Argentina. It is also estimated that at the time of the conquest, the city had over one hundred thousand families.

The Temple of the Sun in Cuzco was the most sacred structure in all the Incan empire; first built in the twelfth century, it was enlarged several times. Much of the golden treasure Pizarro took from Cuzco came from this temple.

Today a Catholic church uses part of the Temple of the Sun as a wall. The curved rocks were placed together without cement and have withstood earthquakes and other damages, an excellent example of Incan engineering skill. Many streets in Cuzco are still lined with walls built by the pre-Columbian peoples. Others who came afterward have built on top of these walls to form the modern buildings seen today.

PISAC

The fortress of Pisac, outside Cuzco, is interesting because of the Inithuatana ("sun clock"), the temples and rooms, and the finely polished surface of the masonry.

TIAHUANACO

The highest and most remarkable basin in the Andes is Tiahuanaco, in which lies Lake Titicaca, the highest navigable water in the world, 12,506 feet above sea level. This lake is transversed by a steamboat and has no drainage system except by overflow to Lake Poopo. The basin is divided between Peru and Bolivia, with the great ancient ruins of Tiahuanaco on the Bolivian side. The Aymara Indians who make their home here depend on potatoes, quinoa, and oca for food. This is the homeland of the llama and alpaca.

The center of this culture was probably localized in this area until the early ninth and tenth centuries, when it expanded and spread to the coastal areas. Tiahuanaco itself was a ceremonial center, and the civic organization appears to have been in the hands of a few noble families who inherited their offices through lineage. They understood the processes of irrigation, utilizing canals and other public works.

The major structures of the ruins of Tiahuanaco occupy about a sixth of a square mile on a unique site. No adobe was used; all the ruins are of stone, and there are few walls. The masonry is considered to be the most skillful in Peru. The great monolith known as the Gateway of the Sun, carved of a single block of andesite, is about ten feet high and twelve and a half feet wide.

The blocks of stone were notched for strength and fitted together by copper clamps, something unusual in Peruvian masonry. T-shaped grooves were carved into adjacent sides of the rocks, and either copper was pounded into these indentations or molten copper was poured into it and allowed to cool and harden.

These huge basalt and sandstone blocks, weighing up to a hundred tons each, were moved some distance and put into place by these ancient craftsman. The art of polishing, cutting, and clamp-tying these huge stones together is one of the most amazing feats of the world.

Tiahuanaco was also famed for its great human statuary. The largest found so far has been taken to La Paz and erected in a plaza there. The age of this civilization is difficult to determine, but it is thought that the supreme god, Viracocha, created man here.

POSSIBLE PHOENICIAN INFLUENCE

At the turn of the century a few historians timidly suggested that perhaps the ancient Vikings had landed in North America, but until the 1960s these few were a definite minority. Their only evidences were a few vague hints in ancient Norse and Icelandic literature referring to "Vinland." Then in 1964 a well-documented article was published in a national magazine concerning archaeological and other proofs confirming not one but several Viking expeditions to North America as early as A.D. 986. (Helge Instad, "Vinland's Ruins Prove Vikings from New World," *National Geographic*, November 1964, pp. 708-34.)

As archaeological exploration expanded in the Americas after World War II, other discoveries came to light. For instance, pottery dating from the Jomon period in Japan was discovered in Ecuador, establishing the possibility of Japanese voyages to America in the third millennium before Christ. (Gordon, *Before Columbus*, p. 68.) Scholars searching old Chinese documents found mention of Hai King who, about 2250 B.C., described a crossing of the "Great East Ocean" and a long southward trip from his landing place.

Hwue Shin, a Chinese Buddhist priest in the fifth century A.D., described a long voyage in a junk to a land called "Fusang." His description could fit Mexico and Central America. (Ibid., p. 142.) From 1932 to 1967 Roman coins dating from the second century A.D. were unearthed in scattered locations in Kentucky. A stone bearing some inscriptions, found near Bat Creek, Tennessee, has recently been reexamined and the descriptions determined to be Hebrew. This stone has been dated at approximately A.D. 135. (Ibid., pp. 175, 185.)

One author insists that America was discovered before Columbus by Romans, Chinese, Irish, Vikings, Welshmen, and Portuguese. (Boland, *They All Discovered America.*) He makes a strong claim for visits by the Phoenicians. While no one is certain where the original Phoenicians came from, they were a Semitic people with close cultural, racial, and linguistic ties with the ancient Hebrews. (Easton, *The Heritage of the Past*, p. 120.) They did not call themselves Phoenicians; it was the Greeks who later applied that name to them, a name derived from the Phoenicians' use of dark red or purple dyes on their cloth. (Christensen, *Transoceanic Crossings to Ancient America*, p. 4.)

As early as 3000 B.C. Egyptian vessels, called "bybloships," were trading with Byblos and other Phoenician cities for cedars of Lebanon and dyed cloth. (*Everyday Life in Bible Times*, pp. 231-32.) The Phoenician culture was centered mainly in what is now Lebanon, the principal cities being Tyre, Sidon, Byblos, Ugarit, and, later, Carthage. Though all Phoenician city-states possessed a common basic culture and the same group of gods and goddesses, there was little political unity; each city was self-governed.

The Phoenicians are best remembered for two important achievements: (1) the oldest known alphabet, derivatives of which were later adopted by the Greeks, has been found at Ugarit, dating from about 1400 B.C., and (2) their great seafaring exploits. Phoenician cities were geographically limited to areas of poor soil and, except for the famous cedars of Lebanon, few natural resources. The people were forced to turn to the sea for avenues of prosperity.

The Phoenicians were the leading traders of the Mediterranean even in the third millennium before Christ. The downfall of the Philistine empire about 990 B.C. freed them for more extensive voyages and probably accounted in part for the friendship existing between Hiram, king of Tyre, and David, whose Israelite armies had crushed the Philistines. Long before the Greeks and Romans built great civilizations, the Phoenicians were sailing through the pillars of Hercules and into the Atlantic, trading purple cloth and exquisite glassware for tin in England and other raw materials in Spain and West Africa. (*Everyday Life in Bible Times*, p. 132.) Cadiz, on the

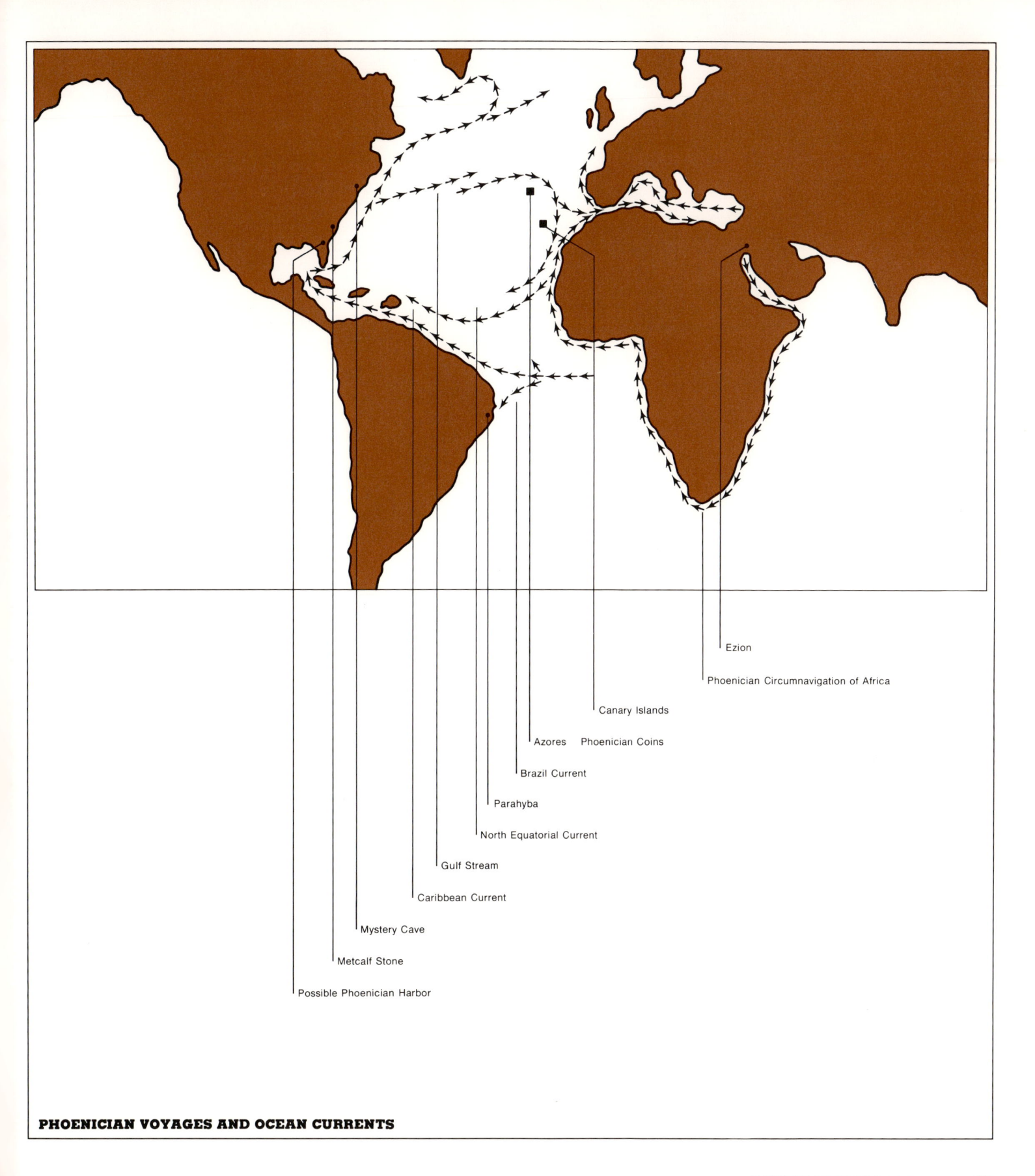

Ezion
Phoenician Circumnavigation of Africa
Canary Islands
Azores   Phoenician Coins
Brazil Current
Parahyba
North Equatorial Current
Gulf Stream
Caribbean Current
Mystery Cave
Metcalf Stone
Possible Phoenician Harbor

PHOENICIAN VOYAGES AND OCEAN CURRENTS

POSSIBLE PHOENICIAN INFLUENCE 65

southwest coast of Spain, the city from which Columbus would later sail, was settled first by the Phoenicians.

Phoenician sailors were often used by other Mediterranean powers for trade and exploration. About 600 B.C. Necho, one of the last pharaohs in Egypt, commissioned Phoenician sailors to circumnavigate Africa, sailing from the Red Sea to the Nile. Later, Hanno of Carthage sailed down the west coast of Africa, establishing colonies as he went.

The Phoenicians enjoyed a close relationship with at least two Hebrew kings, David and Solomon: "And Hiram king of Tyre sent messengers to David, and cedar trees, and carpenters, and masons: and they built David an house." (2 Samuel 5:11.) We read in 1 Kings how this same Hiram helped Solomon build his temple, supplying raw materials and craftsmen. Solomon paid for these supplies and services on an installment plan of "twenty thousand measures of wheat [about 125,000 bushels] . . . and twenty measures of pure oil [about 1,162,000 gallons]" per year. (1 Kings 5:11.) After twenty years Solomon still owed a debt to Hiram, and he finally deeded him several coastal towns in western Galilee.

Solomon also built a navy, based at Ezion-geber near the Red Sea port of Elath. The heart of his navy was Phoenician merchant ships and galleys, which sailed once every three years on voyages lasting a year or more to many ports of call, including fabled Ophir, trading for gold, precious stones, and almug wood (possibly sandalwood) for harps and lyres, spices, peacocks, and apes. *(Everyday Life in Bible Times*, pp. 247-48.) In this way Israel benefited from Phoenicia's control of the seas, while the Phoenicians took advantage of Israel's control of the caravan routes.

How good were the vessels of the Phoenicians and how skillful were the sailors? Were they capable of transoceanic voyages? The prophet Ezekiel gives us a good description of the ships:

"Thy borders are in the midst of the seas, thy builders have perfected thy beauty.

"They have made all thy ship boards of fir trees of Senir: they have taken cedars from Lebanon to make masts for thee.

"Of the oaks of Bashan have they made thine oars; the company of the Ashurites have made thy benches of ivory, brought out of the isles of Chittim.

"Fine linen with broidered work from Egypt was that which thou spreadest forth to be thy sail; blue and purple from the isles of Elishah was that which covered thee." (Ezekiel 27:4-7.)

These vessels were twice the size of Columbus's ships, propelled by sails and oars, and carried crews of warrior technicians expert in architecture, agriculture, metallurgy, and mathematics. ("A First for Phoenicia?" *Newsweek*, May 27, 1968, p. 62.)

With such vessels, Phoenician voyagers quite possibly possessed the skills to cross the Atlantic. We know they sailed into the North Sea at least as far as England, and around Africa, a feat not duplicated until the fifteenth century. The men and ships of Prince Henry the Navigator of Portugal tried for years to find a trade route to India by way of the circumnavigation of Africa. Several voyages failed, and it was not until after the death of Henry in 1460 that Vasco da Gama succeeded. Interestingly, it was while on one of these later voyages that Pedro Alvarez Cabral was blown off course from Africa to Brazil. Would it not have been possible for an ancient Phoenician ship, sailing the same waters, to have been blown over the same course? A study of the oceanic currents of the mid and southern Atlantic leads to speculation that this may have occurred many times. Indeed, Columbus, sailing from the ancient port of Cadiz, followed these same currents and finally did open up the New World for European colonization. (Of interest also is the voyage of Thor Heyerdahl's *Ra II*. See *National Geographic*, November 1964, pp. 708-24.)

Then, one may ask, why did these inventors of the alphabet leave no written record of their exploits? The Phoenicians were extremely jealous and secretive about their trade routes and ports of call. On one occasion, a Phoenician merchant captain discovered that he was being followed by a Roman ship. Rather than betray his destination, he lured the Roman onto shoals, wrecking both vessels.

Yet, according to many scholars, a number of records do exist. In the fourth century B.C. a Greek writer named Theopompus mentioned an enormous continent outside the Old World, inhabited by exotic people living the "strangest life style." In the same century, Aristotle wrote of an island discovered by the Carthaginians, some of whom stayed and colonized. Plato described a great landmass that he called Atlantis, an island west of the Pillars of Hercules and larger than Africa and Asia combined; it was originally reported by Solon, who heard the story from an Egyptian priest. In the first century B.C. a Sicilian writer, Diodorus, told of the discovery by the Phoenicians of a vast island many days' travel to the west of Africa. (Gordon, *Before Columbus*, pp. 38-39, 43.)

In 1929 a map found in the old Imperial Palace in Constantinople caused great excitement. Painted on parchment, it was dated in the Moslem year 919 (1513 on the Christian calendar) and signed by an admiral of the Turkish navy named Piri Ibn Haji Memmid (known today as Piri Reis). The map gives correct longitudinal placement of South America and Africa, an almost impossible feat in the sixteenth century. In fact, the admiral states that he based his map on one drawn by Columbus and twenty other maps, some dating all the way back to the time of Alexander the Great, or 330 B.C. (Hapgood, *Maps of the Ancient Sea Kings*, Preface.) From a perusal of this map it appears that someone knew much more about the shape of South America than was known in Europe before the seventeenth century.

What, if anything, survives in the New World to hint that ancient Phoenicians touched base there? There are many clues, but a complete story is not yet known. Some of the more important findings are listed here:

1. Many cultural and other similarities between Mesoamerican cultures and Mediterranean cultures, including

human sacrifice, relation of science to religion, intentional facial deformation, burial customs, architecture, and religious rites. (Irwin, *Fair Gods and Stone Faces.*)

2. The existence of cotton in the New World, which, according to botanists, could only have originated as a product of hybridization of the Old and New Worlds. There is also a similarity between Old and New World looms. (Gordon, *Before Columbus*, p. 145.)

3. Wheeled toys found in Veracruz and Oaxaca, similar in design to toys found in Phoenician tombs. (Irwin, op. cit., p. 133.)

4. The famous Ruz tomb at Palenque uncovered in 1952, containing a sarcophagus shaped with rounded head and flattened base, almost identical with those found in Phoenician tombs. In one hand of the remains buried in the Ruz tomb was a bearded face carved in jade—a face that would not have been out of place in a Phoenician gallery. (Ibid., p. 95.)

5. Pre-Columbian chickens, sweet potatoes, and other produce probably of Old World origin. (Riley, *Man Across the Sea.*)

6. The voyage of Thor Heyerdahl's *Ra II*, a craft similar in most ways to the reed boats still seen on Lake Titicaca in Peru and Bolivia.

7. Two New England sites that may have been Phoenician: Mystery Caves (Pattee's Caves) near New Salem, New Hampshire, where several acres of stone ruins include a "sacrificial stone with blood grooves," and a carving of a possible Phoenician ship exposed in Assawompset Pond in Massachusetts in 1957, when a severe drought lowered the pond's water level. (Boland, op. cit., p. 52.)

8. A cache of Phoenician coins uncovered in the Azores, dating from the fourth and third centuries B.C. (Irwin, op. cit., p. 241.)

9. Ancient Phoenician carvings associated with the ruins of several stone structures forty miles southwest of Albuquerque, New Mexico. The translation of these engravings yields an archaic form of the Ten Commandments. (*The Lapidary Journal*, April-May 1961, pp. 92-94.)

10. The Metcalf Stone, discovered in 1966 near Fort Benning, Georgia, on which is inscribed a possible system of New East writing dating from the second millennium B.C.—a combination of Aegean syllabary and two letters or symbols of the Phoenician alphabet. (Gordon, op. cit., p. 90.)

11. Circular harbor works found on the south shore of the Miami River, similar in design to Carthaginian harbor construction. (Berlitz, op. cit., p. 93.)

12. Aztec and Mayan legends, particularly a portion of a Mayan book attributed to Votan, a Mayan deity, telling of a voyage by Votan from a distant land beyond the Eastern Sea. The journey is detailed enough that at least one scholar believes it to be the account of a voyage from the Mediterranean, by way of the Canary Islands, the island of Hispanicia, and finally to Central America, up the Usumacinta River, and up one of its tributaries where Votan founded Palenque. (Irwin, op. cit., pp. 97-98.)

It is from Parahyba, Brazil, that the most spectacular discovery of recent years has come. Professor Jules Piccus of the University of Massachusetts acquired a scrapbook containing a letter from Ladislau Netto to Wilburforce Eames about the Phoenician inscription from Parahyba, Brazil. The inscription, discovered in 1872, has long since been lost, but a copy was contained in this letter. Professor Piccus sent a photo copy to Dr. Cyrus H. Gordon, an expert in Phoenician languages. At the time of the discovery the inscription was declared a fraud because of several "errors." Dr. Gordon, though, found these "errors" to be consistent with recently discovered Ugaritic texts and declared the inscription to be genuine, saying it represented a Sidonian script used in the fifth and sixth century B.C. (*Orientalia 37* [1968].) He found the style could not have been known to a nineteenth century forger, stating, "The alternatives are either that the inscription is genuine, or that the guy was a great prophet." (*Time*, May 24, 1968, p. 62.)

The translation of the text is as follows:

"We are Sidonian Canaanites from the city of the merchant king. We were cast up on this distant island, a land of mountains. We sacrificed a youth to the celestial gods and goddesses in the nineteenth year of our mighty King Hiram and embarked from Ezion-geber into the Red Sea. We voyaged with ten ships and were at sea together for two years around Africa. Then we were separated by the hand of Baal and were no longer with our companions. So we have come here, twelve men and three women, into the Island of Iron. Am I the admiral a man who would flee? Nay. May the celestial gods and goddesses favor us well." (Gordon, *Before Columbus*, pp. 124-25.)

There is evidence that Phoenician or other Mediterranean contact was made with the New World long before the Nephites landed there in 590 B.C. The Popol Vuh, a Mayan sacred book, mentions the ancestry of the Mayans coming from across the sea (where the sun rises). Many stories in the Popol Vuh parallel the Old Testament scholars, but the Pearl of Great Price is clear on this point. (Compare Genesis 1 and 2 with Moses 2 and 3.) The flood is mentioned in both the Popol Vuh and the Old Testament, but more important perhaps is the great stress placed upon the confusion of tongues in the Popol Vuh. (Goetz and Morley, *Popol Vuh.*)

Let us compare this with the Book of Mormon: "Jared came forth with his brother and their families, with some others and their families, from the great tower, at the time the Lord confounded the language of the people, and swore in his wrath that they should be scattered upon all the face of the earth: and according to the word of the Lord the people were scattered." (Ether 1:33.) The memory of such an event would have lingered strong in the memories of the Jaredites, and it is only to be expected that such a story would be preserved in the legends of descendants and those with whom they came in contact. (Irwin, op. cit., pp. 59-60.)

About 600 B.C., at about the time the Phoenicians were sailing around Africa from the port of Ezion-geber in Israel, two groups of Hebrews fled from Jerusalem several years apart and unknown to each other. The Book of Mormon details the preparations made by one party led by Lehi.

Of the other group we know nothing except that they were led by Mulek, a son of King Zedekiah of Jerusalem, and that Mulek was the only son of Zedekiah to escape execution by the Babylonians. Let us suppose that as a Hebrew, Mulek would have had little contact with the sea, and yet he desired to put as much distance as possible between himself and the Babylonians. To whom would he have turned for help? Let us also suppose this young prince would have had considerable money. Whom might he have hired? Had he fled northward, he would have been likely to head for a Phoenician city. Had he, instead, chosen to flee into the south, he might have come to the port Ezion-geber. It is not stretching the imagination to picture Mulek's group bargaining with a Phoenician sea captain for passage. It is also possible, with Phoenicia herself threatened by the Babylonians, that Mulek picked up Phoenician refugees. The first contact between Nephites and Mulekites occurs in the book of Omni, where no mention is made of the national origin of the followers of Mulek. We know the Nephites were unable to read the Mulekite records or understand their language. Is it possible the Mulekites originally spoke Phoenician? Unfortunately there is no definite answer, but a few other clues are available.

The city of the Mulekites, Zarahemla, became the capital of the Nephite civilization as the two peoples merged and became Nephites. (Omni 19.) The chief river in Zarahemla, not named until the second chapter of Alma, was the river Sidon, possibly named by the Mulekites in honor of their city of origin, Sidon.

Alma 63:4-10 identifies a shipbuilder named Hagoth who sponsored a Nephite migration northward. Hagoth is never identified as a Nephite. Perhaps he was a descendant of the Mulekites, possibly of Phoenician origin, whose shipbuilding skills might have been handed down from father to son. (Christensen's *Transoceanic Crossings to Ancient America* has much information on this subject.)

ANCIENT WRITING AND LANGUAGE

In 1830 Joseph Smith said that the ancient inhabitants of the Western Hemisphere were of Hebrew origin and that they had left a number of metallic plates inscribed with their language—a language that he was able to translate by the power of God. This claim was considered by most to be nonsensical, not only because of disbelief concerning the ostensible source of these materials, but also because it didn't happen to fall within the pale of current archaeological opinion. Scientists of the time insisted that the ancient peoples of North and South America were not of Hebrew origin, did not leave a written language, and, if they had, they would certainly not have left it on metal plates.

Since that time a number of artifacts have been discovered that seem to substantiate Joseph Smith's claim, but people have rather steadfastly refused to accept these artifacts as proof of the existence of literacy among the pre-Columbian Americans. Recently, however, Dr. Cyrus H. Gordon of Brandeis University said that people who were possibly of Jewish origin may have made transoceanic voyages and landed in America one thousand years before Columbus, leaving evidence of their existence on an inscribed stone that was discovered in Tennessee and named the Tennessee Stone. Although somewhat less assured in his contention than was Joseph Smith over a hundred years earlier, Dr. Gordon seems to have said essentially the same thing. The only apparent difference lies in the public and scholarly responses to the idea, for Dr. Gordon's supposition, unlike Joseph Smith's, was greeted with interest and belief.

After nearly 180 years, the public and scholars are finally beginning to concede the possibility that writing did indeed exist among the ancient Americans. While I have been waiting for this shift to occur among those who do not believe in the Mormons' concept, I have been collecting every available evidence to support my own belief in the existence of such writing. My findings and the findings of others not only establish the fact that writing did exist in ancient America, but they also indicate that metal plates were frequently used as a medium for this writing and that the writings themselves often denote Old World, and specifically Hebrew, origins.

Cortez recorded how the Indians kept a form of writing "which was inscribed in written characters and pictures of a kind of paper they have by which they make themselves understood." (MacNutt, *Hernando Cortes*, 1:94.) Several Mexican books were written in hieroglyphics on paper, which was about the consistency of light pasteboard. Peter Martyr described them as folding tablets. (Ibid., pp. 170-71.)

The Italian humanist Pietro Martire D'Anghiera could not say enough about "the two books such as the Indians use." He remained "wrapped in astonishment," for to him the books were a greater index to the quality of this new civilization than the gold. "The Indians of the golden land write in books," he said in his letters to other humanists as he analyzed the technique of the book and the hieroglyphics, ". . . which almost resemble those of the Egyptians. . . . Among the figures of men and animals are those of kings and great lords. . . ." (Von Hagen, *The Ancient Sun Kingdoms*, p. 14.)

Although the existence of writing in the Eastern Hemisphere has been traced as far back as 3000 B.C., for the most part archaeologists in America have found it necessary to rely on nonwritten artifacts in order to reconstruct the family life, government, and religious beliefs of the ancestors of the American Indian. The only other sources of information concerning these people have been the writings of the early Spanish chroniclers and the observations of Indians.

Joseph Smith's 1830 declaration, then, was archaeologically significant, not only for the American continent, where it was assumed that no ancient written language existed, but also for the entire world, because ancient writings had never before been found on metal plates. Since that time hundreds of examples of writing on metal plates have been discovered. (Wright, *Metallic Documents of Antiquity*, p. 457.) In addition, writings in various forms—linear symbols, glyphs, alphabet, picture—have been found in all parts of America on a variety of media ranging from stone tablets to crude forms of paper. As early as 1842 nine men signed an affidavit that attested to the discovery at Kinderhook, Illinois, of six bellshaped metal plates with writing on them.

A pamphlet distributed in 1878 declared the authenticity of the Cincinnati Tablet, a tablet found in 1841 that featured some pictoglyphic symbols. It is five inches long, three inches wide, and about one-half inch thick.

In 1952 the Arizona State Museum acquired two quarter-inch-thick slabs of hard quartzitic sandstone that had peculiar signs carved on their surfaces. Both stones were found at a ruin on the south side of the Animas River, opposite the settlement of Flora Vista, New Mexico, and both appear to have come from a cave site rather than from an open area. The find was made before 1910, and the slabs themselves have been dated at approximately A.D. 1100, based on an association analysis with potsherds. The writing on the tablets is a picture-and-glyph combination that includes a pictographic elephant.

Pictoglyphs and petroglyphs are pictorial symbols that record certain events. Examples of this form of writing are found throughout the southwestern United States. Many interpretations of the symbols are available; however, no key exists which provides exact definitions for all these colorful character-glyph writings.

Other artifacts have been unearthed in areas as widely diverse as Michigan and the Southern States. In 1966, Manfred Metcalf discovered a stone in Georgia that was called to the attention of the Columbus Museum of Arts and Crafts. A Mr. Mahan of the museum staff concluded that the inscriptions were produced by the Yuchi Indians, who had oral legends that implied a transoceanic origin. His

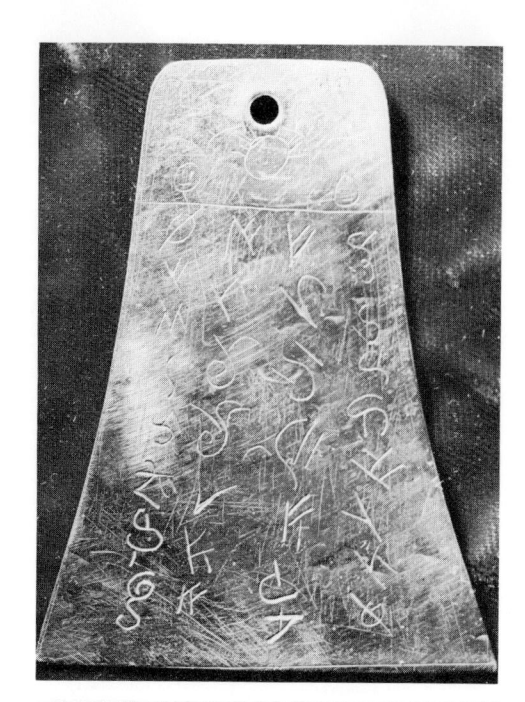

Top: One of six metal plates discovered at Kinderhook, Illinois. *Bottom:* The New Mexico Stone, dated approximately A.D. 1100. These findings, added to numerous other examples of writings on stone and metal discovered in the past century, indicate that pre-Columbian Americans did indeed have a written form of communication. Various forms of writing, such as linear symbols, alphabets, glyphs, and pictures, have been discovered all over North and South America.

research placed the arrival of the Yuchi tribe from the Mediterranean near the middle of the second millennium B.C. Dr. Cyrus Gordon concurred with Mahan's theory about a possible connection between the inscriptions on the stone and the Aegean linear script. He made further news recently by expressing the opinion that the Phoenicians at one time landed in Brazil and left inscriptions on what is now called the Parahyba Stone. (Gordon, *Before Columbus*, pp. 119-27.)

Other areas of the South have been fruitful in producing written artifacts of pre-Columbian America. Stephen Peet reported finding hieroglyphics on tablets near the banks of the Mississippi River, as well as discovering picture writing in Tennessee in the 1890s. Recent publicity has been given to the Bat Creek Stone, found in London County, Tennessee. This engraved stone was discovered in 1885 during a Smithsonian mound exploration program under the direction of Cyrus Thomas. The recent publicity was due to the fact that Dr. Gordon suggested that the inscription was made between A.D. 70 and A.D. 135 and that the language on the stone could be linked with the Roman Empire during the first and second centuries A.D. (*Science*, May 1971, pp. 14-16.)

Other southern artifacts include the Grave Creek and Wilson tablets, found in West Virginia, which have long been controversial objects and which contain characters considered to be Phoenician, Libyan, Celtiberic, and Runic. (*Western Reserve Historical Society Tracts*, No. 9, February 1872.)

At Newark, Ohio, a man named Wyrick discovered two stones covered with old Hebrew inscriptions; and M. E. Cornell published an undated manuscript at Battle Creek, Michigan, that has several drawings of caskets and tablets found near of Wyman, Michigan. Many of these objects have inscriptions on them. (Skinner, *Key to the Hebrews*, p. 55.) The January 1969 edition of *Science Digest* reports the finding of Runic messages on stones discovered at Kensington, Minnesota; Poteau, Oklahoma; Bourne, Massachusetts; and the Canadian province of Nova Scotia.

This impressive, not to say convincing, catalog of North American finds may be equaled, if not surpassed, by a similar listing of artifacts uncovered in Central and South America. Hieroglyphics cut into stone were part of the Mayan culture, and inscriptions on the lintels of buildings in Chichen Itza, as well as the tablets at Palenque and the stelae, or stone slabs, of Tikal, expain certain calendrical and astronomical hieroglyphics.

Recently in Tlatilco, Mexico, a roller stamp was found that bore clay designs forming three registers with sequences of arbitrary symbols that could well have been part of a writing system among the ancestors of the American Indian, specifically of the Olmec culture. (*SEHA Newsletter* 112.0.)

In 1968 in Lima, Peru, I saw a thin gold plaque that bore an interesting embossed design which, upon clear observation, revealed eight distinct symbols. This plate has since been examined by several experts in the United States and has undergone neutron, X-ray, and spectographic analysis to determine its composition. It was found to be 90 percent gold. Although some have labeled this plate a fake, others are less skeptical, and studies to determine its authenticity continue. Striking similarities are re-

This roller stamp found recently in Tlatilco, Mexico, may have been part of an ancient American, specifically Olmec, writing system.

vealed by a comparison of the markings from this plate with certain characters from an ancient Old World text, the *Cyprite*, taken from a study by Luige Palma Cresnola.

In January 1970 I learned of the existence of seven inscribed metal plates belonging to a Catholic priest in Ecuador. I visited this gentleman and secured photographs of the plates, six of copper and one of an alloy of copper, gold, and zinc or tin. Tests and analyses to establish the authenticity or invalidity of these plates will take time, but the prospects are encouraging.

On May 17, 1960, a United Press International report released by the Colombian Anthropology Commission stated that Hebrew and Chinese letter-characters had been found in the La Macarena Mountains. Ten years later the Miami *Herald* reported the finding of Mayan-like hieroglyphics in a cave on the Dutch Antilles island of Bonaire.

Paper was also a notable medium for writing in ancient America. Montezuma reportedly kept his revenue records on books made of a type of paper called *amatl*, and the Toltecs,

Mixtecs, Zapotecs, and Totonacs were also known to have had paper and writing. (Von Hagen, *The Ancient Sun Kingdoms of the Americas*, p. 38.) Furthermore, a type of paper has been found that dates back to the pre-Columbian period in Mexico. In 1968 Thomas Stuart Ferguson discovered a scroll of paperlike material with inked characters inscribed on it. In his book *The First Americans*, G. H. S. Bushnell discusses the findings of manuscripts painted on barkcloth, which was sized with lime and screen-folded. These manuscripts, called codices, contain bar and dot numerals and other glyphs. The various codices on display in major museums have been declared to be a stylized form of writing, and certain pictographic representations in the New World Codex Vaticanus, one of the remaining New World manuscripts, have been interpreted to include the characters of Adam and Eve, Cain, Abel, and a serpent.

Perhaps the most interesting discoveries have been the inscriptions on bowls found near Guadalajara, Mexico, and artifacts found in Peru that depict Mochica couriers carrying small sacks apparently containing incised lima beans painted with strange markings. Other painted pottery portrays men studying such beans. These persons are believed to have been decoders, and the markings, a form of communication.

As this study indicates, scholars have apparently been hasty in claiming that there was no writing among the ancient inhabitants of the New World, just as they were hasty in scoffing at the idea of possible Hebraic origins and the use of metal as an instrument for the preservation of written language. Joseph Smith's account of reading inscriptions on golden plates does not sound so far-fetched today as it did many years ago.

LANGUAGE IN THE ANCIENT AMERICAS

Some archaeologists believe that no relationships between any American Indian languages and the Old World languages have ever been satisfactorily demonstrated. However, "in view of the rapid progress which has been made in recent years in linguistic studies, . . . it is a distinct possibility that Old World and New World languages will be proven related eventually. . . ." (Willey, *An Introduction to American Archaeology* 1:16.)

The Book of Mormon records that a language was taught to the people: "And he appointed teachers of the brethren of Amulon in every land which was possessed by his people; and thus the language of Nephi began to be taught among all the people of the Lamanites." (Mosiah 24:4.)

"And now, behold, we have written this record according to our knowledge, in the characters which are called among us the reformed Egyptian, being handed down and altered by us, according to our manner of speech.

"And if our plates had been sufficiently large we should have written in Hebrew; but the Hebrew hath been altered by us also; and if we could have written in Hebrew, behold, ye would have had no imperfection in our record.

"But the Lord knoweth the things which we have written, and also that none other people knoweth our language; therefore he hath prepared means for the interpretation thereof." (Mormon 9:32-34.)

If the Book of Mormon is an English translation of a record written by a people originally from a Hebrew-speaking community, it seems there should be found within its pages oddities of expression, thinking processes, and grammatical constructions that would be used infrequently in the English tongue. An idiom is defined in its broadest sense as any peculiar character of a language. Nephi states that his father, Lehi, was a native of Jerusalem. (See 1 Nephi 1:4.) Since Hebrew was the language of that city, we can suppose that Lehi spoke Hebrew. There are indications that one thousand years after Lehi's time, his descendants on the American continent were acquainted with that language. (Mormon 9:33.)

A cursory count of the vocabulary of the Book of Mormon reveals approximately 2700 word roots. In the Book of Mormon, adjectives are rarely used. This is one of the characteristics of Hebrew. Hebrew syntax is relatively simple because of the ever-recurring "and." "And" often stands before words or phrases in series in the Book of Mormon. Genesis 20:14 and 1 Samuel 13:20 illustrate the same usage in the Bible.

The style of enumeration in the Book of Mormon follows the principles of Hebrew extensively. Numbers composed of tens and units, such as 23, usually appear in the older writings with the larger number first and the two numbers joined by "and": twenty and three. (Davidson, *Hebrew Syntax*, p. 54.) There are examples in the Book of Mormon of this form. (Jacob 1:1, Enos 1:25, Omni 1:3.)

The use of prepositions and prepositional phrases meets the requirements of correct Hebrew usage. "Before the wind" (1 Nephi 18:8 and 9) and "into an exceeding high mountain" (1 Nephi 11:1) are phrases also found in the Old Testament. (See Exodus 24:12; 24:13; Numbers 27:12; Deuteronomy 10:1.)

In the Book of Mormon, a man marries a woman and records it in characteristic Hebrew; e.g., "his sons should take daughters to wife. . . ." (1 Nephi 7:1.) In Hebrew a man does not marry a woman, but he "takes her to wife" or "she is given to him to wife." (McFadyn, *Key to Introductory Hebrew Grammar*, p. 13.)

"By the hand of" is found in the singular form many times. (1 Nephi 5:14; 13:26; 2 Nephi 1:5, 6; Jacob 1:18.) This interesting Hebrew phrase shows instrumentality and is common in the Old Testament.

The construct form of adjectival phrases, such as "an iron rod," is handled differently from the English manner. In Hebrew the correct form would be "rod of iron." The translation of the small plates of the Book of Mormon is rather consistent in this respect. "Rod of iron" is used eight times in this fashion and never as the "iron rod"; "house of Laban" and "the daughters of Ishmael" are other examples. It can be said that the construct form in Hebrew is a very common grammatical structure:

". . . if we find . . . that there is more

than the customary resort, as English practice goes, to the equivalent form with an apostrophe to denote the possessor, that fact will put the Book of Mormon on a basis which is distinctly Jewish in this particular aspect, and tends strongly to show that no English author wrote that book." (Brockbank, "Hebrew Idioms and Analogies in the Book of Mormon," *Improvement Era*, 1914, p. 1061.)

One observes in the Book of Mormon an unusual practice of making many nouns plural that would seem to require the singular form. This practice is not alien to proper Hebrew usage. One example of plural nouns found in the Book of Mormon is 1 Nephi 16:21 where Nephi writes that the wooden bows had "lost their springs." This is the Semitic use of a plural for a noun of quality.

The grammatical principle of the compound subject is illustrated in the Old Testament and the small plates, such as "I and my brethren" (1 Kings 1:21; 1 Samuel 14:40; Genesis 43:8; 1 Nephi 3:9, 10; 5:20; 7:2, 3, 22; 22:31). This is immediately recognized as being poor English grammatical construction, but it can be defended by its Hebrew origin. The expression "and it came to pass" is as frequently used in the Hebrew text of the Old Testament as in the Book of Mormon.

In support of the theory that the Indians are descendants of the Hebrew nation, Elijah M. Haines summarizes the opinion of many archaeologists:

"The languages of the Indians and of the Hebrews . . . are both found without prepositions, and are formed with prefixes and suffixes, a thing not common to other languages; and he says that not only words, but the construction of phrases in both are essentially the same. The Indian pronoun, as well as other nouns, . . . are manifestly from the Hebrews. The Indian laconic, bold, and commanding figures of speech, . . . exactly agreeing with the genius of the Hebrew language." (Haines, *The American Indian*, p. 99.)

Concerning these, the writer is cognizant that most students of this problem realize that there is no such language as "Indian." There are many languages among the various tribes. The great variety of Indian languages—although they diverged through the millennia from a smaller number of parent tongues of ancient times—also bespeak many people. It has not yet been determined how many different languages and dialects have been spoken in the Americas. Many tongues have become extinct. Linguist Morris Swadesh believes that when the whites arrived in the New World, Indians were speaking some 2200 different languages, many of them possessing regional variations. Other students have estimated that there were at least 200 mutually unintelligible languages among the native peoples north of Mexico, at least another 350 in Mexico and Central America, and considerably more than 1,000 in the Caribbean and South America. (Josephy, *The Indian Heritage of America*, p. 12.)

Roy Cheville has written: "A greater variety of languages existed in North America than in all the Old World put together; and a greater variety in South America than North America. The most conservative guesses put the number of mutually unintelligible languages in North America at from 500 to 1000 and in South America to at least twice that." (Cheville, *Scriptures from Ancient America*, p. 106.)

QUIPU

The only so-called book in Peru that has been found thus far is a system of knotted cords called *quipu*—a series of knots tied on different colored strings, with the knots varying in size and shape, which constituted the record-keeping system of the ancient Peruvians.

The Incan government kept all its tax records with a *quipu*, and there was even a symbol for zero. Some scholars believe the use of the zero among the pre-Columbian Indian preceded its use in the Old World.

The number of the knots on the string and the placement of the knots constituted a formula that produced the results. While some would wonder why this is classified as writing, it must be remembered that if messages of mathematical importance were sent from place to place, as was evidently

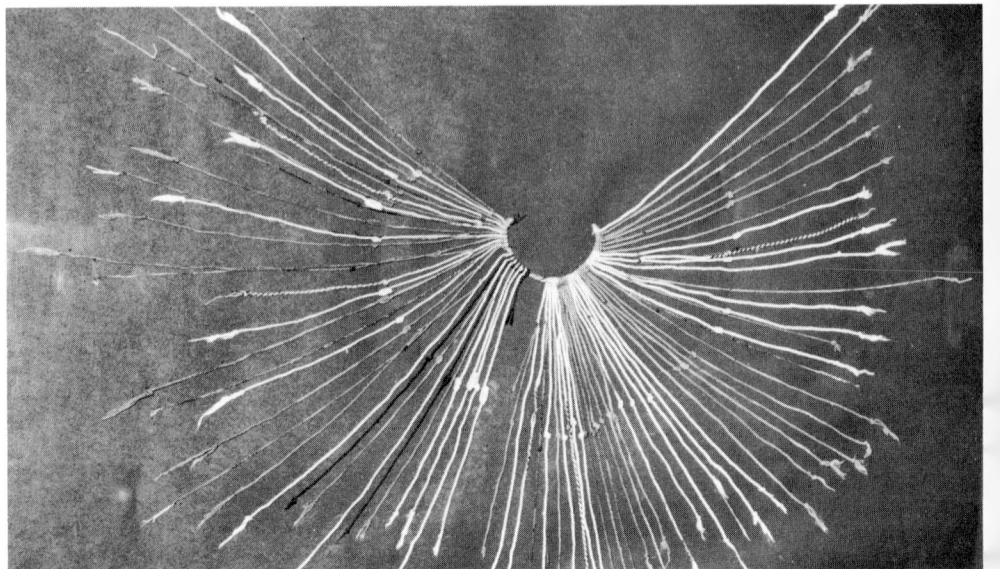

Right: A quipu, the Incan record-keeping system, comprised of a series of knotted cords. Number and placement of knots on the strings had special significance. They may have provided the key to a mathematical formula, or perhaps constituted a method of recording names, dates, and places. Opposite: Petroglyphs of "Newspaper Rock" in Monticello, Utah. Although no successful translation of petroglyphs has been made, one theory is that they were a type of trail marker. The footsteps pictured here might have shown ancient Americans where to go for good hunting.

done, this would constitute a form of communication.

It has also been conjectured that the form of the knot and its placement constituted a method of recording names, places, and events. Professional "rememberers" who knew the meaning of every knot were possibly employed as interpreters. The *quipu* is an outstanding example of the inventiveness of the Incas.

Among the Aztec and Mayan Indians, a numbering system of dots and dashes developed. An Indian could dip his hand in paint and use a finger dot for a number and make a stroke for another digit, and combine these for a system of numbering.

PETROGLYPHS

The fascinating forgotten past of the ancient American inhabitants is written in the rocks of the Americas in the form of petroglyphs, which dot the face of the land from Canada to Mexico and from California to Maine.

Petroglyphs date from the Olmec culture (800 to 400 B.C.) northeast of Acapulco, Mexico, to post-Columbian times. Dating techniques include the degree of erosion on pigment paintings and the growth of lichens on rocks. The petroglyphs consist of stick figures, straight and wavy lines, numerous types of animals (birds, deer, the feathered serpent), and the sunburst in a number of designs. Pictoglyphs differ from petroglyphs in that they are drawings or paintings using pigmented compounds, while petroglyphs are scraped or chizzled into the rock surface. Petroglyphs are better preserved than pictoglyphs because they are part of the rock.

Although many symbols and characters are well preserved, no one has succeeded in translating their meaning. A theory has been suggested that perhaps the petroglyphs were symbols used by travelers as a type of trail language, since stick figures pointing in many directions have been found.

In a recent publication, *America B.C.*, Professor Barry Fell of Harvard University asserts that there are many examples of Old World writing in the New World. His claims involve the translation of some of these findings.

BAPTISM AND SACRAMENT

To their great amazement, the early Spanish explorers and colonizers found among the ancient civilizations in Central and South America many rites and ceremonies resembling Christian practices. The Spanish writers did not believe that what they saw could in any way have been a remnant of full Christian worship by civilizations that existed hundreds of years earlier. Most of them summed up what they saw in the same manner as did Jose de Acosta when he said, "In what manner the Devil hath laboured in Mexico to counterfeit the feast of the Holy Sacrament and Communion used in the holy Church." (Acosta, *The Natural and Moral History of the Incas*, p. 356.)

What the early writers described would serve as evidence that these natives did at one time have and practice certain elements of Christianity as we know it today. Basis for a belief that the people practiced the ordinance of baptism is found throughout the Book of Mormon. Only one reference is given here, for the purpose of background and illustration:

"Behold, ye shall go down and stand in the water, and in my name shall ye baptize them.

"And now behold, these are the words which ye shall say, calling them by name, saying:

"Having authority given me of Jesus Christ, I baptize you in the name of the Father, and of the Son, and of the Holy Ghost. Amen.

"And then shall ye immerse them in the water, and come forth again out of the water." (3 Nephi 11:23-26.)

One of the earliest Spanish writers, Bishop Diego de Landa, observed as he went among the natives that they were practicing a type of baptism for which the Mayan word *caputchil* was used, meaning "to be born again." (Willard, *Lost Empires*, p. 422.) Bishop Landa, as quoted by Daniel G. Brinton, said also that this rite of baptism had an "appalling similarity to their own, connected with imposing a name, done avowedly for the purpose of freeing from inherent sin; believed to produce a regeneration of the spiritual nature, may in more than one instance be called by an indigenous word signifying 'to be born again.'" (*Myths of the New World*, pp. 147-48.)

Father Jose de Acosta wrote that although he felt the devil had instigated the ordinances among the Indians, "the Indians had an infinite number of other ceremonies which resembled the ancient law of Moses . . . and some approached near to the law of the Gospel, as their baths or OPACUNA, as they call them; they did wash themselves in water, to cleanse them from their sins." (Acosta, p. 369.)

One of the earliest of the writers, Sahagun, observed that those Indians who were well off had the most elaborate baptismal ceremonies. He made no mention of baptism among the poor people, but went into some detail describing the ceremonies of the lords and leading nobles of the villages. *(Florentine Codex* 2:39.)

Hubert Howe Bancroft, however, in quoting Sahagun and others, states that *all* the people had to be baptized. He states further the name given to this ordinance of baptism is *zihill*, which means "to be born again." This ordinance caused the individuals to "receive a purer nature, and the individuals were protected against evil spirits and future misfortunes." The ordinance was administered to everyone between the ages of three and twelve, and was a prerequisite for marriage. The baptism was to take place on a day of good omen. The father of the person being baptized and those he had chosen to assist fasted for three days prior to the ceremony. After the period of fasting, the baptism followed with much pageantry and ceremony and was concluded with a banquet and gifts for those who had assisted in the ritual. (*The Works of Hubert Howe Bancroft* 5:682.)

Early explorers of the Americas observed practices resembling baptism among many of the natives. This structure, found in Pachacamac, Peru, is possibly a baptismal font.

74 THE WORLD OF THE BOOK OF MORMON

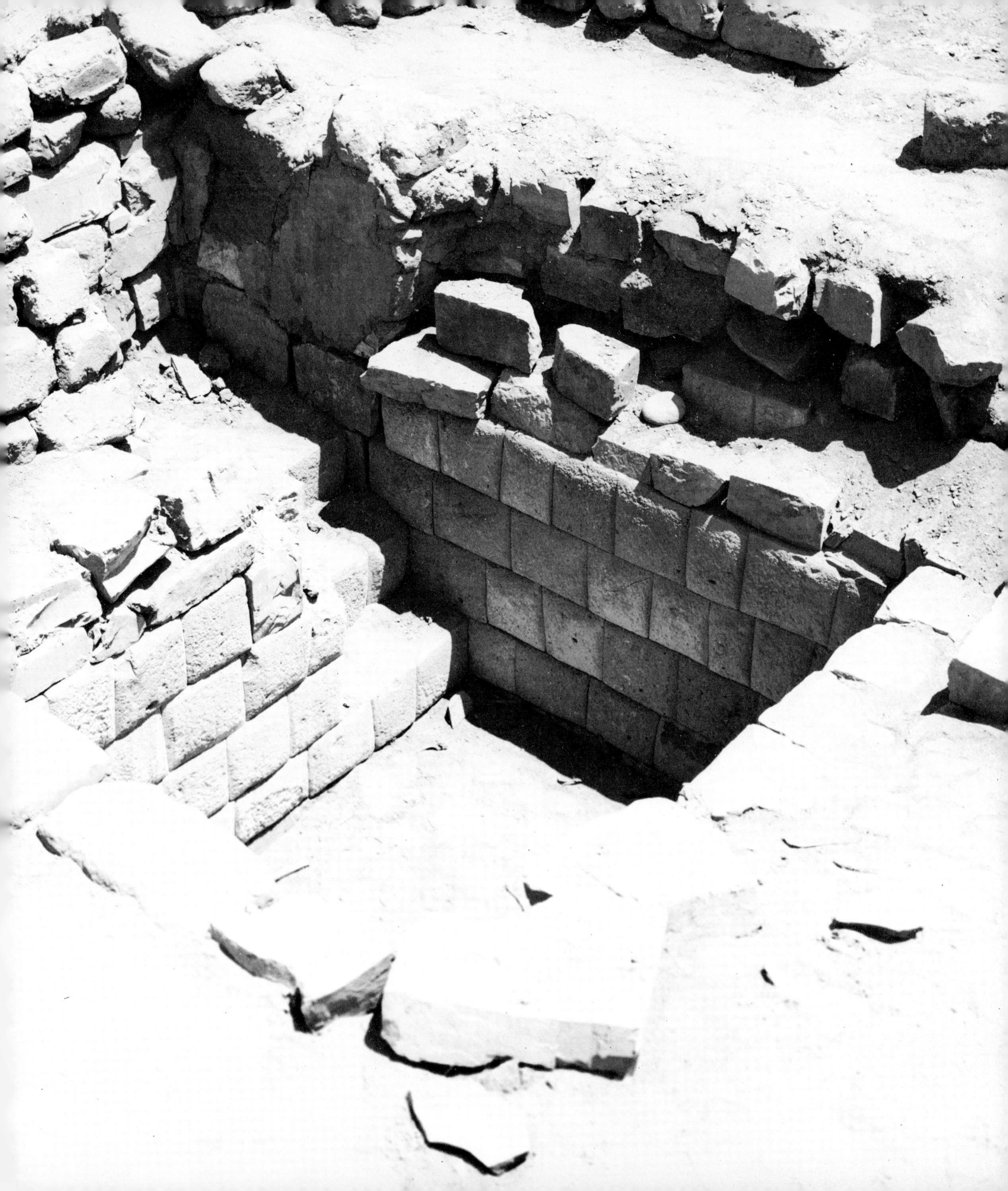

Bancroft tells of two baptisms that occurred among the Indians. One was performed at birth by the midwife who delivered the child. Bancroft states that the midwife completed the ceremony by dipping the child in water and saying, ". . . let it wash thee; let him cleanse thee that is in every place, let him see good to put away from thee all the evil that thou hast carried with thee from the beginning of the world, the evil that thy mother and father have joined to thee." The second baptism took place on the fifth day after birth and was performed also by the midwife. This baptism included the blessing of each part of the child's body. (Ibid., 3:369-76.)

Bancroft tells of a type of baptism that occurred at a marriage ceremony. On the fourth night of the ceremony, the night when the marriage was consummated, the couple sat on a mat of green reeds and were baptized by the priest pouring water over them. "Nobles received four ablutions with water in honor of the goddess of water and four of wine in honor of the goddess of wine." (Ibid., 2:260.) Bancroft does admit that these many rites and ceremonies among the nations of ancient America were similar to others observed by Jews and Christians of the Old World. Evidently the views of the early Spanish writers convinced him concerning the origin of the ordinances.

Pierre Honore describes a baptism recorded by some early Spanish chroniclers. The baptism took place in one of the temples of Tenochtitlan when a child was sprinkled with water and given a name. The priest said, "Take and receive, for on this earth you will live on water; water makes you grow and flourish, water gives us what we need for our life—receive this water." The Spanish writers also saw Aztec priests forgiving sins during baptism. (In Quest of the White God, p. 34.)

Rivero, in his history of Peru, finds that "baptism was general among all of the Peruvian nations west of the Andes." (Peruvian Antiquities, p. 180.) De Roo confirms that baptism took place in Yucatan before the Spaniards arrived. (America Before Columbus, p. 467.)

What appear to be baptismal fonts have been found in the Old World in numerous places, including a basin found beneath the Church of the Annunciation at Nazareth, Israel; a font at Qumran; and one at Ephesus. In the New World, fonts are thought to have been located in the Yucatan and near Lima, Peru.

Unlike the abundance of material written concerning baptism, very little is found concerning the practice of communion or the sacrament as we know it today. What has been found, though, indicates that a type of communion was practiced. Acosta, for example, writes of a ceremony among the Incas of Peru. In June the nuns of the sun made little loaves of bread from the flour of maize and the blood of white sheep. The priests gave everyone a morsel of these loaves, which were carried in silver and gold platters appointed for that use, "and all did receive those pieces thanking the sun infinitely for so great a favour which he had done them, speaking words and making signs of great contentment and devotion; protesting that during their lives they would neither do nor think anything against the sun or the Inca." (Acosta, pp. 345-54.)

May was the month of a similar ceremony among the Indians of Mexico. This was one of their principal feasts, and was made to their god Uitzilipuztli (also spelled Huitzilopochitli). Two days before the feast an image of the god made of the beet seeds and maize, molded with honey, was carried to the top of the temple and placed in "a little lodge of roses." The people stood in the court in reverence and fear. Pieces of the paste-type materials of which the idol was made were also used to fill the lodge. These morsels, called the flesh and bones of the god, were blessed by ceremonies of singing and dancing and distributed to everyone. Those who partook said they did eat the flesh and bones of God. People who were sick and could not attend had the sacrament brought to them. The ceremony ended with an old man of authority preaching the laws and ceremonies from a high place on the temple. (Ibid., pp. 356-60.)

Sahagun, describing probably the same ceremony, affirms that the dough was made into the form of the god, Uitzilopochtli (as he spelled it), and was broken up into pieces and given to all to eat in remembrance of the god. They said as they ate it, "the God is eaten." (Florentine Codex 3:5-6.) Bancroft, in describing much the same ceremony, says the name of the ceremony was teozualo, which meant "The god is eaten." (Works 3:440.)

No type of ceremony was found in my research that would correspond to partaking of the water as we do in our sacrament today. Christoval de Molina does mention that many elements of the Hebrew Passover and the Lord's Supper were found in the Feast of the Situa, the Incan Passover. He does not mention what these elements are, however, so it is not known if both a bread and water communion were available. (The Rites and Laws of the Incas, p. 21.)

STONE BOXES

Joseph Smith's account of the visitations from the angel Moroni indicate that his first experience occurred September 21 and 22, 1823. During the night of September 21, 1823, he was visited three times by this heavenly messenger. The following day he received a fourth visit, with specific instructions to meet Moroni on a nearby hill. In Joseph's own words we read of his fifth visit with Moroni:

". . . On the west side of the hill, not far from the top, under a stone of considerable size, lay the plates, deposited in a stone box. This stone was thick and rounding the middle on the upper side, and thinner towards the edges, so that the middle part of it was visible above the ground, but the edge all around was covered with earth.

"Having removed the earth, I obtained a lever, which I got fixed under the edge of the stone, and with a little exertion raised it up. I looked in, and there indeed did I behold the plates, the Urim and Thummim, and the breastplate, as stated by the messenger. The box in which they lay was formed by laying stones together in some kind of cement. In the bottom of the box were laid two stones crossways of the box, and on these stones lay the plates and the other things with them. . . ." (Joseph Smith 2:51-52.)

Joseph then stated that he returned to this spot, as commanded, each year for four years. In the fourth year he was permitted to take the plates from the stone box. He retained the plates, except for short intervals, until the messenger called for them; when he then delivered the plates to the messenger, he remarked, ". . . he has them in his charge until this day, being the second day of May, one thousand eight hundred and thirty-eight." (Joseph Smith 2:60.) We are not told of the exact date when the plates were returned, only that it was sometime prior to May 2, 1838.

Brigham Young said that Oliver Cowdery was with Joseph when he returned the plates:

"Oliver Cowdery went with the Prophet Joseph when he deposited these plates. Joseph did not translate all of the plates; there was a portion of them sealed, which you can learn from the Book of Doctrine and Covenants. When Joseph got the plates, the angel instructed him to carry them back to the Hill Cumorah, which he did. Oliver says that when Joseph and Oliver went there, the hill opened, and they walked into a cave, in which there was a large and spacious room. He says he did not think, at the time, whether they had the light of the sun or artificial light; but that it was just as light as day. They laid the plates on a table; it was a large table that stood in the room. Under this table there was a pile of plates as much as two feet high, and there were altogether in this room more plates than probably many wagon loads; they were piled up in the corners and along the walls. The first time they went there the sword of Laban hung upon the wall; but when they went again it had been taken down and laid upon the table across the gold plates; it was unsheathed, and on it was written these words: 'This sword will never be sheathed again until the kingdoms of this world become the kingdoms of our God and his Christ.'" (Journal of Discourses 19:38.)

Oliver Cowdery wrote eight letters to W. W. Phelps concerning the translation of the record of the Book of Mormon and the visit of Moroni. In an article published in the *Messenger and Advocate*, he related that the letters were written with the help of Joseph Smith, who offered to assist him in this effort to present a history of the Church. (*Messenger and Advocate*, October 1834, p. 13.) The following is Oliver's description of the stone box that contained the plates:

"The manner in which the plates were deposited: First, a hole of sufficient depth, (how deep I know not,) was dug. At the bottom of this was laid a stone of suitable size, the upper surface being smooth. At each edge was placed a large quantity of cement and into this cement, at the four edges of this stone were placed, erect, four other, their bottom edges on the first stone. The four last named, when placed erect, formed a box, the corners, or where the edges of the four came in contact, were also cemented so firmly that the moisture from without was prevented from entering. It is to be observed, also, that the inner surface of the four erect, or side stones, was smooth. This box was sufficiently large to admit a breastplate, such as was used by the ancients to defend the chest, etc., from the arrows and weapons of their enemies. From the bottom of the box, or from the breastplate, arose three small pillars composed of the same description of cement used on the edges; and upon these three pillars was placed the record of the children of Joseph, and of the people who left the tower far, far before the days of Joseph or a sketch of each, which had it not been for this, and the never failing goodness of God, we might have perished in our sins, having been left to bow down before the altars of the gentiles and to have paid homage to the priests of Baal!

"I must not forget to say that this box, containing the record, was covered with another stone, and the bottom surface being flat and the upper, crowning; but these three pillars were not so lengthy as to cause the plates and the crowning stone to come in contact. I have now given you according to my promise, the manner in which this record was deposited; though when it was first visited by our brother, in 1823, a part of the crowning stone was visible above the surface while the edges were concealed by the soil and grass, from which circumstance you will see, that however deep this box might have been placed by Moroni, at first, the time had been sufficient to wear the earth so that it was easily discovered, when once directed, and yet not enough to make a perceivable difference to the passer-by. . . ." (*Messenger and Advocate*, October 1835, pp. 196-97.)

Edward Stevenson, an early member of the Church and a friend of the Prophet, was shown the Hill Cumorah by an old gentleman in 1873 and wrote the following:

"He pointed out the spot of ground where the stone box was placed, near the summit, and on the west side of the point of the hill. He likewise stated that soon after the rumor so widely spread regarding 'Joe' Smith finding a gold bible, that there was great excitement throughout the whole country, and that it was about this time the Rochester Company located and searched for hidden treasure.

"Questioning him closely he stated that he had seen some good sized flat stones that had rolled down and lay near the bottom of the hill. This had occurred after the contents of the box had been removed and these stones were doubtless the ones that formerly composed the box. . . ." (*Reminiscences of Joseph, the Prophet*, pp. 28-29.)

In recent years other similar boxes have been discovered in Central and South America. Some contained tools, clothing, and jewelry; others appear to have been used for burial purposes. In each case, however, it is evident that these stone boxes were used to preserve something very valuable.

E. Wyllys Andrews of Tulane University states that stone boxes were used anciently as hiding places for food and supplies. He has found such boxes in Mexico that contained a variety of raw materials used in making jewelry. Some of the boxes were constructed by inverting one metate over the other. He also said that the boxes were occasionally sealed with plaster. (Letter dated April 20, 1964.)

Another interesting stone box, measuring approximately 1½ feet by 1 foot (inside) and 2½ feet by 2½ feet (outside), was found in Bolivia on the island of Titicaca. A fine tapestry poncho was found inside the box, but there is no positive means of dating it. A few stone boxes about 7 inches to 9 inches long have been found in Peru. These belonged to the Mochica culture, dating near the time of Christ.

Many of the stone boxes found in Mexico are carved with intricate designs. Some of the carved figures are believed to have represented gods, and there are evidences in the carvings that the people practiced blood sacrifice. Hieroglyphs, the quetzal bird, and other figures are seen. It is believed by some experts that cremation may have been practiced, and that the boxes were not only used to hold the remains of the dead, but also to preserve some of their worldly possessions.

At the ruins of Chichen Itza in Merida, the writer photographed a stone box with a lid rounded on the top, similar to the description of the box Oliver Cowdery said was the vessel for the gold plates of the Book of Mormon.

Prior to 1823, when Joseph Smith first saw the stone box containing the plates, no record had been found describing any type of stone box from any ancient period. Only in recent years have archaeologists confirmed that this method of storing valuable articles was commonly used in ancient cultures.

What would have been more valuable to the leaders of the Book of Mormon period than a history of their own people? What better way to preserve this precious record than in a stone box? Joseph Smith's and Oliver Cowdery's description of the stone box containing the golden plates stood alone for nearly a century as the only account involving ancient stone boxes. Today the validity of this description is strengthened by numerous discoveries of stone boxes in a variety of shapes and sizes.

A few of the nearly 50 stone boxes found to date in various locations. Ancient Americans apparently used these boxes to store their valuables in, keeping them safe from the elements and from warring tribes. Many times the boxes consisted simply of two *metates*, stones used for grinding corn, fitted together. Others were more eleborate, built carefully with more room for storage. It was in just such a stone box that Joseph Smith found the gold plates of the Book of Mormon, along with a breastplate and the Urim and Thummim.

STONE BOXES 79

HIGHWAYS

The Book of Mormon records the following on the highways of pre-Columbian America:

"And behold, now it came to pass that it was upon a tower, which was in the garden of Nephi, which was by the highway which led to the chief market, which was in the city of Zarahemla; therefore, Nephi had bowed himself upon the tower which was in his garden, which tower was also near unto the garden gate by which led the highway." (Between 23 and 20 B.C., Helaman 7:10.)

"And many highways shall be broken up, and many cities shall become desolate." (6 B.C., Helaman 14:24.)

"And it came to pass that there were many cities built anew, and there were many old cities repaired. And there were many highways cast up, and many roads made, which led from city to city, and from land to land, and from place to place." (A.D. 28, 3 Nephi 6:7-8.)

"And the highways were broken up, and the level roads were spoiled, and many smooth places became rough." (A.D. 34, 3 Nephi 8:13.)

From these scriptures we can deduce the following and then look for verification in archaeological evidences: (1) Highways existed in the Americas between 23 B.C. and A.D. 34, when they were "broken up" by earthquakes. (2) It is possible that no highways were constructed after this time, since no subsequent mention of highway construction occurs. (3) The remains of the highways would not be intact today. (4) We do not know what materials were used. (5) Cement is not mentioned. (6) Many highways and roads were constructed.

The history of modern road building goes back only two hundred years to Pierre-Marie Jerome Tresaquet, a French engineer who "made it possible for Napoleon to build great systems of French highways...." (Oglesby, *Highway Engineering*, p. 538.) This could explain why the explorers were surprised to discover pre-Columbian highways in Central and South America, for they believed that only the Old World possessed the technology to build highways. Several Spanish explorers left descriptions of highways in their records. The following is a literal translation of an extract from the manuscript *Relacion de Sarmiento*:

"One of the things that I admired most contemplating and noting the things of these kings was to think how they could make such big and superb roads as the ones we saw and what human strength was necessary to make them and with what tools and instruments they could level the mountains and break off the peaks to make them wide and fine like they are.... Some roads were fifty, an hundred, and two hundred leagues (1 league = 3 miles). One was eleven hundred leagues long, all excavated through mountains so great and fearful that looking down one lost sight and some of the straight cliffs were so abrupt that the road surface had to be cut into the rock and supported with wood to make the road wide and level enough, all of which was done with fire and tools; in other parts there were grades so sharp and extreme that they made stairs from the bottom to get to the highest point, interspersed at various points with rest areas for people to refresh themselves; in other parts there were mountains of snow that were to be feared, and these places were made to secure access through the snow...." (Prescott, *Conquest of Peru*, pp. 478-79.)

Cortez wrote on November 8, 1519: "In the morning the conquistadors arrived at a causeway that would lead them across a lake, a causeway so broad and strong that eight horsemen could ride along it abreast." (Irwin, *Fair Gods and Stone Faces*, p. 7.)

In 1548 Pedro Cieza de Leon noted in his diary:

"Accordingly the Inca constructed the grandest road that there is in the world as well as the longest, for it extends from Cuzco to Quito and was connected from Cuzco to Chile—a distance of 800 leagues (2,400 miles). I believe since the history of man there has been no other account of such grandeur as is to be seen on this which passes over deep valleys and lofty mountains, by snow heights, over falls of water, through the living rock and along the edges of tortuous torrents. In all these places, the road is well constructed, on the inclining mountains well terraced, through the living rock cut along the river banks supprted by retaining walls, in the snowy heights built with steps and resting places, and along its entire length swept cleanly and cleared of debris with post stations and storehouses and Temples of the Sun at appointed intervals along its length." (Von Hagen, *Highway of the Sun*, p. 3.)

The Mayan roads were reported by some to have been far superior to Roman highways: "Roman roads, proverbial for their permanence, have disappeared, can be traced today only with difficulty, or not at all. Our modern roads will, if left to the forces of nature, have completely disappeared without leaving a trace in 500 years, but this great Mayan road has withstood the passage of centuries, in a country of heavy rainfall and luxuriant vegetation, and with the exception of its cement facing, is almost the same now as it was the day when the last Maya trod its smooth level surface." (Hunter and Ferguson, *Ancient America and the Book of Mormon*, pp. 261-62.)

Alexander von Humboldt, in an 1802 scientific study of the highways in Ecuador, remarked: "The roads of the Incas were the most useful and stupendous works ever executed by man. . . . The solemn impression which is felt on beholding the deserts of the Cordinlleras is increased by the remarkable and unexpected fact that in these very regions there still exist wonderful remains of the great road of the Incas, that stupendous work. . . ." (Von Hagen, *Highway of the Sun*, p. 3.)

Cement appears to have been used in construction of roads and buildings: "Curiously enough, a fine variety of cement was known in those days which was used for covering houses and pyramids and for the making of roads. . . . In ancient times Chichen Itza and all the great and lesser cities of the Yucatan peninsula were linked by a network of smooth, hard-surfaced highways. The Mayas of today call these old roads Zac-be-ob, or white

Preceding page: Ancient road out of Pachacamac, Peru. *Above:* Pre-Columbian road of the Yucatan peninsula. Some 3,000 miles of ancient roads such as these stretch between Ecuador and Peru. The ingenuity of the ancient peoples is evident in their bypassing of natural obstacles with bridges and tunnels. *Opposite:* A stopping place for the chasqui runners, messengers of the Incas who comprised a relay-type communication system.

ways." (Widtsoe and Harris, *Seven Claims of the Book of Mormon,* p. 82.)

In South America there were two main north-south roads, one along the coast and one through the highlands. Transverse roads connected these, and minor roads connected each village. The north-south road started in Colombia and ended in Chile and was approximately 3,000 miles long. The roads followed a straight line wherever possible and zigzagged up slopes. Many were paved and were from three feet wide to one hundred feet wide. It has been estimated that there were 9,500 miles of road in the ancient South American system. Causeways were built in marshy places and over streams, and bridges and even tunnels have been found. Some suspension bridges were supported by ropes sixteen inches in diameter.

There is much conjecture regarding the purposes for which the pre-Columbian people built highways. Researchers believe that they were used for ceremonial purposes, for a communications system, and for military transport.

Most scholars agree that ancient highways were built for foot travel, but the dimensions of the roads indicate another purpose: "The Maya had no wheeled vehicles and no beasts of burden, so the road was used only by travelers on foot or in litters, and for them a road six feet wide would have been ample; the unusual width must have been for ceremonial pageantry: A procession of priests decked in jade and all their splendor with their overwhelmingly impressive spectacle of barbaric pomp." (Wauchope, *They Found the Buried Cities,* p. 341.)

Whenever communities start inhabiting larger and larger areas of land, the result is a greater separation from one another. Thus, for any kind of civilization to exist, a communications system is necessary.

"The Incas had an admirable communications system based on the chasqui runners. The Incas invented a system of posts which was the best that could be thought of . . . and so well was this running performed, that in a short time they knew, at a distance of three hundred . . . or even eight hundred leagues (2,400 miles) the message. The chasqui stations were built from half league to half league. . . . The roads were lined with these small houses at regular intervals. In each house the order read that there should be two Indians stationed there with provisions. The chasqui then ran with great speed, without stopping, each one for his half league. . . . Messages sent by relay runners reached Cuzco from Quito in five days, a distance of 1,230 miles." (Williams, *Americological Corner*, part IV.)

Concerning military use of highways, the Book of Mormon can be used to enlighten us, because these people were constantly at war.

"And it came to pass in the seventeenth year, in the latter end of the year, the proclamation of Lachoneus had gone forth throughout all the face of the land, and they had taken their horses, and their chariots, and their cattle, and all their flocks, and their herds, and their grain, and all their substance, and did march forth by thousands and by tens of thousands, until they had all gone forth to the place which had been appointed that they should gather themselves against their enemies." (A.D. 17.—3 Nephi 3:22.)

This type of mass migration would be a tremendous ordeal unless the people could travel on highways capable of such volume.

If the soldiers used chariots, they could take advantage of time and speed to defeat their enemies. Though scholars are not yet satisfied that the wheel was used in the New World until after the Spanish arrived (see Chapter 18), in recent years archaeologists have unearthed many wheel-type objects that seem to indicate the pre-Columbians understood the principle of the wheel. If so, it is only logical to assume that they would have used that knowledge to their advantage.

With thousands of years of highway building to their credit, it is likely that the ancients developed an expertise that paralleled or even surpassed modern road-building technology.

"Having described how these roads ran and how good they were, I shall tell how easily they were built by these people, without the work occasioning death or undue hardship. When a Lord-Inca had decided on the building of one of these famous highways, no greater provisioning or levies or anything else was needed except for the Lord-Inca to say, 'Let this be done.' The inspectors then went through the provinces, laying out the route and assigning Indians from one end to the other to the building of the road. In this way, from one boundary of the province to the other, at its expense and with its Indians, it was built as laid out, in a short time; and the others did the same, and, if necessary a great stretch of the road was built at the same time, or all of it. When they came to the barren places, the Indians of the lands nearest by came with victuals and tools to do the work, and all was done with little effort and joyfully, because they were not oppressed in any way, nor did the Incas put overseers to watch them." (Von Hagen, *The Incas of Pedro de Cieza de Leon*, p. 137.)

The ancients built their highways perfectly straight and overcame obstructions in ingenious ways, such as filling in ravines, building bridges, constructing dikes and tunnels, and terracing along canyon walls. Sometimes they would zigzag up and down mountainsides. In desert areas adobe block walls, bound together with mud, lined the roadsides to keep the road clear of drifting sand.

Research literature continually refers to the use of cement as a means of obtaining a smooth surface on ancient American highways. Cement, which has adhesive and cohesive qualities, chemically interacts with water to bind the mixture into a solid mass. Such a cement was used anciently as a plaster to smooth over a rough surface made of mortar and egg-sized aggregate.

The cement or plaster layer, however, was not the element that contributed to the strength of the road. It was, rather, the mixing of mortar and egg-sized stones, the mortar being the cement; when this was mixed with the aggregate and water, it formed a hardened composition that we know as concrete.

Durability is one of the most important factors in the quality of roads and pavement in any time. In Central and South America the weather is generally warm, humid, and rainy, conditions that usually have an adverse effect on the durability of highways. This problem is overcome somewhat when the concrete can be kept moist during the early stages of construction, to prevent the evaporation of the water in the concrete. The durability of the ancient roads seems to have been due to the moderate weather, which would almost eliminate the problems of freezing and thawing, heating and cooling so destructive to highways in less moderate areas today.

The ancient highways in damper climates included drainage systems to discourage the deteriorating effects of water on the roads. In the cities of Central and South America there are still drainage canals, ditches, and pipes where water was brought down the mountains for drinking, bathing, and irrigation.

Though the pre-Columbian engineers built their highways under difficult conditions, they produced adequate highways for their time, using practical know-how rather than sophisticated theory. Because of the many similarities between these roads and those of the Old World, it appears obvious that the builders' knowledge came with their ancestors from the Old World.

THE WHEEL

The only reference to the wheel in the Book of Mormon is in 2 Nephi 15:28, which is a quotation from Isaiah. However, use of wheels in the ancient Americas is inferred from seven references to chariots.

The wheel, a basic mechanical device, is regarded by most scholars as one indication of a higher civilization. The earliest known use of the wheel is the depiction of one on a limestone relief in Mesopotamia, indicating the use of a cart dating about 3500 B.C. (Singer, Holmyard, and Hall, *A History of Technology* 1:205.) This reference dates the presence of the wheel in the Old World considerably earlier than any reference for the New World. Recently, however, some artifacts have been found that are of serious interest to the student in this field.

POTTER'S WHEEL

Most archaeologists contend that the potter's wheel was not known in ancient America because the pottery uncovered appears to have been made by hand. There is, however, ample indication that pottery was made both by hand and by wheel in the Old World, and that many pots were manufactured there commercially and produced rapidly. It is also possible that these Old World techniques were taken at some time to America, either anciently or in more modern times.

W. N. Holmes reports an interpretation of an ancient American custom from which one may infer the use of the wheel in America: "In modeling a clay vessel, a bracket may be used as a support and pivot thus becoming an incipient form of the wheel. It may be used equally well in shaping of the bodies of vessels, thus assuming in a limited way the functions of a mold." (*20th Annual Report of the Bureau of American Ethnology*, p. 69.) This report notes that a device similar to a roulette wheel was used during the pre-Columbian period, and that such items were found near the mouth of the Missouri River.

In 1895 Henry C. Mercer observed a true though simple potter's wheel used by native potters of Merida, Mexico. Although this could have been a tool resulting from Spanish influences, its peculiar mechanism and mode of operation distinguish it from any similar wheel thus far known, in ancient or modern times, anywhere in the Old World. The natives even called the device by a Mayan name, *kabal*. Mercer is convinced that this device is indigenous to ancient Yucatan. (*The Bulletin of Free Museum of Science and Art* 1:63-69 [1897, no. 2].)

Lu Fawson concluded, after nine years of research, that the *kabal* of the Mayan civilization was a potter's wheel and that it was used prior to the arrival of the Spanish. (Fawson, "A Study of Documents That Substantiate the Existence of a Potter's Wheel in Ancient America.") Samuel K. Lothrup writes that he saw what appeared to be a potter's table in Peru. (Caso, *Sobretiro del Cuadernos Americanos*, p. 25.)

WHEELED TOYS

Researchers report that miniature animal-like clay articles apparently with wheels have been unearthed in Mesopotamia, and their counterparts have been found in Mexico. Because of their size, these artifacts are called toys. In Mesopotamia, miniature carts and chariots as well as full-size vehicles have been found. One large cart of a practical design has been discovered in Mexico. The absence of numerous larger artifacts has led some archaeologists to conclude that practical uses for the wheel were not known. Their assumption rests on the absence of stone or metal wheels. However, if wooden wheels were used, they would probably have been decomposed by now.

In 1880 the French explorer Desire Charnay, exploring an Indian cemetery in Popocatepetl, Mexico, found a toy dog or coyote with four disks that fit perfectly as wheels. In 1940 Matthew Stirling discovered eight in Tres Zapotes, Veracruz. The wheels appeared to be clay disks used to make the pottery toys mobile. Found alongside the wheels were a pottery dog and a pottery jaguar, each with two

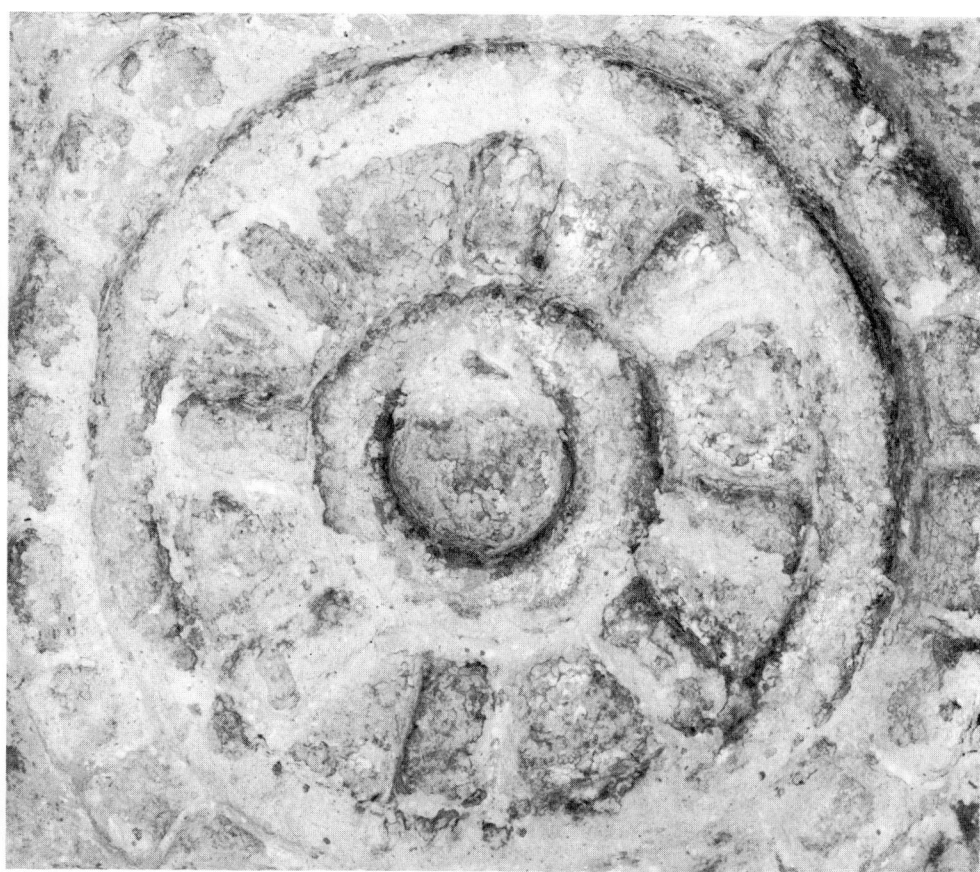

Wheeled toys and other wheel-shaped artifacts such as those pictured here indicate that the pre-Columbian Americans did have a knowledge of the principle of the wheel. Thus far, most archaeologists have believed that the wheel was not introduced to America until the arrival of the Spanish, but the increasingly numerous discoveries are calling that theory into question.

THE WHEEL 85

adobe tubes attached to the feet. The wheels were held together by wooden axles that passed through the tubes, which were attached to the animals' front and rear legs. On a second expedition Stirling found twelve more similar disks. He concluded that it apparently didn't occur to the people that they could use the wheel in a more general way. (Caso, *Sobretiro del Cuadernos Americanos*, p. 5.)

Some small metal dogs with circular perforations in their forefeet were once displayed in the National Museum of Mexico. Dr. Alfonso Caso classified them as Panamanian. In more recent years in Mexico and even in the southern United States, numerous adobe wheels with center perforations have been found. They could have been used as disks for sewing on clothing, in hairdos, or for spindle whorls or wheels.

Dr. Gordon P. Ekholm, a director of the American Museum of Natural History in New York, reports:

"During the winter of 1942, while I was making some excavations in Panuco and in the vicinity of Tampico, I found a certain number of small disks that I suspected of having been the wheels of rolling toys like those found by Dr. Stirling in Tres Zapotes and in Charnay in Popocatepetl. In the excavations of Panuco I felt most happy when my helper informed me of the finding of a complete toy with wheels just after having left the place myself and only a few meters from my excavation. This finding, together with the other known examples, convinced me that the Mexican Indians, before the conquest, had made small vehicles with wheels in the form of animals and therefore had some knowledge of the principle of the wheel." (Ibid., p. 8.)

In 1960 Hasso Von Winning reported the discovery in Central America of eighteen figurines that had presumably been mounted on wheels. In addition to these, the author has noted two more figurines now in the Museum of the American Indian in New York, five wheeled toys in the Stendahl collection at Los Angeles, three in the Los Angeles County Museum, and two in his own collection. Another survey in El Salvador recently has revealed an additional fifteen wheeled toys. (Contributions to Mesoamerican Anthropology, Miami, Florida, Pub. 1, 1973.) It is estimated that there are at least thirty examples of pre-Columbian wheeled toys that have been unearthed in Central America.

It is unlikely that the toys used a basic mechanical principle that was not used in a larger model. If we consider the nearly universal use of dolls, which are miniatures of people or animals, and of other small items common to everyday life, it is worth noting that we have not found any toys in a culture that were not at least partial replicas of larger, practical models.

The remarkable highways uncovered in Peru and northern Yucatan suggest the use of the wheel or rollers. South America has a system of highways measuring over nine thousand miles. Some archaeologists argue that the pre-Columbian Indians did not use the wheel, but that they did use rollers to carry loads. (Josephy, *The Indian Heritage of America*, p. 20.) That they constructed such huge highways for roller transportation and did not see the wheel principle in those rollers seems inconceivable. (See Chapter 17, "Highways.")

The concept of using the wheel to represent calendrical material is doubtless pre-Columbian, according to J. Eric Thompson, a renowned researcher. (Caso, *Sobretiro del Cuadernos Americanos*, p. 5.)

Smooth circular disks have been found throughout Mexico and the southern United States that could be spindle whorls or small wheels. If they are whorls (and some of them are attached to spindles), they could be construed to represent the wheel and axle principle.

William Salazar of Lima, Peru, discovered some metal disks, which are generally called mace heads. The mace was common in ancient America, but true maces were constructed of heavy metal or stone pieces, and they would form formidable weapons of war. What is most interesting concerning the pieces is that they were *not* made heavy, but were purposely made light. Near the periphery, openings were cut into the metal to lighten it. As a matter of fact, they seem to be early examples of our present gear principle, with an axle hole and precision-made gear-like teeth.

Other types of revolving objects with widespread use among the American cultures might have contributed to the discovery of the wheel principle. These include the pump drill, the top, the buzz disc, and possibly even the roller. Portions of the carvings on the pre-Columbian "Newspaper Rock" found in Indian Creek Canyon near Monticello, Utah, bear a marked resemblance to wheels.

Another interesting finding is a large circular stone with a hole in the center, thought to have been used for the ball game so common throughout Central America. Since the center hole is not as large as most of the game baskets, other uses are possible. In Copan, Honduras, the writer saw a sculptured stone slab with a figure resembling a wheel. The doughnut-shaped hoop used in the ball game of the ancient Americans indicates the idea of a circular unit. The large reservoirs of the Cuzco area of Peru are arranged in circular compartments. Even the large Aztec calendar stone suggests the idea of a wheel.

With the number of wheeled objects that have been found and the evidence of additional wheel-like units, it seems probable that archaeologists will soon recognize the wheel as an instrument used in ancient America. And since the Book of Mormon specifically mentions chariots, which implies the use of the wheel, we shall eagerly await future research to uncover more evidence of practical uses of this principle.

ARTS AND CRAFTS

The native Mesoamericans were particularly adept in certain arts and crafts, and many examples of their fine workmanship in pottery, metallurgy, and jewelry making are available for study.

Most of the pottery that has been unearthed appears to have been hand modeled by the coil method. The basic shapes are bowls, plates, jars, and bottles. Such items as whistles, rattles, earplugs, roller and flat stamps or seals, pipes, and spindle whorls were also made. Ceramic decorative techniques included modeling, incising, carving, and painting. Negative painting, an unusual process for decorating pottery, appeared early in Mesoamerica.

In ancient Peru, the Mochica civilization produced pottery that was exquisite in its recreation of lifelike figures. Many of these vessels, which date back to the first six centuries A.D., were probably modeled after portraits of actual persons.

The finest pottery in Peru is dated between 800 B.C. and A.D. 500. The surface of most of this pottery is black, brown, or red. The most common shape was the stirrup-spouted jar. Tripod dishes were also made, as well as the common low-level types. Serpents, monkeys, jaguars, birds, and supernatural beings embellished the pottery.

Though many of the pieces of pottery from 300 B.C. to A.D. 500 were made in molds, duplicates were rare. Portrayed on the pottery were humans engaged in different types of activities, animals, vegetables, houses and boats, deformations, and mutilations.

Most of the metallurgy of the ancient Americas consisted of a combination of gold, silver, and copper. The techniques included hammering, embossing, annealing, welding, soldering, strap joining, incising, cut-out designing, and the manufacturing of bimetal objects. Gold was cast by the lost-wax or wax-model method, and made into exquisite jewelry. Gold and silver ornaments from Peru include such items as pendants, tweezers, crowns, ear and nose ornaments, cuffs, pins, plaques and disks, earspools, and beads. Some of the gold objects were painted with a colored pigment. Iron has been found only in Peru, and there are few examples of this extant, probably because of the oxidation property of iron.

Atahualpa, the Inca leader, told his Spanish captors that if they would release him, he would fill a room twenty-five feet long, fifteen feet wide, and nine feet high with gold within sixty days. His offer indicates the ready availability of gold. The objects that were brought as part of Atahualpa's ransom were only part of the gold the Peruvian empire had gathered. Even today there is perhaps more gold still undiscovered than has been found. It is believed that the color of gold was sacred to the ancient peoples because it resembled the sun, symbol for the Incan god. The people built temples to their sun god and made objects of gold that resembled the sun.

Scholars believe gold was not used as money or a medium of exchange, but for ornamental purposes. Sheet gold was used on the inside walls of buildings, and small pieces were sewn on garments for decoration. Animals of gold and silver were sculptured. These metals were so plentiful that they were even used to make pots, pans, and dishes. Gilding was done with gold leaf, but the process used is not known today. Welding was used at low heat levels with some kind of chemical mixture.

Tumbaga, a gold and copper alloy, was very popular in Colombia. When hammered, it becomes almost as hard as bronze or soft steel. One of the items valued greatly by collectors of ancient artifacts is the pre-Columbian gold cup, handwrought in all sizes and all shapes and with varying gold content. Some authorities believe that tin and platinum were used as alloys. Bronze was used, but brass objects have not yet been found. Alloys were used to make blades for digging sticks, mace heads, and lance points. It is believed that metalworking started in South America several hundred years earlier than in Central America.

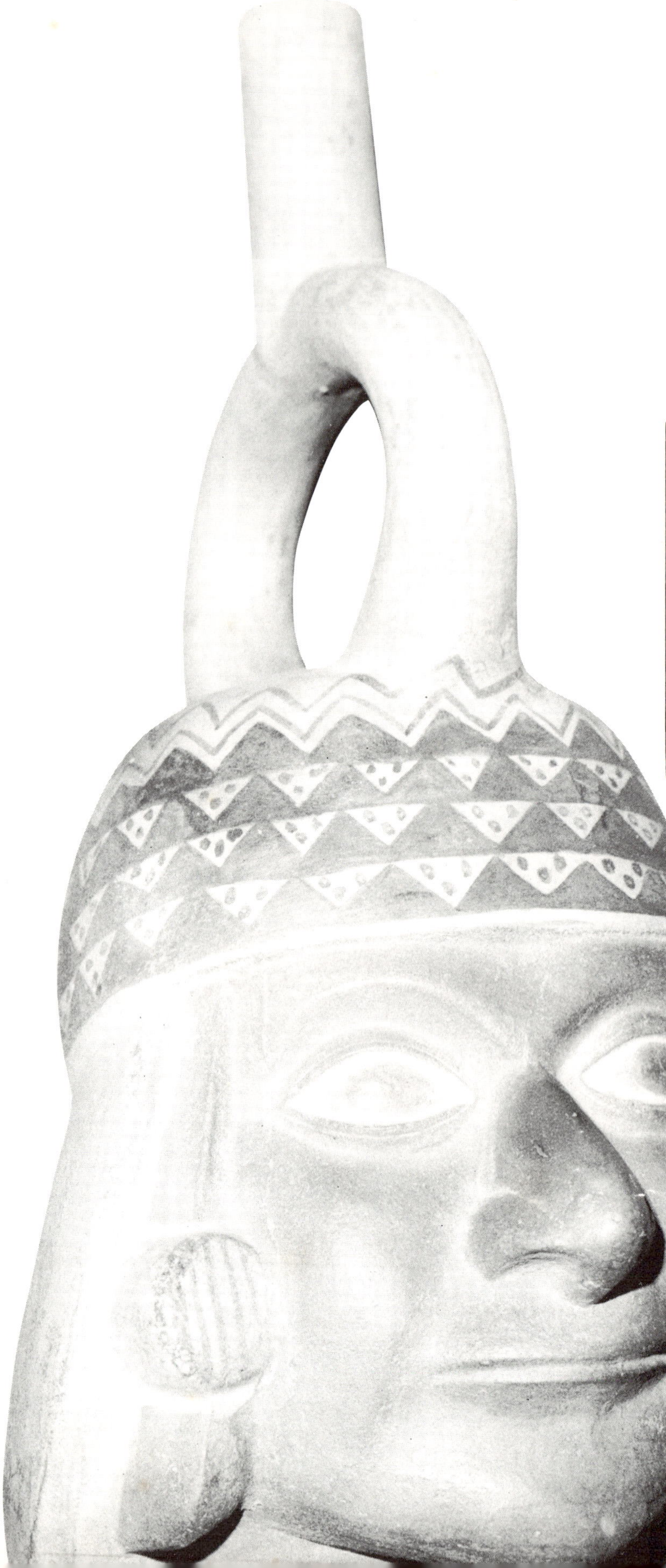

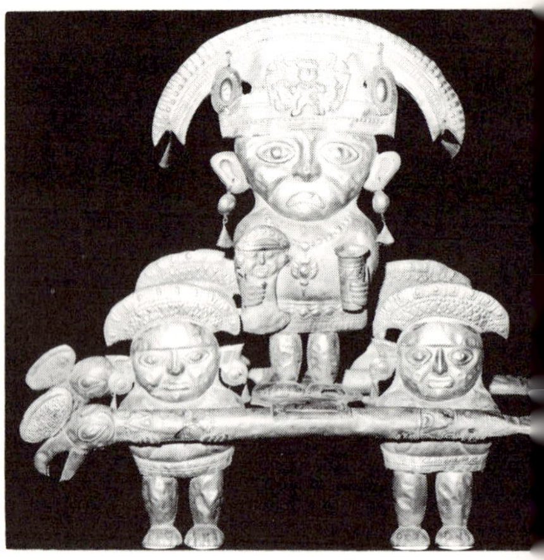

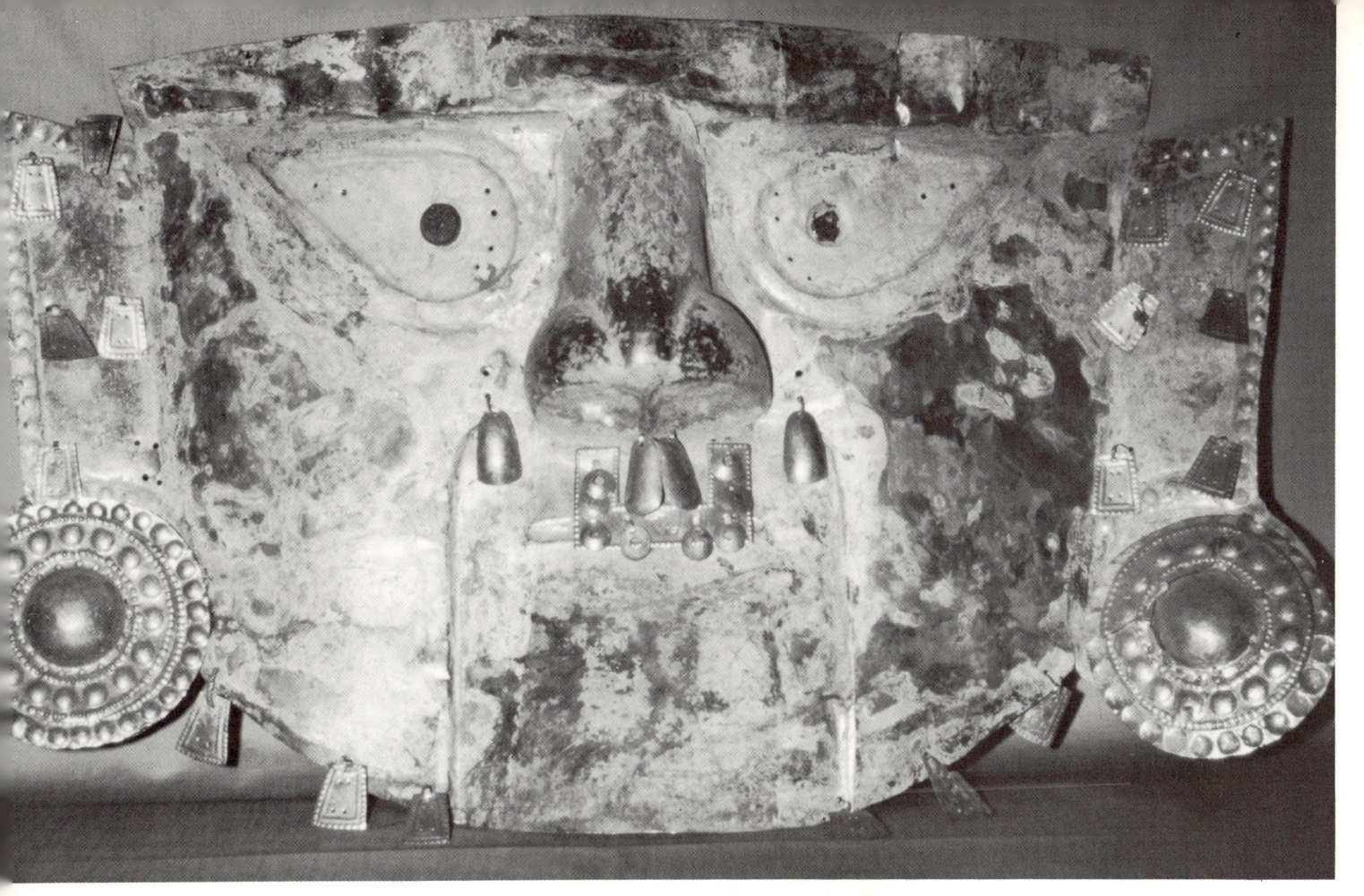

Opposite: Portrait jar from the Mochica culture of Peru. This beautiful, lifelike pottery form, which took the place of photographs anciently, reached its zenith with the Mochica. *Opposite above:* Gold statue from Peru, now a part of the Hugo Cohen collection. *Above:* Gold face mask from Peru. Gold was plentiful in pre-Columbian times and was used for ornamentation rather than as a medium of exchange. *Left:* This pottery, of the Nasca culture, is unusual in its shape and design. Nasca pottery is noted for its polychromatic, or multicolored, style.

ARTS AND CRAFTS 89

As early as 800 B.C., the Peruvians were masters in the art of fashioning jewelry from turquoise, quartz, lapix luxuli, and other hard stones. Bone, shells, and wood were also used in the creation of such items as beads, pendants, rings, and combs.

Central America's most valuable stone during the Maya civilization was green jade, a semiprecious jewel considered more valuable than gold. Mirrors of silver, copper, and pyrite have been found in ancient burial areas, along with tweezers made of copper, silver, and gold. Inlaid teeth have been found, as well as ancient hairpins, thorn combs, rings, and costume jewelry.

The carving was a slow, painstaking process, using crude drills, stone saws, strings, stone and copper chisels, and rubbing stones with sand as an abrasive.

The ornaments of the common people appear to have been limited to nose rings and earrings. The jewelry of the more elite was made from wax molds.

This piece of pottery from Mexico demonstrates one style that reached beyond the realistic to the fantastic. It has not been dated.

THE WORLD OF THE BOOK OF MORMON

HORSES

The existence of horses in the pre-Columbian Americas has been a point of debate among Book of Mormon and scientific researchers. Ample evidence has been found in an archaeologically sound context to show beyond doubt the horse was once in the Americas. But the skeletal remains, as interpreted by scientists, show that the horse died out about ten to eleven thousand years ago, or sometime near the end of the Pleistocene Age.

The horse is often cited by scientists as an example of how the theory of evolution works. Eohippus, a small animal about the size of a dog, is named as the forerunner of the modern horse. It is Eohippus that has been found in excavation, and Eohippus that died out ten thousand years ago. But though the supposed evolutionary generations of Eohippus may have been found in strata from different geological ages, we can, by pointing out some inconsistencies in the evolutionary theory, show that Eohippus does not have to be related to the horse.

George Gaylord Simpson, a prominent paleontologist, points out a major flaw in the theory and suggests there was no need for this animal to evolve into anything else: "Eohippus was *not* an imperfect model that needed to have the teeth, feet and other parts rebuilt to make it into equus [modern horse]. Eohippus was a going concern on its own, a well-adapted animal that got along very well in its own world and following its own habits." (Simpson, *Horses*, p. 230.)

Scientists have also claimed that the modern one-toed horse has descended from Eohippus, which was a five-toed type. They say this happened in stages of five toes, then four, three, and one, with no trace of two ever having been found. If this theory is to hold up, we should not be able to find in modern times any variety of three-toed horses (that supposedly being the last evolutionary link to modern horses, and transpiring about eight million years ago).

In 1922 the *Guide to the Specimens of the Horse Family*, published by the Department of Zoology, British Museum of Natural History, had a discussion on three Shire horses, each of which was "said to be a veritable three-toed horse." With all three horses exhibiting the same characteristic, we might assume that it is representative of the breed, not a mutation or recidivism.

Another example of multitoed horses in relatively recent times is given by Richard S. Lull: "Pliny the Elder, a naturalist in A.D. 79, tells us in his Natural History: 'It is also said that Caesar the dictator had a horse which would allow no one to mount him but himself, and that its forefeet were like those of a man.' Unquestionably this description is somewhat highly colored, but a multitoed horse without doubt forms that basis for the legend." ("The Evolution of the Horse Family," *American Journal of Science*, 23 [1907]: 166-67.)

There are several other flaws in the evolutionary theory with regard to brain, teeth, and size, but these passages will suffice for our discussion here. The flaws in the theory of evolution of the horse have not been pointed out to discredit science, but rather to help free the mind from traditionally accepted scientific theory that may tend to stifle creative thinking.

The Book of Mormon mentions the horse fourteen times, in 1 Nephi 18:25; 2 Nephi 12:7 and 15:28; Enos 1:21; Alma 18:9 (twice), 18:10, 18:12, and 20:6; 3 Nephi 3:22, 4:4, 6:1, and 21:14; and Ether 9:19.

What do we have by way of external evidence that horses existed in America in pre-Columbian times?

A Catholic priest in Cuenca, Ecuador, keeps a large collection of metal plates and panels purchased from local Indians. The plates and panels were dug up by the Indians. One of the many pictures on the panels clearly depicts a horse.

Some claim there were no pre-Columbian horses because there were no roads that the horses could walk on. However, networks of thousands of miles of roads have been discovered in South America. (See Chapter 17.)

Research by M. F. Ashley Montague indicates that the horse never became extinct in America. His argument is that the horse is a slow breeder and that its size in the post-Columbian period shows the stock drawn upon was primarily the native American horse. (*American Anthropologist*, 1944, pp. 568-69.)

Some bones found in 1953 near Midland, Texas, have been identified as those of a horse. Dating places this find at eight thousand years old. (Josephy, *The Indian Heritage of America*, p. 44.)

Victor Von Hagan reports that a story recorded by two chroniclers related the finding of a hide and the jaw of an animal, which both sources said looked like those of a horse. (Von Hagan, *The Desert Kingdoms of Peru*, p. 135.)

Rock art of the American Indian depicting horses can be found in Kansas, Utah, and Colorado. Many of these figures were no doubt made after the Spanish arrived, but there is still the possibility that some were carved earlier. It is very difficult to determine the age of this type of inscription.

Ancient horse bones have also reportedly been found in Argentina. (*National Geographic*, October 1969, p. 473.) Evidences of extinct horses have also been reported at Fells Cave on the Straits of Magellan (Clark, *World Prehistory*, p. 272) and at Tule Springs, northwest of Las Vegas, Nevada (Reed, *The Ancient Past of Mexico*, p. 3).

When the Book of Mormon was published in 1830 it was generally believed that the horses introduced by the Spanish were the only ones ever known to America; however, it has since been proved that horses appeared on the western continent ages ago and that they had disappeared almost completely at the time of Columbus. The exact date of their extinction is not known; remains of horses are found in the most recent geological formations, and they continued here after the introduction of man. Professor W. D. Matthew of the American Museum of History believes it probable that they were destroyed by early hunters. He implies that few of them may have lived to the time of Columbus.

"All of these horses became extinct [in] both North and South America. Why, we do not know. It may have been that they were unable to stand the cold of the winters, probably longer continued and much more severe during the Ice Age than now. It is very probable that man—hunters—played a large part in extinguishing the race. The competition with the bison and the antelope, which had recently migrated to America, may have made it more difficult than formerly for the American horse to get a living. Or, finally, some unknown disease or prolonged season of drought may have extinguished the race. Whatever the cause, the horse had disappeared from the New World when the white man invaded it (unless a few individuals still lingered on the remote plains of South America), and in his place the bison had come and spread over the prairies of the North." (Matthew and Chubb, *Evolution of the Horse*, p. 13.)

The University of Nebraska reports the discovery of man and horse bones together in the Guadalupe Mountains of New Mexico, and remains at Burnet Cave and Hermit's Cave have been declared several thousand years old. The researchers conclude that the horse was used only as food. (*University of Nebraska News Museum Notes*, January 1963.)

Leo Deuel says his research points to the fact that horses were found in ancient America, leading him to conclude that "we had found the first evidence that this ancient horse was hunted and eaten by the early natives of South America." (Deuel, *Conquistadores Without Swords*, p. 538.)

A display in the British Museum indicates that the horse originated in the Americas and traversed the Bering Straits to Europe and Asia. This theory is not new; it has been stated by several anthropologists.

Readers of the Book of Mormon have found that although horses are mentioned fourteen times, no one is reported to have ridden on one. Most of the references are in connection with the use of a chariot. Another clue of the purpose of the horse may be in 3 Nephi 4:4, where we read that horses, cattle, and flocks were gathered by the Nephites so they "might subsist" for the space of seven years. Perhaps horses were used for food until they became extinct—which would seem a logical explanation for the lack of their presence at the time of the Spanish conquest.

Lucy Mack Smith, mother of Joseph Smith, reports he related how the ancient inhabitants of this continent had animals "upon which they rode." (*History of Joseph Smith by His Mother*, p. 83.) This reference could not be considered as evidence to the non-Mormon, but the things the Prophet said are today proving to be true.

CALENDAR SYSTEMS

A calendar system is a system of thought dealing with the passing of time and not necessarily a physical object, such as the circular Aztec calendar stone. Some references to ancient calendar systems do, however, refer to a physical object.

No calendar stone has been found that would date back to the early Classic or pre-Classic Mayan period:

"Archaeologists have concluded, from this total absence of examples showing the earlier stages in the development of Mayan hieroglyphic writing and chronology, that both originally must have been recorded on some medium other than stone; that the first Mayan monuments were, in fact, made of some perishable material like wood, excellent hard varieties of which are to be found in greatest abundance throughout the Peten forest; and which the Mayan hieroglyphic writing and chronology were carved, have all been destroyed by the moist climate and heavy rains of the Peten lowlands." (Morley, *The Ancient Maya*, p. 46.)

This discussion will not be dependent upon the actual physical structure of the Mayan calendar; rather, it will deal only with the calendar system. For convenience, however, it is assumed that the physical Mayan calendar was similar to the common Aztec calendar stone.

Most authorities believe that the ancient American calendar system was developed independently of external influences. One authority writes:

"The passage of time, seen in finer and finer degree in the course of human life, the succession of summer and winter, the waxing and waning moons, the alternation of day and night, the upward and downward sloping of the sun and the swing dial of the stars, is a phenomenon that no human group has failed to notice." (Spinden, *Civilizations of Mexico and Central America*, pp. 96-97.)

Sylvanus G. Morley believes that the Mayan chronological system is the product of a single mind:

"The Maya chronological system is so complex, so delicately built and balanced, that it is difficult to believe it could have developed slowly, part here, part there, until it gradually took final form. On the contrary, it seems more than probable that it was the work of a single mind, possibly working with a few associates, some ancient Maya Hipparchus, who brought the Maya chronological system to perfection in his own lifetime, although the solar and lunar data upon which it was based doubtless had been accumulating for a number of centuries before this time." (Morley, *The Ancient Maya*, pp. 46-47.)

If Morley's reasoning is correct, his idea lends weight to the thought that the Mayan chronological calendar system is more accurate than our own Gregorian calendar. Alvin Josephy confirms this: ". . . we can unravel all the intricacies of their [Mayas] calendric calculations which are quite impressive—their calendar in general use was one ten-thousandth of a day per year more accurate than is ours now." (*The American Heritage Book of Indians*, p. 19.)

Lehi, of the Book of Mormon, could have introduced the principle of the Mayan calendar system to ancient America. There seem to have been influences from both the Hebrew and Egyptian calendar systems. Though he lived in Jerusalem, it is possible he had knowledge of the Egyptian calendar system because of the large amount of trade between Egypt and Israel during that period. If it is true that Lehi did know of both calendar systems, it would follow that, if he were establishing a new society, he would take the best ideas from each system and form one new system. The reader should keep in mind that we are not attempting to establish that Lehi did, in fact, bring the principle of the Mayan calendar to the Americas, but that he, or anyone in a similar situation, *could* have brought it to the Americas. The point is that there seems to be distinct Old World influence on the Mayan calendar system.

Both the Egyptians and the Mayas used a year as a unit of time. This point may seem rather insignificant,

CALENDAR SYSTEMS 93

but the particular type of year (lunar-solar) has considerable importance.

"This original lunar calendar of the Middle Americas appears to have been more or less identical with the lunar calendars of other early people, such as those of the ancient Egyptians and Israelites. Like them its months were moon or lunations of 29 or 30 days each, counted from new moon. Its year began very probably on the day following the appearance of the first new moon after the spring equinox, the natural point of beginning for an agricultural and astronomically minded people such as the ancient Middle Americans." (Jakeman, *The Ancient Middle-American Calendar System—Origin and Development*, pp. 6-7.)

Both the Mayas and the Egyptians were aware of the fact that there are more than 360 days in a year.

"They understood that there were more days in the true solar year by 5¼ days. They seemed generally to have ignored the ¼ day altogether, and using the same arrangement as the Egyptians, placed the five extra days, which they counted as evil days, on the end of one year and the beginning of the next. . . .

"Not all nations adhered to this procedure. Though they had a 30-day month and recognized that it did not keep in step with the seasons or the solar year, they rectified this by adding an extra month every 6 years. So 5 days each year × 6 equals 30 days." (Mahoney, *Symposium of the Archaeology of the Scriptures*, pp. 87, 93.)

Concerning the quarter-day mentioned above, we read in the *Encyclopedia Britannica* (4:626): "There is evidence, not accepted by all students, that the Maya calculated the error between their year of 365 days and the solar year of 365.242199 days which had accumulated in nearly 4,000 years since the starting point of their count. Such corrections were recorded in separate entries, they were not an integral part of the calendar."

Both the Egyptians and the Mayas placed emphasis on the extra five days: "For the Egyptians the five days were for fasting and celebrations. For the Mayas they were evil days—no

94 THE WORLD OF THE BOOK OF MORMON

serious undertaking was performed during the five days—no marriages, no important journeys, etc." (Mahoney, p. 93.)

A seven-day week seems to have been characteristic of both the Mayan civilization and that of the Old World. Dr. Jakeman writes that there is "evidence of an early 7-day count in the Maya area—i.e., the period known as the week in the Ancient Mesopotamian, Israelite and Christian calendars of the Old World." (The Ancient Middle-American Calendar System, p. 7.)

"The Mayas and the Egyptians both had a religious calendar apart from the civil one, and both had it under the direction of their priesthood." (Ibid., p. 90.) The Mayan sacred calendar year was probably the more popular of the two:

"In all probability the only part of their highly elaborate calendar and chronology with which the common folk, the corn farmers, the hewers of wood and drawers of water, were familiar was the sacred year of 260 days, the tozolkin or 'count of days.' This time-period was the most fundamental fact of their religion, since it determined for everybody the very pattern of his or her ceremonial life. The ancient Maya, man or woman, . . . regarded his or her birthday not as the position in the tropical year [civil year], that is the month-day upon which he was born, as we do but the day of the tozolkin, or 260-day sacred year upon which he was born. The god of the particular day of this 260-day period upon which a man was born was his patron saint, his guardian diety, his celestial godfather, so to speak." (Morley, The Ancient Maya, pp. 265-67.)

The history of the Egyptian calendar system is obscure, and even more obscure is any information pertaining specifically to the Egyptian religious calendar. Mahoney writes: "Up to now I have found only a statement that Egypt also had a sacred calendar, apart from the civic calendar, which was perhaps more correct and stable as to seasons than the civic calendar. . . . Here also the priests were in charge because their calendar called for feasts and rituals." (Op.

Opposite: **Maya month- and day-sign glyphs. Symbols like these are found carved on stones in many ruins, such as Palenque. The Mayan calendar system, highly elaborate and very accurate, bore many similarities to that of the Egyptians.** *Above:* **This sun-dial stone, which provided the ancients with a method of determining time, is found on top of Machu Picchu.** *Left:* **Gold disc calendar from Peru. This calendar is of the Chavin culture, c. 800 B.C. to A.D. 200.**

cit., p. 90.) This statement is not documented, so there is little possibility of learning where Mahoney got his information. Further investigation leads to the possible conclusion that this Egyptian religious calendar is the ancient astronomical or mythological calendar. However, this is only a theory. One author presents the hypothesis that "the twelve Egyptian months and the twelve signs of the zodiac formerly corresponded—the one as a vulgar or civil, the other as an astronomical or mythological calendar—to each other, and to a form of year commencing in autumn. . . ." (Mure, A Dissertation on the Calendar and Zodiac of Ancient Egypt, p. 61.)

Mahoney makes no reference to the length of the religious year, but if it is correct to theorize that he was referring to the ancient Egyptian Zodiac calendar, then it would appear that the Egyptian religious calendar has the same number of days as the civil calendar, in contrast to the 260-day Mayan religious calendar. The Mayan time system was broken up in the following way:

Kin = day
Uinal = twenty days, or a month
Tun = 360 days
Katun = twenty Tuns, or 7,200 days
Baktun = twenty Katuns, or 144,000 days
Pictun = twenty Baktuns, or 2,880,000 days
Calabtun = twenty Pictuns, or 57,600,000 days
Kinchiltun = twenty Calabtuns, or 1,152,000,000 days
Alautun = twenty Kinchiltuns, or 23,040,000,000 days
(Lorang, Footloose Scientist in Mayan America, p. 193.)

Another important basic unit of the

CALENDAR SYSTEMS 95

calendar system is the Mayan number system, a decimal system with 10 as a basic unit. Certain South American calendrical systems that have been found show that these people also had a knowledge of astronomy. A sun dial at Machu Picchu has been found, as well as a gold disc calendar of the Chavin culture (c. 800 B.C. to A.D. 200).

German Arciniegas summarized the status of the Mayan calendrical system well when he stated:

"The Maya invented a hieroglyphic writing, the oldest known texts of which correspond to the beginning of the Christian era. They used a very advanced numbering system, superior to Europe's because it made use of the zero. This enabled them to leave an accurate chronology in their codices. Their year of 365 days was divided into nineteen months: eighteen of twenty days each, and one of five. Their metric system was vigesimal, that is, it was based on the number twenty. They used their calendar to advance their knowledge of astronomy more than to record their political history. The Mayan manuscript known as the Dresden Codex is an almanac for divination. The date with which their chronology begins must be a reference to a myth of the creation of the world. The Mayan priests recognized the difference between the year of 365 days and the solar year, and remedied the difference by means of a secondary series." (Arciniegas, *Latin America: A Cultural History*, p. 8.)

Here one might ask, Are the similarities between the Mayan and the Old World systems simply coincidental, or is there some connection between them? It is possible that some of the similarities are due to astrological observations; yet one may question the similar handling of the extra five days, the seven-day week, the dual calendar system, and the number systems. Though the evidence is not yet conclusive, I believe that the evidence presented shows that the Old World theory of origin of the Mayan calendar system is a feasible one.

The chart on this page, compiled by Pierre Honore (*In Quest of the White God*, pp. 93-94), shows a comparison of the most important calendars.

Year of introduction	Country or people	Division of the year	Duration of year in days
2772 B.C.	Egypt	Calendar of 10 months and 365 days	365.000
2500 B.C.	Mesopotamia	Calendar of 360 days	360.000
2025 B.C.	Mesopotamia	Cycle of moon and sun of 19 years—12 with 12 months each, 7 with 13 months each	
1200 B.C.	Babylonia	Sun year with 12 months and 12 signs of the zodiac	
1200 B.C.	Judea	Moon year of 345 days with irregular intercalations of varying length	345.000
715-672 B.C.	Rome	Numa Pompilius introduces moon calendar with 355 days, 12 months, and intercalations of varying length	355.000
46 B.C.	Rome	Julius Caesar introduces Calendar of the Sun year, 365 days with intercalary day every four years (still used in Russia, which explains why the Russian New Year is 13 days after ours)	365.250
A.D. 1582	Rome	Pope Gregory reforms Julian calendar and establishes the one valid today	365.424,400
App. A.D. 300	Maya	18 months with 20 days each plus 5 blank days	365.242,129

Exact length of the astronomical year: 365.242,198

96 THE WORLD OF THE BOOK OF MORMON

MEDICINE

When the conquistadores of Spain arrived in the Americas, they found a civilization that was advanced in many areas. But in their attempt to Christianize the conquered peoples, most of the natives' valuable writings were destroyed, including their medical books. Fragments that were left gave some insight into their knowledge of medicine; even more has been and is being discovered through archaeological findings.

Europe is indebted to Mexican doctors for balsam, copal, liquid amber, sarsaparilla, and other plants that have been used in medicine. Diuretic agents, sneezing powders, medicine to combat fever, salves, ointments, infusions, plasters, and other medicinal items were sold in the marketplace, as Cortez and Diaz testified in their accounts. (Ramirez, *Medicine Pre-Cortesiana, the Stelae of Monte Alban,* pp. 25-26.)

From a few scriptures in the Book of Mormon we learn that the ancient Americans knew enough about medicine that they could successfully treat their wounded and combat diseases with special plants and roots. Concerning the health of the people, the Book of Mormon records: "And there were some who died with fevers, which at some seasons of the year were very frequent in the land—but not so much so with fevers, because of the excellent qualities of the many plants and roots which God had prepared to remove the cause of diseases, to which men were subject by the nature of the climate—But there were many who died with old age." (Alma 46:40-41.)

When the Spanish arrived in the New World in 1519, they found the Aztecs using roots and herbs to cure their invalids. Avocado seeds were mixed with plantain water to help stop diarrhea, while a cathartic agent from the quauhay chuachtli herb helped stop constipation. Jimson weed was useful in treating asthmatic spasms. A variety of herbs and resins from trees helped in preventing psoriasis and other skin ailments. The flowers and bark of the Mexican magnolia tree were used to treat heart cases, working in much the same manner as modern-day digitalis. The Aztecs were also advanced in the use of anesthetics, such as mescaline from peyote and marijuana. (Ramirez, *op. cit.,* pp. 64-73.) The Incas also discovered an anesthetic, cocain, from the coco bush. (Thorwald, *Science and Secrets of Early Medicine,* p. 294.)

Sarsaparilla was used in treating kidney and bladder ailments, as a medicine for internal treatment of rashes, and as a gargle. Acayall leaves were rolled around a little stick and smoked to produce a state of tranquillity. Pulverized tobacco leaves were used to treat headaches, dizziness, stupor, and maladies of the nostrils; the tobacco powder was used by sniffing.

Tonic, a beverage of the Aztecs, was made by boiling powder made from the bean of the cacao bush in water with vanilla, honey, and pepper. Mouthwash was made by combining salt and the leaf of a certain aromatic plant. Toothpaste was created from wood ashes and honey. Antiperspirant was produced by mixing herb juice with human bone and dog bone ground up with sweet-smelling flowers.

The milk and resin of a tree called mulli yielded a dried latex used as a plaster to help heal wounds and as a suppository to treat intestinal worms. White milk from a tree called hoje, which grows in the area of Pucallpa in the Peruvian jungle, is a powerful coagulant and stops bleeding almost immediately.

Curare was used for a muscle relaxant. Cinchona bark was a source of quinine often used to treat fevers. Cascara sagrada was discovered to be a laxative.

Datura was valuable as pain reliever. Ephedra was a nasal remedy.

A common religious practice among the Aztecs was to offer human sacrifices to their gods. For practical if not compassionate reasons, the priest dulled the senses of the victim with narcotics given at dawn on the day of sacrifice. Later, before he was flung onto the sacrificial stone, a second narcotic, in the form of a powder, was blown into his face. This narcotic was extracted from the plant yoyotti. (Schendel, op. cit., p. 17.)

Steam baths were used to relieve rheumatism, paralysis, and neuralgia. Water was poured over hot stones, and the patient's body was lashed with maize leaves. Rubber was applied in the form of large plasters to relieve rheumatism and pleurisy.

The Indians had specialists in bleeding, called the tecoani. Instead of using leeches, they used thorns of the maguey or lancets of obsidian to open veins.

Treatment for broken bones was similar to that used today. The broken bone was carefully set and the limb placed between splints of wood and tied tightly with cord. A plaster was then applied to the break. It was composed of gum from the acozotle tree, resin, and feathers. The limb and splints together were then encased in a second covering of rubberlike gum.

For arthritis, the patient was directed to find an anthill and let the ants bite his ailing hands. Sometimes the hands were soaked in warm water in which the leaves of a bitter astringent had been crushed.

One Aztec treatment for diarrhea was an enema followed by a suppository composed of soot, oil, and allspice. Treatment for fever consisted of drinking part of a jar of water in which willow leaves were soaked, pouring the remainder of the liquid over the patient's head, rubbing the patient's body with a cooling lotion, and administering a cold enema. Quinine was given in severe cases.

A common burn ointment of the Aztecs was composed of the yolk of a raw egg, the juice of a nopal cactus, and honey. The Mayans used egg yolk and lime juice.

Ulcers were cured with extract of the bark of the guava tree, which has an astringent property. A tea brewed from chiranthodendron pentadactylon was sipped as a tonic for the heart.

The people wore amulets to protect against disease—an arm stricture, a nose ornament, a lucky shell or stone.

Dr. C. Martinez Duran, professor of the history of medicine at Guatemala University, says that the Indians still believe that illness is due to a spell. He further states that the surgical instruments of the Guatemalan Indians in pre-Hispanic times were made of obsidian. From pottery he has analyzed, he concludes that tuberculosis was found in America anciently.

Medical and dental scientists at Case Western Reserve University in Cleveland, Ohio, have examined many skeletons in Ohio and have concluded that the pre-Hispanic Indian was plagued by arthritis. Investigation also shows chronic bone infections and numerous bone tumors. (Medical Tribune, August 15, 1968, p. 3.)

Dr. Abner I. Weisman, clinical professor of obstetrics and gynecology at New York Medical College, has demonstrated through his research that the pre-Columbian Indian possibly had rickets, asthma, brain tumors, skin infections, and skeletal disease resulting in poor posture and edema.

Dr. Mario Perez Ramirez has studied in Monte Alban on stelae found among the ruins. Other scholars suggest that the figures represent priests, warriors, or dancers, but Dr. Ramirez interprets these stelae as depicting medical disorders. I think the stone carvings possibly represent a textbook to help with certain diagnoses. An early missionary, Father Clavigero, relates that the medical arts were passed from father to son. Such information as the use of medicine, a knowledge of herbs, and also degrees of sickness was taught. (Ramirez, Medicine Pre-Cortesiana, pp. 22-25.) Pictorial representations on pottery indicate that abnormal pregnancies, broken limbs, and perhaps certain dental abnormalities were also diagnosed.

Gordon Schendel suggests there were two categories of physicians among the Aztecs. The first were those who specialized, such as bloodletters, internists, dentists, obstetricians, surgeons, and general practitioners. The second group were the so-called "witch doctors," who cured with charms and magical devices. (Schendel, Medicine in Mexico, pp. 46-54.)

Sahagun, the padre historian, says the Indians taught him that they practiced medicine. He records: "The good physician [is] a diagnostician, experienced—a knower of herbs, of stone, of trees, of roots. He has [results of] examinations, experience, prudence. [He is] moderate in his acts. He provides health, restores people, provides them splints, sets bones for them, purges them, gives emetics, gives them potions; he lances, he makes incisions in them, stitches them, revives them, envelopes them in ashes." (Historia General 10:30.)

Dr. Abner I. Weisman has studied pre-Columbian medicine for many years and has further classified the ancient doctors as follows:

"Type I. The High Priest Healer.—He relied almost exclusively on religious invocations and ceremonials, using only the minimum of scientifically sound medication. He was expert in laparotomy and thoracotomy for sacrificial surgery.

"Type II. The Clinical Pharmacologist.—The herbalist utilized myriads of physiological medicaments based on years of pharmacologic use and clinical observation, but he also relied on religious adjuncts.

"Type III. The General Practitioner.—The rural doctor supplemented pharmacologic preparations with magical incantations and ceremonials. He had some knowledge of minor surgery.

"Type IV. The Surgical Specialist.— He had received training in the technical skills of operative surgery. Some belonged to the super-specialized group of brain surgeons. All surgeons called upon the deities.

"The high priest was basically a priest and secondarily a medicine man. He was one of the most important members of the tribe who led the religious worship and supplications. His resort to medicine and surgery was probably in a consulting capacity when the ordinary doctor had been unable to achieve a result. It was his task to supervise and conduct the human sacrificial offerings to the gods. It was he who was able to reach the pericardial sac, excise the human heart and hold the still-beating heart aloft to the gods for their approval.

"The clinical pharmacologist was the forerunner of the internist and medical clinician. He had studied herbs, roots and leaves extensively, studying under masters in the field.

There are no evidences of medical schools in pre-Columbian edifices, so it must be assumed that he received his information via the preceptor method. It was the clinical pharmacologist who was pharmacist, pharmacologist and clinical physician, all in one.

"The *small village rural doctor* was the general all-round medicine man to whom the members of the community appealed for help before resorting to the high priest. This type of practitioner was probably most common throughout Middle America and each small group of families undoubtedly had access to such a practitioner. Some historians prefer to term him a *shaman* or ordinary witch doctor, but he was probably more than that. One must remember that the land in which these people lived was highly productive in vegetable life and, from all the evidence at hand, it appears that he must have used a number of potent herbs and roots together with his magic. He probably also knew how to splint a fracture, open boils and remove an infected tooth.

"The *surgical specialist* was undoubtedly a separate individual from the others, who had received special training in incisions of all kinds. But despite his surgical background, he probably was closely associated with a priestly rank in the tribal religion. It is difficult to imagine the average medicine man attempting brain surgery or amputations. He surely must have had a very intensive training in these undertakings, not only with sterility and anesthesia but also with control of bleeding. There were probably times when the high priest, also a specialist in the use of the obsidian scalpel, would do brain surgery and when the surgical technican would extirpate beating hearts in sacrificial offerings. However, since trephinations were so commonly performed, it would appear that the brain surgeon would have enough to keep him busy without often resorting to thoracotomies in ritualistic ceremonies." (Abner Weisman, in *International Surgery* 47:3-4 [1967, no. 1].)

It is possible that at one time medical knowledge and the power of the priesthood were used concurrently, but being cut off from the Spirit caused great prostitution of past medical and spiritual practices.

DISEASES AMONG THE ANCIENT AMERICANS

Among the diseases suffered by the Indians of Peru were malaria, cancer, diarrhea, rheumatism, obesity, dropsy, gout, leprosy, inflammation of the nerves, kidneys, and lungs, tuberculosis, severe glandular disturbances, and possibly syphilis. *Micous leishmaniasis* was a cancerlike malady transmitted by the bite of flying insects. *Verruga* caused pain in the throat and bones, and the whole body became covered with red bumps. Later these bled and the patient died from loss of blood.

Because the Indians of Peru thought that sin was a cause of disease, the doctors sometimes sucked the victim's blood in an attempt to suck out the evil spirits causing the disease. A priest diagnosed the nature and course of diseases from the position of coca leaves that he cast on the ground. The doctors rubbed a guinea pig over the body of the sufferer until it touched the spot where the most intense pain was felt. The animal was then killed by a quick twist of its neck. After opening the abdomen of the guinea pig, the priest examined the condition of its inner organs, especially those abnormal in shape or charged with blood. From this the doctors determined the hidden seat of the disease.

The Aztes believed that sickness and disaster were consequences of sin against heavenly powers. Certain citizens were assigned to do medical research; bodies of people who had been sacrificed were used for dissection, study, and research.

Among the Indians of Mexico, the following physical infirmities have been diagnosed: dropsy, syphilis, harelip, tumors, small pox, yellow fever, arthritis, diarrhea, asthma, fevers, burns, ulcers, heart trouble, vitamin deficiency, elephantiasis, and caesarean section.

TREPHINATION

Although surgery is not specifically mentioned in the Book of Mormon, there is much evidence that trephination, a type of surgical procedure, was practiced by the ancient Americans. Trephination, as defined in *Stedman's Medical Dictionary* (p. 444), is "the removal of a disc of bone from the skull." It is considered to be "one of the oldest surgical operations, and was extensively practiced by prehistoric people everywhere in the world at all periods of time, starting from the New Stone Age or even perhaps earlier than this."

The word *trepanation* comes from the Greek word *trypanon*, which means "a borer," and dates back to classical times. Today the French word *trephination* is used. Essentially, both *trepanation* and *trephination* have the same meaning: to make a depression or perforation in the skull. In a broad sense it includes making a depression—not a hole—in the skull in one or both tables of the cranium and removing bone fragments already present from trauma or infection. The hole or depression is usually made by scraping, rasping, and cauterizing, but may also be accomplished by drilling, boring with a gimlet or knife tip, cutting, or sawing. (Brothwell and Sandixon, *Diseases in Antiquity*, p. 673.)

Trephination was practiced for many different reasons. In some primitive cultures it was performed as a religious rite. It was used to cure severe headaches, epileptic fits, para-

Trephination, "the removal of a disc of bone from the skull," was widely practiced among the ancient Americans. The operation was performed for a variety of reasons: religious, psychological, and medical.

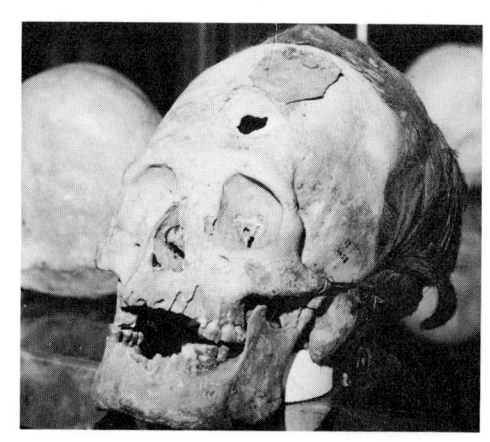

lytic conditions, mental derangement, pain, and unconsciousness, and to remove bone that might have been pressing against the brain because of an injury. It was also used to release evil spirits or to obtain amulets for decorative purposes.

Often the earlier man did not regard death and disease as natural phenomena. Such common maladies as colds or constipation were accepted as part of existence and dealt with through herbal remedies. Serious and disabling diseases, however, were thought to be of supernatural origin, the work of a demon or an offended god who had projected some object into the body or extracted something from it. The aim of the treatment, therefore, was to rid the body of the evil spirit or object. One method was to drill a hole in the skull of the victim. (*Encyclopedia Britannica*, 1973 ed., s.v. "Medicine and Surgery, History of.")

With regard to trephining for the sake of obtaining amulets, it has been said: "The wearing of amulets made from sections of skulls was a common custom among the earlier inhabitants of the world. They were mostly obtained post-mortem, but some were evidently removed from living captives, possibly with the idea that they were more potent as talismans against disease, or that they conferred on the wearer the physical or mental powers of the original owner." (Freeman, "Primitive Surgery of the Western Hemisphere," *Journal of the American Medical Association* 70:443.)

A great paleopathologist, R. L. Moodie, characterized the ancient Peruvian surgery thus: "I believe it to be correct to state that no primitive or ancient race of people anywhere in the world had developed such a field of surgical knowledge as had the pre-Columbian Peruvians. Their surgical attempts are truly amazing and include amputations, excisions, trephining, bandaging, bone transplants, cauterization, and other less evident procedures." (Mason, *The Ancient Civilization of Peru*, p. 222.)

Questions arise as to how these people obtained their knowledge of medicine, how they knew about preventing hemorrhaging, how they were able to avoid cutting the temple arteries, how they prevented postoperative infections. From the evidence of the skulls that have been uncovered, we can see that somehow they did find ways to avoid these fatal hazards.

In 1962 Dr. Francisco Grana, a Peruvian brain surgeon who had spent a great deal of time studying trephined skulls, attempted to perform the operation on a live human being in the same manner that he believed it to have been done in ancient times. His patient was a thirty-one-year-old man whose face had been paralyzed on the right side after an accident. A blood clot under the cranium was exerting pressure upon several of the motion centers in the brain, and removal of this clot would eliminate the paralysis.

Dr. Grana used modern anesthetics in an antiseptic environment, but otherwise the operation was performed essentially the same as if an early Peruvian doctor had done it, and used only the ancient instruments of the early Peruvians. The patient recovered without complications.

Trephination was not used exclusively for medicinal purposes. It was also used for supernatural causes. Leonard Freeman writes: "The supernatural diseases were supposed to have originated in various ways: by the casting of spells, by contact with some objectable person or thing, or by the presence of something in the system, such as an evil spirit, a stone, a piece of wood, a worm or an insect." According to Dr. Freeman, ". . . a medicine-man was not only a physician in our sense of the word, but was also a sort of priest, prophet, magician and all-around dealer in the mysterious." (Freeman, *op. cit.*, p. 443.)

"The medicinemen of Peru," says W. T. Corlett, "were most famed for their treatment of certain diseases by trephining." He quotes an incident from Dr. Moodie, who comments on the use of heat as a means of exorcising the demon of disease while trephining:

"By the use of our power of imagination we see in a secluded spot in the highlands of Peru, a primitive blanket or skin clad shaman holding the head of his demented woman on his knee while he very roughly cuts her scalp with a flint knife, first a long anteroposterior incision, then transversly across the obelion in the form of a Latin cross. Nearby on a slow, wood fire is an earthen pot containing the fat of a llama. As soon as the incisions are made the surgeon tenses the scalp so as to make the wound gape, then with the wisp of vegetable fiber he applies some of the bubbling oil to the wound. The application of boiling oil to the wound would result in an instant and hearty response, and the patient would have an instant, though possibly temporary, relief from the demon of insanity. The shaman, still holding the patient's head, urging her to control her wild yells of pain, applies to the cauterized wound a quid of cocoa, which he had been quietly chewing during the operation, and binds it in place with cooling leaves by means of dirty strips of blanket or other cloth. The riotous infection which followed gave rise to the pathology which is present on the skull, but the woman recovered and lived many years after the healing of her surgical wound. There is no indication that she ever had another attack of melancholia. The memory of the boiling oil was too vivid." (Corlett, *The Medicine Man of the American Indian and Cultural Background*, p. 229.)

Judging from the number of trephined skulls that have been found, we might say that the Incan surgeons considered trephining a sort of cure-all. But we might also bear in mind that head wounds were unquestionably the most common injury received by men who wielded such weapons as axes, clubs, maces, and slings.

Some of the surgical instruments used in trephining have been found in graves of Indians. They were usually made of obsidian, bronze, or copper, with a wooden handle attached to the blade by the means of a cord.

To deaden the pain, the natives of Peru and Bolivia could have used cocoa leaves, the chewing of which was habitual in these countries. Cocoa, a narcotic, would serve as a good local anesthesia, but trephining would probably have required a general anesthesia. Little is known about the use of anesthetics and narcotics among the Peruvians except the types of narcotics that were available to them.

After the operation, a silver or gold plate would often be inserted over the opening, the edges of which would eventually be overgrown with new bone. The skull would be bandaged with dressings made of layers of cotton and cotton string.

The Aztecs of Mexico had a little different trephining procedure from that of the Incas. Their technique was to punch a series of small holes in the skull, outlining a fracture or the area to be removed. Then they cut between these small holes and lifted off the depressed section of the cranial bone. The exposed brain was subsequently protected with a thin plate of hardwood and cotton pads. (Gordon Schendel, *Medicine in Mexico*, p. 57.)

Most of the evidence of trephining on the American continents is in either Central or South America, with very little evidence of it in North America. Interestingly enough, some primitive South American cultures still practice it today as they did centuries ago. Adolph F. Bandelier, in an article titled "Aboriginal Trephining in Bolivia" (*American Anthropologist* 6:441), remarks that trephining is presently being practiced by Bolivia's Aymara Indians. He notes, however, that it is difficult to get the Indians to reveal any information about the practice. "Why the operation is kept secret is not ascertainable," he laments. Leonard Freeman writes, "In the mountains of Peru, Chile and Bolivia, trephining for fractured skulls is still practiced occasionally by native medicinemen." (*Art and Archaeology* 8:21.)

It is thought by most scholars that the medical knowledge of the Incas came from previous cultures. We cannot at present say whether the Incas enlarged on the knowledge of the past cultures or debased it. Until further light is shed upon the subject, we can only speculate.

CONCLUSION

Oliver Cowdery once gave a speech to the Delaware Indians. He stated:

"Once the red men were many; they occupied the country from sea to sea—from the rising to the setting sun; the whole land was theirs; the Great Spirit gave it to them, and no pale faces dwelt among them. But now they are few in numbers; their possessions are small, and the pale faces are many.

"Thousands of moons ago, when the red men's forefathers dwelt in peace and possessed this whole land, the Great White Spirit talked with them, and revealed His law and His will, and much knowledge to their wise men and prophets. This they wrote in a Book, together with their history and the things which should befall their children in the latter days.

"This Book was written on plates of gold and handed down from father to son for many ages and generations....

". . . here is a copy of the Book which we now present to our red friend, the Chief of the Delawares, which we hope he will cause to be read and known among his tribe; it will do them good."

The Indian chief's reply: "We feel truly thankful to our white friends who have come so far and been at such pains to tell us good news, and especially this new news concerning the Book of our forefathers; it makes us glad in here. . . ." (*History of the Church* 1:183-85.)

The Book of Mormon story tells of a people who, when they were righteous, were the happiest people on earth. (See 4 Nephi 16.) When they transgressed, they were destroyed.

The ruins of the ancient Americans stand as monuments to a people who had once known God and had rejected him. The Book of Mormon was brought to us as a guide to Jesus Christ and his message of peace. Through a search of its religious teachings a person will receive a more thorough insight into true happiness.

Those who travel in Central and South America find themselves in awe as they face evidence of the greatness in past American civilizations. When the Book of Mormon was published, its contents were almost totally unconfirmed by scientific means. Since then many evidences have come forth to substantiate it. Nothing has ever been found to disprove it, and artifacts come forth almost daily in support of its historicity.

From the Book of Mormon we see that there were among the pre-Columbian peoples those who prayed in our generation's behalf. They pled for the preservation of the record of their people so we might benefit from their mistakes. They kept their record in the hopes of convincing all that Jesus is the Christ. It comes to us like a voice of one crying from the dead, even one speaking out of the dust.

While in Jerusalem Jesus Christ told the people there were "other sheep" who were not of that fold. He said he would visit them. The Book of Mormon records that the people of the Western Hemisphere were among those other sheep. Christ's dealings with these other sheep constitute the main theme of the Book of Mormon and became the record that witnesses with the Bible that he is the Savior of the world.

An ancient prophet from the Book of Mormon wrote: "I speak unto you as the voice of one crying from the dust. ..." (2 Nephi 33:13.) As one sees the ruins of a magnificent civilization, it does seem probable that these silent edifices are not the only remains of the past. Surely ancient historians have recorded the tremendous activities of these people. The book containing the abridgment of the history of some of these people, written by Mormon, Moroni, and others, gives us a record that helps us understand the lessons that come from such a great civilization. It records the peoples' relationship with God and his commandments to them.

In reference to claims made in the Book of Mormon concerning the people, the way they lived, and other aspects of their ancient culture, there are too many evidences forthcoming in our day and time that reinforce these claims. It is, rather, almost unbelievable for modern scholars to declare such massive findings as fake—findings so far removed from each other geographically that they all could not possibly have been planted as a hoax. These evidences should not be considered merely as coincidences. The Book of Mormon is in very deed a record written by these early Americans.

BIBLIOGRAPHY

Acosta, Jose de. *The Natural and Moral History of the Incas.* London: Hakluyt Society, 1880.

Aldred, Cyril. "The Rise of the God-Kings." *The Dawn of Civilization.* Edited by Stuart Piggott. New York: McGraw Hill, 1961.

Arciniegas, German. *Latin America: A Cultural History.* New York: Alfred A. Knopf, 1967.

Baldwin, Gordon C. *America's Buried Past.* New York: G. P. Putnam's Sons, 1962.

Bancroft, Hubert Howe. *The Native Races of the Pacific States of North America.* San Francisco: A. L. Bancroft and Co., 1882.

———. *The Works of Hubert Howe Bancroft.* 5 vols. San Francisco: San Francisco History Co., 1887.

Banks, Florence A. *The Coins of Bible Days.* New York: Macmillan, 1965.

Barrett, Ivan J. *Joseph Smith and the Restoration.* Provo, Utah: Brigham Young University Press, 1967.

Bauer, Edward E. *Plain Concrete.* 3rd ed. New York: McGraw Hill, 1949.

Berlitz, Charles. *Mysteries from Forgotten Worlds.* Garden City, New York: Doubleday, 1972.

Bernal, Ignacio. *Mexico Before Cortez: Art, History, and Legend.* Garden City, New York: Doubleday, 1963.

Birrell, Verla. *The Book of Mormon Study Guide.* Salt Lake City: Birrell Book Co., 1948.

Boland, Charles Michael. *They All Discovered America.* New York: Pocket Books, 1963.

Bourbourg, L'Abbe Brasseur de. *Relations des Choses de Yucatan de Diego de Landa.* Edited by Auguste Durand. Paris, 1864. (Original published in Spanish, 1566.)

Boyd, W. C. *Genetics and the Race of Man, an Introduction to Modern Physical Anthropology.* Boston: Little, Brown, 1950.

Braden, Charles S. *Religious Aspects of the Conquest of Mexico.* Durham, N.C.: Duke University Press, 1930.

Brinton, Daniel G. *American Hero-Myths.* Philadelphia, 1882. As cited in Milton R. Hunter, *Christ in Ancient America.* Salt Lake City: Deseret Book, 1959.

———. *Myths of the New World.* Philadelphia: D. McKay, 1896.

———. *The Native Calendar of Central America and Mexico.* Philadelphia: MacCalla & Co., 1893.

———. *Ancient Nahuatl Poetry.* New York: Ams Press, 1969.

Brooks, Melvin R. *LDS Reference Encyclopedia.* Salt Lake City: Bookcraft, 1960.

Brothwell, Don, and A. T. Sandison. *Disease in Antiquity.* Springfield, Ill., and Baltimore: C. C. Thomas, 1935.

Brown, F. Martin. *America's Yesterday.* Philadelphia: Lippincott, 1937.

Bushnell, G. H. S. *The First Americans.* London: Thomas and Hudson, 1968.

Cannon, George Q. *Life of Joseph Smith the Prophet.* Salt Lake City: Deseret Book, 1958.

Caso, Alfonso. *Sobretiro del Cuadernos Americanos.* Mexico City: Imprenta Mundial, 1946.

Cheville, Roy A. *Scriptures from Ancient America.* Independence, Mo.: Herald House, 1964.

Christensen, Ross T., comp. *Progress in Archaeology.* Provo, Utah: Brigham Young University Press, 1963.

———. *Tranoceanic Crossings to Ancient America.* Provo, Utah: Brigham Young University Press, 1970.

Clark, Grahame. *World Prehistory.* 2nd ed. New York: Cambridge University Press, 1969.

Clavigero, *The History of Mexico.* Philadelphia: Thomas Dodson, 1817.

Coe, Michael D. *Mexico.* Mexico City: Ediciones Lara, 1962.

Corlett, W. G. *The Medicine-Man of the American Indian and Cultural Background.* Springfield, Ill., and Baltimore: C. C. Thomas, 1935.

Cortez, Hernando. *Five Letters 1519-1526.* Translated by F. Bayard Morris. London: George Routledge & Sons, Ltd., 1908.

Cottrell, Leonard. *The Bull of Minos.* New York: Rinehart, 1958.

Covarrubias, Miguel. *Indian Art of Mexico and Central America.* New York: Alfred A. Knopf, 1957.

Cowley, Matthias. *Wilford Woodruff.* Salt Lake City: Bookcraft, 1964.

Davidson, A. B. *Hebrew Syntax.* 3rd ed. Edinburgh: T. & T. Clark, 1950.

DeHass, Jacob, ed. *The Encyclopedia of Jewish Knowledge.* New York: Behrman's Jewish Book Houdr, 1934.

Del Mar, Alexander. *A History of Money in Ancient Countries.* Bart Franklin Research Source Works Series #227. New York: B. Franklin, 1968.

De Roo, Peter. *America Before Columbus.* New York: J. P. Lippincott Co., 1900.

Deuel, Leo. *Conquistadors Without Swords.* New York: St. Martin's Press, 1967.

D'Harcourt, Raoul. *Textiles of Ancient Peru and Their Techniques.* Seattle: University of Washington Press, 1962.

Diaz del Castillo, Bernal. *The Discovery and Conquest of Mexico, 1517-1521.* London: George Routledge & Sons, Ltd., 1800.

Dixon, Riley L. *Just One Cumorah.* Salt Lake City: Bookcraft, 1958.

Dockstader, Frederick J. *Indian Art in South America.* Greenwich, Conn.: New York Graphic Society Publishers, Inc., 1967.

Duran, Fray Diego. *The Aztecs—The History of the Indies of New Spain.* Translated with notes by Doris Heyden and Fernando Horcastes. New York: Onion Press, 1964.

Easton, Stewart. *The Heritage of the Past.* New York: Holt, Rinehart and Winston, 1955.

Emerson, Ellen R. *Indian Myths.* Minneapolis: Ross & Haines, Inc., 1965.

Encyclopedia Britannica. Chicago: William Benton.

Enock, Charles Reginald. *Mexico.* New York: Scribner, 1909-10.

Evans, John Henry. *Message and Characters of the Book of Mormon.* Salt Lake City: n.p., c.1929.

Everyday Life in Bible Times. Washington, D.C.: National Geographic Society, 1967.

Fell, Barry. *America B.C.* New York: Demeter Press, Quadrangle/New York Times, 1976.

Ferguson, Thomas Stuart. *One Fold and One Shepherd.* San Francisco: Books of California, 1953.

Filson, Floyd Vivian, and George Earnest Wright, eds. *The Westminster Historical Atlas to the Bible.* Chicago: The Westminster Press, R. R. Donnelly & Sons Co., 1945.

Fletcher Robert. "On Prehistoric Trephining and Cranial Amulets." In *Contributions to North American Ethnology*, vol. 5. Edited by J. W. Powell, 1882.

Gamboa, Sarmiento de. *History of the Incas* (1572, in works issued by the Hakluyt Society, Series No. XXII, Cambridge, 1907). As cited in Milton R. Hunter, *Christ in Ancient America.* Salt Lake City: Deseret Book, 1959.

Garst, Doris Shannon. *Three Conquistadores: Cortes, Coronado, Pizarro.* New York: M. Messener, 1947.

Gorenstein, Shirley. *Introduction to Archaeology.* New York: Basic Books, 1965.

Gordon, Cyrus. *Before Columbus.* New York: Crown Publishers, 1971.

Grant, Carter E. *The Kingdom of God Restored.* Salt Lake City: Deseret Book, 1955.

Hammond, Fletcher B. *Geography of the Book of Mormon.* Salt Lake City: Utah Printing Co., 1959.

Hapgood, Charles. *Maps of the Ancient Sea Kings: Evidence of Advanced Civilization in the Ice Age.* New York: Chilton Books, 1966.

Hasting's Encyclopedia of Religion and Ethics. Edinburgh: Charles Scribner & Sons, 1951.

Helps, Sir Arthur. *The Life of Pizarro.* London: G. Bell & Sons, 1896.

Heyerdahl, Thor. *Sea Routes to Polynesia.* Chicago: Rand McNally, 1968.

———. *American Indians in the Pacific.* London: George Allen and Unwin Ltd., Ruskin House, 1952.

Hickman, Josiah E. *The Romance of the Book of Mormon.* Salt Lake City: Deseret News Press, 1937.

Holmes, W. N. *20th Annual Report of the Bureau of American Ethnology.* Washington, D.C., 1898.

Honore, Pierre. *In Quest of the White God.* London: Hutchinson & Co., Ltd., 1961.

Hoyle, Rafael Larco. *Checan. Studie uber die erotischen Darstellungen in der peruanischen kunst.* Munich: Deutsch Bearbeitung von Enrique Lift, 1965.

Humberto, Valquez Machicado. *Manual de la Historia de Bolivia.* La Paz: Gilbert and Cia, 1958.

Hunter, Milton R. *Christ in Ancient America.* 2 vols. Salt Lake City: Deseret Book, 1959.

———. *Great Civilizations and the Book of Mormon.* Salt Lake City: Bookcraft, 1970.

Hunter, Milton R. and Thomas S. Ferguson. *Ancient America and the Book of Mormon.* Oakland, Calif.: Kolob Book Co., 1950.

Irwin, Constance. *Fair Gods and Stone Faces.* New York: St. Martin's Press, 1963.

Jakeman, M. Wells. *The Ancient Middle-American Calendar Systems—Origin and Development.* Provo, Utah: Brigham Young University, 1947.

———. *Discovering the Past.* Provo, Utah: Brigham Young University, 1954.

_____. *The Origin and History of the Mayas, Part I*. Los Angeles: Research Publishing Co., 1945.

Jenson, Andrew. *Historical Record*. Historical Department Library of The Church of Jesus Christ of Latter-day Saints, Salt Lake City.

Johnston, Thomas Crawford. *Did the Phoenicians Discover America?* London: James Nisbet & Co., 1913.

Josephy, Alvin M., ed. *The American Heritage Book of Indians*. New York: American Heritage Publishing Co., 1961.

_____. *The Indian Heritage of America*. New York: Alfred A. Knopf, 1968.

Journal of Discourses. 26 vols. and index. London: Albert Carrington, 1872.

Kelley, Francis C. *Blood-Drenched Altars*. Milwaukee: Bruce Publishing Co., 1935.

King, Mary Elizabeth. *Ancient Peruvian Textiles*. Greenwich, Conn.: New York Graphic Society, 1965.

Kirkham, Francis W. *A New Witness for Christ in America*. Independence, Mo.: Zion's Printing and Publishing Co., 1942.

Klaw, Hasteen. *Navajo Creation Myth*. Santa Fe, N.M.: Museum of Navajo Ceremonial Art, Bulletin No. 1, 1945.

Landa, Friar Diego de. *Landa's Yucatan 1949-79*. Translated with notes by William Gates. Baltimore: The Maya Society, 1937.

_____. *Relation des Choses de Yucatan*. Paris: A. Durand, 1864.

Landstrom, Bjorn. *Columbus*. Translated from the Swedish by Michael Phillip and Hugh W. Staff. New York: Macmillan, 1967.

LaSueur, James W. *Indian Legends*. Independence, Mo.: Zion's Printing and Publishing Co., 1929.

Leon-Portillia, Miguel. *Aztec Thought and Culture*. Translated by Jack David. Norman: University of Oklahoma Press, 1963.

Leonard, Jonathan Norton. *Ancient America*. New York: Time-Life Books, 1967.

Linee, Sigvald. *Treasures in Mexican Art*. Stockholm: Nordisk Rotogravyr, 1956.

Lizana, Bernardo de. *History of Yucatan and Spiritual Conquest*. Cited in T. A. Willard, *Kukulcan the Bearded Conqueror*. Hollywood, Calif., 1941. Impresa en 1633 y ahora nuevamente por el Museo nacional de Mexico, Mexico City, 1893.

Loeb, E.M. *The Blood Sacrifice Complex*. Menosha, Wisc.: George Banta Publishing Company for the American Anthropological Association, 1923.

Lorang, Sister Mary Corde. *Footloose Scientist in Mayan America*. New York: Scribner, 1966.

Ludlow, Daniel H. *A Companion to Your Study of the Book of Mormon*. Salt Lake City: Deseret Book Co., 1976.

Lundwall, N.B. *Masterful Discourses and Writings of Orson Pratt*. Salt Lake City: N. B. Lundwall, 1949.

_____. *Temples of the Most High*. Salt Lake City: Bookcraft, 1941.

Machicado, Humberto Vasquez. *Manual de la Historia de Bolivia*. La Paz: Gilbert y Cia SA, 1963.

Mallery, Arlington H. *Lost America, the Story of the Pre-Columbian Iron Age in America*. Washington, D.C.: Washington Overlook Co., 1951.

MacNutt, Francisco Augustus. *Cortes Hernando: His Five Letters, Relations to the Emperor Charles V*. Glendale, Calif.: Arthur H. Clark, 1908.

Markham, Clements R. *History of Peru*. Chicago: Sergel and Co., 1892.

Mason, J. Alden. *The American Civilizations of Peru*. Baltimore: Penguin Books, 1957.

McConkie, Bruce R. *Mormon Doctrine*. Salt Lake City: Bookcraft, 1966.

McFadyen, John. *Key to Introductory Hebrew Grammar*. 3rd ed. Edinburgh: T. & T. Clark, 1951.

McGavin, E. Cecil. *Cumorah's "Gold Bible."* Salt Lake City: Bookcraft, 1947.

_____. *Mormonism and Masonry*. Salt Lake City: Bookcraft, 1947.

McGavin, E. Cecil, and Willard Bean. *The Geography of the Book of Mormon*. Salt Lake City: Bookcraft, 1948.

Mead, Charles W. *Old Civilization of Inca Land*. New York: American Museum Press, 1945.

Mead, Philip Ainsworth. *Ancient Civilization of the Andes*. New York: Charles Scribner's Sons, 1931.

Meggers, Betty, and Clifford Evans. *Archaeological Investigations on the Rio Napo, Eastern Ecuador*. Washington: Smithsonian Institution Press, 1968.

Meighan, Clement W. *Archaeology: An Introduction*. San Francisco: Chandler Publishing Co., 1966.

Menzel, Dorothy, John H. Rowe, and Lawrence E. Dawson. *The Paracas Pottery of Ica, a Study in Style and Time*. Berkeley and Los Angeles: University of California Press, 1964.

Mercer, Henry C. "The Kabal—Or Potter's Wheel of Yucatan." *The Bulletin of Free Museum of Science and Art*. University of Philadelphia, vol. 1 (1897), no. 2.

Mertz, Henriette. *Pale Ink*. Chicago: Swallow Press, 1972.

Michael, Henry N., and Elizabeth K. Ralph. *Dating Techniques for the Archaeologist*. Cambridge, Mass., and London: Massachusetts Institute of Technology Press, 1971.

Miller, Medelin S., and J. Lane Miller. *Encyclopedia of Bible Life*. New York: Harper and Row, 1944.

Morley, Sylvanus G. *The Ancient Maya*. Palo Alto, Calif.: Stanford University Press, 1946.

Mure, W., Esq. *A Dissertation on the Calendar and Zodiac of Ancient Egypt*. London and Edinburgh, 1832.

Nibley, Hugh. *An Approach to the Book of Mormon*. Salt Lake City: Deseret News Press, 1957.

_____. *Lehi in the Desert and the World of the Jaredites*. Salt Lake City: Bookcraft, 1952.

Noerdlinger, Henry S. *Moses and Egypt*. Los Angeles: University of Southern California Press, 1956.

Oglesby, Clarkson Hill. *Highway Engineering*. 3rd ed. New York: Jim Wiley, 1974.

Oliver, Douglas L. *The Pacific Islands*. Cambridge, Mass.: Harvard University Press, 1952.

O'Neale, Lila M. *Textile Periods in Ancient Peru II. Paracas Caverns and the Grand Necropolis*. University of California Publications in Archaeology and Ethnology. Berkeley: University of California Press, vol. 39 (1945).

O'Neale, Lila M., and Bonnie Jean Clark. *Textile Periods in Ancient Peru III*. University of California Publications in Archaeology and Ethnology. Berkeley: University of California Press, vol. 40 (1956).

O'Neale, Lila M., and A. J. Kroeber. *Textile Periods in Ancient Peru*. University of California Publications in American Archaeology and Ethnology. Berkeley: University of California Press, vol. 28 (1931).

Osborne, Harold. *South American Mythology*. Middlesex: Hamlyn Publishers Group Ltd., 1968.

Peterson, Frederick A. *Ancient Mexico*. New York: G. P. Putnam's Sons, 1961.

Phillips, E. D., ed. *Greek Medicine*. London: Thomas and Hudson, 1973.

Powell, Guy E. *Latest Aztec Discoveries*. San Antonio: Naylor Co., 1967.

Pratt, Parley P. *Autobiography*. Salt Lake City: Deseret Book, 1938.

Prescott, William. *Conquest of Peru*. New York: A. L. Burt Publishers, 1928.

_____. *History of the Conquest of Mexico*. Vol. 1. New York: Thomas Y. Crowell & Co., 1843.

_____. *History of the Conquest of Peru and History of the Conquest of Mexico*. New York: Random House, 1936.

Ramirez, Mario Perez. *Medicina Pre-Coretsiana, the Stelae of Monte Alban*. Benito, Mexico: Jauezde Uaxaca, 1963.

Rappaport, Samuel. *A Treasury of the Midrash*. New York: KATV Publishing House, Inc., 1968.

Raymond, George, Miguel Angel Asturias, and J. M. Gonzales. *Anales de los Xahil Traduccion y Notes*. Mexico City: Mendoze National University, 1946.

Recinos, Adrian. *Popol Vuh, The Sacred Book of the Ancient Quiche Maya*. Translated by Delia Goetz and Sylvanus G. Morley. Norman, Okla.: University of Oklahoma Press, 1950.

Recinos, Adrian, and Delia Goetz. *The Annals of the Cakchiquels*. Norman, Okla.: University of Oklahoma Press, 1953.

Reed, Alma M. *The Ancient Past of Mexico*. New York: Crown Publishers, 1966.

Reynolds, George. *A Complete Concordance of the Book of Mormon*. Salt Lake City: Deseret Book Co., 1957.

_____. *A Dictionary of the Book of Mormon*. Salt Lake City, 1891.

Reynolds, George, and J. M. Sjodahl. *Book of Mormon Geography*. Salt Lake City: Deseret News Press, 1957.

Richards, Franklin D., and James A. Little. *A Compendium of the Doctrine of the Gospel*. Salt Lake City: Deseret News, 1914.

Ricks, Eldin. *Book of Mormon Commentary*. Vol. 1. Salt Lake City: Deseret News Press, 1951.

Ricks, Joel E. *The Geography of Book of Mormon Lands*. Logan, Utah: Brigham Young College, 1904.

Riley, Carroll L., et al. (eds.) *Man Across the Sea*. Austin: University of Texas Press, 1971.

Rivera y Ustariz, Mariano Eduardo de. *Peruvian Antiquities*. New York: George P. Putnam & Co., 1853.

Rivet, Paul. *Maya Cities*. London: Elek Books, 1960.

Roberts, B. H. *A Comprehensive History of the Church*. Vol. 1. Salt Lake City: Deseret News Press, 1930.

_____. *New Witnesses for God*. Vol. 3. Salt Lake City: Deseret News Press.

Rout, Etti A. *Maori Symbolism*. London: Kegan Paul, Trench and Co., Ltd., 1926.

Sahagun, Fray Bernardino de. *Historia General de los Cosas de Nueva Espana: Florentine Codex*. Translated and edited by Charles E. Dibble and Arthur J. O. Anderson. 12 vols. Santa Fe: The School of American Research, and Salt Lake City: The University of Utah. 1950ff.

_____. *A History of Ancient Mexico*. Vols. 1-3. Translated by Fanny R. Brandilier. Glendale, Calif.: The Arthur H. Clark Co., 1932.

Schendel, Gordon. *Medicine in Mexico*. Austin: University of Texas Press, 1968.

Seler, Edward. *Gesaminelte Abhandlanger*. Berlin: A. Asher and Co., 1904.

Seton, Ernest Thompson. *The Gospel of the Red Man*. Garden City, N.Y.: Doubleday, 1937.

Sharp, Andrew. *Ancient Voyagers in Polynesia*. Auckland and Hamilton, New Zealand: Paul's Book Arcade, 1963.

Simpson, George Gaylord. *Horses*. New York: Oxford University Press, 1951.

Singer, Charles, E. J. Holnyard, and A. P. Hau (eds.). *A History of Technology*. Vol. 1. Oxford: Clarendon Press, 1954.

Singer, Isadore (ed.). *The Jewish Encyclopedia*. Vol. 5. New York: Funk and Wagnalls Co., 1903.

Sjodahl, J. M. *An Introduction to the Book of Mormon*. Salt Lake City: Deseret News Press.

Valliant, George C. *Artists and Craftsmen in Ancient America*. New York: The American Museum of Natural History, 1935.

_____. *Aztecs of Mexico*. Garden City, N.Y.: Doubleday, Doran and Co., Inc., 1944.

VanLoon, Hendrick William. *The Story of the Pacific*. New York: Harcourt, Brace and Co., 1940.

Velasco, Padre Juan de. "Historia Antigua de Quito." *Padre Juan de Velasco*. Puebla, Mexico: Editorial J. M. Cajica Jr. SA, 1960.

Verrill, Hyatt. *America's Ancient Civilizations*. New York: G. P. Putnam's Sons, 1953.

Viranco, Jose Luis Melgarejo. *Totonacapan*. Xalpa, Veracruz: Talleres Traficos del Governo del Estado, 1943.

Von Hagen, Victor Wolfgang. *The Ancient Sun Kingdoms of the Americas*. New York: The World Publishing Co., 1961.

_____. *The Desert Kingdom of Peru*. New York: The New American Library, 1964.

_____. *Highway of the Sun*. New York: Duell, Sloan, Pierce, 1955.

_____. *The Incas of Pedro di Cieza de Leon*. Norman, Okla.: University of Oklahoma Press, 1959.

_____. *Realm of the Incas*. New York: The New American Library, 1961.

Walker, Charles L. *Walker Journal*. Brigham Young University Library.

Washburn, J. N. *Book of Mormon Geography*. Provo, Utah: New Era Publishing Co., 1939.

_____. *From Babel to Cumorah*. Provo, Utah: New Era Publishing Co., 1937.

Wasserman, Jacob. *Columbus, Don Quixote of the Seas*. Boston: Little, Brown, and Co., 1930.

Waters, Frank. *Book of the Hopi*. New York: Ballentine Books, 1969.

Wauchope, Robert. *Handbook of Middle American Indians*. Austin: University of Texas Press, 1965.

_____. *Lost Tribes and Sunken Continents*. Chicago: University of Chicago Press, 1956.

_____. *They Found the Buried Cities*. Chicago: University of Chicago Press, 1956.

Webster's Third New International Dictionary. Springfield, Mass.: G. and C. Merriam Co., 1971.

Wells, Calvin. *Bones, Bodies, and Diseases*. New York: Frederick A. Praeger, 1964.

Wesleyan Bible Commentary. Vol. 1. Grand Rapids, Mich.: Wm. B. Eerdman's Publishing Co., 1967.

Whitney, Orson F. *Life of Heber C. Kimball*. Salt Lake City: Bookcraft, 1945.

Widtsoe, John A. *Book of Mormon Treasury*. Salt Lake City: Deseret Book Co., 1926.

_____. *In a Sunlit Land*. Salt Lake City: Deseret News Press, 1952.

Widtsoe, John A., and Franklin S. Harris, Jr. *Seven Claims of the Book of Mormon*. Independence, Mo.: Zion's Printing and Publishing Co., 1935.

Willard, T. A. *Lost Empires*. Glendale, Calif.: The Arthur H. Clark Co., 1935.

_____. *Kukulcan, the Bearded Conqueror*.

Willey, Gordon R. *An Introduction to American Archaeology*. Englewood Cliffs, N.J.: Prentice-Hall, 1966.

Williams, Nancy C. *After One Hundred Years*. Independence, Mo.: Zion's Printing and Publishing Co., 1951.

Williams, S. C. *Adair's History of the American Indian*. Johnson City, Tenn.: Watauga Press, 1930.

Winsor, Justin (ed.). *Narrative and Critical History of America*. Boston and New York: Houghton, Mifflin, and Co., 1884-1889; 1891-1897.

Winter, George. *Design of Concrete Structures*. 8th ed. New York: McGraw Hill, 1972.

Wright, Curtis. *Metallic Documents of Antiquity*.

INTERVIEWS

Espinosa, Dr., and Daniel Rime, in Huancayo, Peru; recorded October 14, 1965.

Nibley, Dr. Hugh, August 12, 1971.

Smith, Eldred G., Patriarch to The Church of Jesus Christ of Latter-day Saints, Church Administration Building, Salt Lake City, Utah, July 23, 1971.

Williams, Fred, October 17, 1969.

MICROFILM

Patriarchal Blessing Index. Microfilm Room, Brigham Young University.

MISCELLANEOUS PAPERS

Brainward, G. W. Unpublished notes from Department of Archaeology, Carnegie Institute, Washington, D.C., 1940.

Braithwaite, Douglas C. "Continuing Discovery of Ancient Coins." 1973.

Cheesman, Paul R. "Cultural Analysis of the Nephite-Lamanite-Mulekite Civilizations from the Book of Mormon." Brigham Young University, 1968.

Christiansen, Keith. "Southern Yucatan Theory." Provo, Utah, 1969.

Columbus, Christopher. Diary entry of November 6, 1492.

Fawson, Lu. "A Study of Documents That Substantiate the Existence of a Potter's Wheel in Ancient America." Salt Lake City, 1966.

Gordon, Cyrus. Society for Early Historic Archaeology Symposium Lecture, Brigham Young University, 1970.

Haws, Virgil. "The American Indian and the Blood Groups." Provo, Utah: The University Archaeological Society, Miscellaneous Paper No. 18, 1956.

Hirschi, Max G. "Possible Origin of the Polynesian Islands." Summer School, Brigham Young University, 1969.

Lindstrom, Talbot Shaw. Report at Lumpkin, Georgia, Symposium, October 12-13, 1973.

Meha, Stuart. "Maori Origin Told." Provo, Utah: Brigham Young University Library, Special Collections, 1960.

Sperry, Sidney B. "Were There Two Cumorahs?" Topic for discussion on March 31, 1964, Religion 622, Brigham Young University.

PERIODICALS

Abottempo, November 1963.

American Anthropologist. N.S. Vol. 6, 1904; vol. 7, 1905.

American Journal of Science. Vol. 23, 1907.

Antiquity. Vol. 42, 1968.

Archaeology. Autumn 1950, Autumn 1953.

Art and Archaeology. Vol. 8, 1924; vol. 18, 1924.

BYU Studies. Summer 1971.

Children of the Covenant. Published by the Genealogical Society of Utah. 1936-37.

Church News, section of the *Deseret News*. February 27, 1954, p. 2.

Conference Reports. Proceedings of the annual and semiannual conferences of The Church of Jesus Christ of Latter-day Saints. April 1947, April 1962, October 1966.

Deseret News. March 3, 1928.

German Alatrista. LaPrensa, 1963.

Improvement Era. 1897-1970.

Instructor. 1930-1970.

International Surgery. January 1967.

The Lapidary Journal. April-May 1961.

La Prensa. January 20, 1963.

Medical Tribune. August 15, 1968.

Messenger and Advocate. October 1834, July 1835.

Millennial Star. 1840-1970.

National Geographic. February 1970, November 1964, October 1969, January 1971.

Nature. July 15, 1967.

Newsweek. May 27, 1966; May 27, 1968.

Orientalia. Vol. 37, 1968.

San Diego Union. October 9, 1970.
Saturday Review. May 3, 1969; July 18, 1970.
Science. May 1971.
Science Digest. January 1969.
Science News. April 9, 1966.
Society for Early Historic Archaeology Newsletter. 1970.
Southern Workman. September 1928.
Time. May 24, 1968.
Times and Seasons. 1839-1846.
USA Newsletter. No. 46, December 19, 1957.
U.S. Geographical and Geological Survey of the Rocky Mountain Region. 5:8.
Utah Genealogical and Historical Magazine. 1910-1940.
Western Reserve Historical Society Tracts. No. 9, February 1872.

SCRIPTURES

Book of Mormon. Salt Lake City: The Church of Jesus Christ of Latter-day Saints.
Bible. (King James Version.) Cambridge, England: University Press.
Pearl of Great Price. Salt Lake City: The Church of Jesus Christ of Latter-day Saints.

THESES

Allen, Joseph L. "A Comparative Study of Quetzalcoatl, the Feathered-Serpent God of Meso-America, with Jesus Christ, the God of the Nephites." Doctoral dissertation, Brigham Young University, 1970.
Barrett, Gwynn W. "John M. Bernhisel, Mormon Elder in Congress." Unpublished doctoral dissertation. Provo, Utah: Brigham Young University, 1968.
Bramwell, E. Craig. "Hebrew Idioms in the Small Plates of Nephi." Unpublished master's thesis. Brigham Young University, 1960.
Brown, Amanda J. "A Design Study in Costume for Projected Dramatic Productions Prescribing a Book of Mormon Setting Identified Herein as Late Preclassic Mesoamerican Culture." Unpublished master's thesis, BYU, 1970.
Sorensen, John L. "Evidences of Cultural Contacts between Polynesia and the Americas in Pre-Columbian Times." Unpublished master's thesis, BYU, 1952.
Skinner, J. Ralston. *Key to the Hebrews: Egyptian Mystery in the Sources of Measures.* 1875.
Slotki, Judah J. "Numbers," *Midrash Rabbah.* London: The Soncino Press, 1939.
Smith, Ethan. *View of the Hebrews.* Poultney, Vermont: Smith and Shute, 1825.
Smith, Henry A. *Matthew Cowley, Man of Faith.* Salt Lake City: Bookcraft, 1954.
Smith, Joseph. *History of the Church.* 7 volumes. Salt Lake City: The Church of Jesus Christ of Latter-day Saints.
———. *Teachings of the Prophet Joseph Smith.* Compiled by Joseph Fielding Smith. Salt Lake City: Deseret Book Co., 1938.
Smith, Joseph Fielding. *Doctrines of Salvation.* Vol. 3. Salt Lake City: Bookcraft, 1956.
Smith, Lucy Mack. *History of Joseph Smith.* Salt Lake City: Bookcraft, 1956.
Spence, Lewis. *Myths and Legends: Mexico and Peru.* Boston: David P. Nickerson, 1931.
———. *The Myths and Legends: the North American Indians.* Boston: David P. Nickerson, 1932.
Sperry, Sidney B. *Book of Mormon Compendium.* Salt Lake City: Bookcraft, 1968.
———. *The Book of Mormon Testifies.* Salt Lake City: Bookcraft, 1952.
———. *Our Book of Mormon.* Salt Lake City: Stevens and Wallis, 1947.
———. *Science, Tradition and the Book of Mormon.* Salt Lake City: General Board of MIA of The Church of Jesus Christ of Latter-day Saints, 1937.
Spinden, Herbert J. *Ancient Civilizations of Mexico and Central America.* New York: American Museum Press, 1922.
Sprague, L., and Catherine de Camp. *Ancient Ruins and Archaeology.* Garden City, New York: Doubleday, 1964.
Stedman's Medical Dictionary. Baltimore: Williams and Wilkins Co., 1957.
Stephens, John L. *Incidents of Travel in Central America, Chiapas, and Yucatan.* Vol. 2. New York, 1841.
Stevenson, Edward. *Reminiscences of Joseph, the Prophet.* Salt Lake City: Edward Stevenson, 1893.
Stout, Walter M. *Harmony in Book of Mormon Geography.* Las Vegas, Nev.: Chief Litho, 1950.
Talmage, James E. *Articles of Faith.* Salt Lake City: The Church of Jesus Christ of Latter-day Saints, 1913.
Thacher, John Boyd. *Christopher Columbus.* Vol. 2. New York and London: G. P. Putnam's Sons, 1903-04.
Thompson, Edward H. *People of the Serpent.* Boston: Houghton Mifflin, 1932.
Thompson, J. Eric. *Sky Bearers, Colors and Directions in Maya and Mexican Religion.* Contributions to American Archaeology, vol. 2, no. 10. Washington: Carnegie Institute, 1934.
Thompson, J.E.S., H.E.O. Pollock, and J. Chariot. *A Preliminary Study of the Ruins of Coba, Quiztana Roo, Mexico.* Washington: Carnegie Institute, 1932, publication no. 424.
Thorwald, Jurgen. *Science and Secrets of Early Medicine.* New York: Harcourt, Brace and World, Inc., 1963.
Troell, George E. *Composition and Properties of Concrete.* 2nd ed. New York: McGraw Hill, 1968.
Underhill, Ruth Murray. *Red Man's America: A History of Indians in the United States.* Chicago: University of Chicago Press, 1953.
Unger, M.F. *Archaeology and the Old Testament.* Grand Rapids, Mich.: Zondervan Publishing House, 1954.

INDEX

Acosta, Jose De: on Indian legends, 2; on Christian-like practices among Indians, 74, 76
Acropolis of Copan, Honduras, 56-57
Agriculture: cultural parallels in, viii; comparison of, in different accounts, 13, 19; among Mayas, 39
Albuquerque, New Mexico, 67
Alloys, 87
Almagro, Diego de, 58
Altars, 55, 61
Alvarado, Pedro de, 53
Amaru, Tupca, 58
Amatl, 70
American Indian. See Indian
Amulets, 100
Anales de los Xahil, excerpt from, 15
Anatomy, Mayan, 1
Andagoya, Pascal de, 58
Animals, comparison of, in different accounts, 13, 19
Annals of Cuauhtitlan, 12
Annals of the Cakchiquels, 12
Anointing, 16
Arch, true, use of, ix
Archaeological evidences of Book of Mormon, chart of, ix
Archaic period, 35
Architecture: wonders of, 20-21; of Aztecs, 35, 37; of Mayas, 37; of Zapotecs, 41; styles of, found in Copan, 56
Aristotle, 66
Art, 87-90; Aztec, 37; Mayan, 37; Olmec, 39; Zapotec, 41
Arthritis, ancient treatment for, 98
Artifacts: assembling of, viii; of Monte Alban, 48; of Tikal, 53; North American, 70
Assawompset Pond, Massachusetts, 67
Atahualpa, 87
Avenue of the Dead, 49
Aztecs, beliefs of: concerning their origin, 2-3; concerning God and Christ, 7; civilization of, 35, 37; architecture of, 35, 37; calendar of, 37

Ball courts, 42, 46, 47, 49, 52, 55
Bancroft, Hubert Howe: on bearded white God, 7-8; on baptism, 74, 76; on sacrament, 76
Banners, comparison of, in different accounts, 13-14

Baptism in ancient America, 9, 74; as symbol of cleansing, 16, 74; ritual surrounding, 74; examples of, 76
Baptismal fonts, 76
Beans, markings on, 71
Bearded men in ancient America, ix
Bearded white god: universality of, 7; descriptions of, 7, 8. See also Quetzalcoatl
Bernhisel, Dr. John M., 23
Bingham, Hiram A., 61
Bolivar, Simon, 58
Bonampak murals, 8
Book of Mormon: testimony of, must be spiritual, ix, xi, 22; modern scripure testifies of, vii; is record of only three groups, vii, ix, 4; comments on archaeological support for, viii, 21-22, 102; Christ is central figure of, viii; teachings of, concerning origin of American Indians, 2; account of Christ in, 9-10, 11, 15-16; relation of, to accounts of Chroniclers, 13-15; coming of explorers foretold in, 18; geography of, 21-34; five lands in, 28-29; tells of groups fleeing Jerusalem, 67-68; accounts of language in, 71; similarity in language of, to Hebrew, 71-72; account of baptism in, 74; account of highways in, 80; military use of highways in, 83; horses mentioned in, 91; account of medicines in, 97; Oliver Cowdery's introduction of, to Indians, 101
Bountiful, land of, 28, 33, 34
Bridges, 82, 83
Brinton, Dr. Daniel G., 74; on bearded white God, 8; on Itzamna, 10; on names of deity, 11
Broken bones, ancient treatment for, 98
Buchanan, Golden R.: tells story of Papago convert, 3; on Navajo tradition, 3-4; on Indian legends, 5; on the flood myths, 6
Bybloships, 64

Cadiz, 64, 66
Cajamarquilla, 58, 60-61
Cakchiquels, theory of origin among, 14
Calendar systems, ancient, 14; Aztec, 37; Mayan, 37, 93, 95, 96; development of, 93; accuracy of, 93; Old World influence on, 93; calculation of years in, 94; comparison of Egyptian and Mayan, 94-95; calculation of weeks in, 95; sacred, 95; unit breakdown of Mayan, 95
Callis, Charles A., on Joseph Smith and the Book of Mormon, ix
Calpullis, or "clans," 49
Cannon, George Q., on geography, 22
Canoes, 21
Caracol, 42
Cat, symbolism of, viii
Cement, ix, 81, 83
Cenote, or well, 42, 47
Central America, 25
Ceremonial pageantry, roads built for, 82
Chan Chan, 60, 61
Chancay, 58
Chariots, 83
Charts: archaeological evidences and corresponding Book of Mormon refences, ix; comparisons between various calendar systems, 96
Chasqui runners, 82-83
Chastity, Indian standards of, 7
Chavin culture, 58, 60
Cherokees, religious views of, 3, 4
Chiapas, Mexico, viii
Chichen Itza, Yucatan, Mexico, 2, 8, 42
Chilam Balam, 12
Chile, South America, 22, 23, 24
Chimu culture, 60
Cholula, pyramid of, 46
Christ: is central figure of Book of Mormon, viii; figures prominently in
Christ: is central figure of Book of Mormon, viii; figures prominently in Indian legends, 5; account of, in Book of Mormon, 9, 11, 15-16; belief of ancients in, 15; location of appearance of, to Nephites, 27. See also Bearded white god; Quetzalcoatl
Christian-like practices among Indians, 74
Chroniclers: definition of, 12; agreement between, 12; relation of accounts of, to Book of Mormon, 13-15
Cincinnati tablet, 69
Cisterns, 52
Civilization: high degree of, among pre-Columbian people, viii, 13, 20, 35; peak of, was at time of Christ, viii; periods of, in early America, 35
Classic period, 35
Clavigero: on Quetzalcoatl, 11; on size of natives, 18-19
Codz-pop, 47
Coins, Phoenician, 67
Columbus, Christopher, 56; on natives' reception of crew, 10, 18; on animals, 19; on gold, 19
Communications system, 82-83
Communion, 76
Concrete, 83
Convert to Church from Papago reservation, story of, 3
Copan, Honduras, 56-57
Cortez, Hernando, 49; on Indian beliefs concerning their origin, 2; on Quetzalcoatl, 11; on architecture, 20; on city half under water, 21; on writings, 69; on highways, 80
Costa Rican theory of Book of Mormon geography, 33
Cotton, 67
Cowdery, Oliver, 77; on stone box, 77-78; speech of, to Indians, 101
Craftsmanship, 87-90; Aztec, 37; Mayan, 37, 39; Mixtec, 39; Zapotec, 41; in Kaminaljuyu, 55
Creation myths, 5, 16-17
Cuicuilco, 46-47
Cumorah. See Hill Cumorah
Cuzco, Peru, 20, 63

D'Anghiera, Pietro Martire, on Indian books, 69
David, 66
De Roo, Peter: on the Godhead, 5; on the "Divine Book," 6; on baptism, 76
Desolation, land of, 28-29, 34
Devil, belief in, 16
Diodorus, 66
Diseases among ancient Americans, 98, 99
Disks, finding of, 84, 86
"Divine Book" of the Otomis, 6
Dots and dashes, 73
Drainage systems on pre-Columbian highways, 83
Duran, Fray Diego, 12; on determining origin of American Indians, 4
Dyes, manufacture of, ix
Dzibilchaltun, 47

Easter-type feast, 17
Egypt: tracing of civilization back to, 1; cultural similarities of ancient America and, 2; calendar systems of, compared to Mayan, 94-95
El Castillo, 39, 42
El Tajin, 47
Eohippus, 91

INDEX 107

Evolution, 91
Explorers, Spanish, 18
Ezekiel, on Phoenician ships, 66
Ezion-geber, 68

Fasting, 17
Feathered serpent, symbolism of, 11. See also Quetzalcoatl
First inheritance, land of, 28, 29
Five lands of Book of Mormon, 28-29
Flood, Indian legends concerning, 6
Florentine Codex, 13, 14
"Flowing vase," 2
Fonts, baptismal, 76
Fort Benning, Georgia, 67
Fortress of Sacsahuaman, 61
Furlani, Paulo de, 19

Gateway of the Sun, 63
Geography of the Book of Mormon, danger of speculation concerning, 22; theories of, 28-34
Giants, race of, 18
Giron-Gagal, 13
God: would instruct *all* His children, viii; figures prominently in Indian legends, 5
Gold, 19-20, 87; plate of inscriptions made of, 70; room full, as ransom for Incan king, 87
Gordon, Dr. Cyrus H., 4, 67, 68, 70
Government, 14
Governor's Palace, Uxmal, Mexico, 51
Grammatical structure, comparison of, in Hebrew and Book of Mormon, 71-72
Guadalajara, Mexico, 71
Guatemala, history of, 53; ruins in, 53-54

Hagoth, 68
Hai King, 64
Harbors, 67
Harlot, definition of, 14
Headache, curing of, 14
Heaven, degrees in, 17
Hebrew: inscriptions of, found in Tennessee, 4, 64, 68; inscriptions of, found in Ohio, 26, 70; Joseph Smith claimed ancient Americans were, 68; similarity of, to Book of Mormon language, 71-72
Herbs, medicinal use of, 97
Heyerdahl, Thor, 4, 67
Hieroglyphics, vii, 56-57, 70
High priest healer, 98
Highways in pre-Columbian America: descriptions of, 80-81; comparison of, with Roman highways, 81; two main north-south, 82; total miles covered by, 82; purposes for, 82-83; building of, 83; durability of, 83; drainage systems of, 83; use of wheel suggested by, 86
Hill Cumorah, 24-25, 34; story of old man on way to, 24; as great battleground, 24-25
Hiram, King of Tyre, 64, 66
Holy Ghost, Indian legends concerning, 5
Homes, different types of, 14
Honduras: history of, 56; ruins in, 56-57
Honore, Pierre: on white God, 11; on baptism, 76
Hopis, creation myth of, 3
Horses: existence of, in pre-Columbian America, 91-92; mention of, in Book of Mormon, 91; discovery of bones of, 92; pictures of, 91, 92; extinction of, 92; possible early uses of, 92
House of Turtles, Uxmal, Mexico, 51-52
Hwue Shin, 64

Immortality, 17
Incas: legendary origin of, 2; beliefs of, concerning God, 8; history of, 58, 60; highways of, 80, 81; chasqui runners of, 82-83
Indians, American: theories of origin of, 1-4; evidence of Oriental and Near-Eastern background of, 1; were credited with being first to use zero, 1; philosophy of future of, 7. See also Aztecs; Incas; Mayas; Pre-Columbian peoples
Inithuatana, "sun clock," 63
Internal geography theory of Book of Mormon, 34
"Ipalneomani," 11
Irrigation systems, 19, 63
Islands, peopling of, 26
Israelites: list of reasons why Indians might have been, 6; Quiche Maya claimed to be, 13
Itzamna, 8, 10
Ixtlilxochitl, Fernando de Alva, vii, 12, 13, 15; similarities between account of, and Book of Mormon, 15

Jade, 90
Jaguar: painting of, in Kukulcan, 42; statue of, in Uxmal, 51; Temple of the Giant, 53
Japanese voyages to America, 64
Jaredites, 33, 67; landing of, 24, 26
Jerusalem, 33
Jewelry, 87, 90

Kabah, Mexico, 47
Kabal, or potter's wheel, 84
Kaminaljuyu, Guatemala, ix, 55
Kenko, 61
Ketchikan, Alaska, 8
Kinderhook, Illinois, 69
Knotted cords, 72-73
Kon Tiki expedition, 4
Kukulcan, temple of, 8, 39, 42

La Venta, 47
Labna, 48
Lake Titicaca, 10, 63
Landa, Bishop Diego de, 12, 13; on baptism, 9, 74; on scripts, 9
Land Northward, 29
Lands, five, of Book of Mormon, 28-29
Language, relationship between New and Old World, 71; accounts of, in Book of mormon, 71; diversity of, among Indians, 72
Laws, 19
Lee, Harold B., on Lehi's landing, 24
Legends, Indian: of two sets of brothers who fought, 3-4; of premortal existence, 5; of creation of planets and man, 5; of the Godhead, 5; of biblical occurrences, 5-6; of the flood, 6; of Votan, 67
Lehi: theories concerning course of, 22-24; possible introduction of calendar system by, 93
Lima, Peru, 58, 70
Limited Tehuantepec theory of Book of Mormon geography, 29

Mace heads, 86
Machu Picchu, 61-63
Magician, Temple of the, 51
Manco Capca, 2
Manti, Utah, 25
Manuscripts, ancient, 71
Map dated 1513 showing longitudinal placement of South America and Africa, 66
Marriage: Indian customs of, 7; baptism at time of, 76
Masonry, 63
Mathematical reckoning, ix, 72
Mayas: civilization of, 37, 39, 56; sense of community among, 37; religion of, 37; writing of, 37; farming among, 39; class system of, 39; dress of, 39; highways of, 81; calendar system of, 93-96

Medicine: various types of, 97-98; account of, in Book of Mormon, 97; practitioners of, 98-99
Mendez, Colonel Modesto, 53
Mesoamerica: definition of, 35; six cultures of, 35
Metal plates, writings on, 69, 70
Metallurgy, 19-20, 51, 87
Metcalf Stone, 67, 69
Mexico, civilizations of, 42-52
Migration: possible routes of, 1; speculation concerning, 1; traditions surrounding, 14, 15
Military use of highways, 83
Milky Way, 2
Mitla, Mexico, 48
Mixtecs, civilization of, 39
Mochi culture, 60
Monoliths, 55, 63
Monte Alban, Mexico, 48
Montezuma, 2
Monuments: of Cuicuilco, 46-47; of La Venta, 47; of Copan, 56
Moroni, angel, 77
Mosaics, 47, 48, 52
Mulek, 68
Mystery Caves, New Hampshire, 67

Narcotics, 97
Narrow neck of land, 29, 33, 34
Narrow pass, 29, 33
Nasca culture, 60
Navajo Indians, legends of, 3-4, 6
Navy of Solomon, 66
Necho of Egypt, 66
Nephi, 15
Nephi, land of, 28, 33, 34
Nephites, twelve, called by Christ, 26
New York-Panama theory of Book of Mormon geography, 33-34
"Newspaper Rock," 86
Nibley, Dr. Hugh, 23
North America, populating of, 26
Numbering systems, 73
Nunnery, the, 51

Ollantaytambo, 61
Olmecs, culture of, 39, 47
Otomis Indians, 6

Paccaritambo, 2
Pachacamac, 63
Palace of Six Patios, Yagul, Mexico, 52
Palenque, 48-49, 67; Temple of the Inscriptions in, 2, 49
Papago convert, story of, 3
Paper, use of, anciently, 70-71

Papyri, translation of, 23
Paracas, 63
Parahyba, Brazil, 67
Parahyba stone, 70
Parallels: between Mesoamerican and Near-Eastern cultures, viii-ix; between Mayans and Egyptians, 1-2; between Chroniclers' and Book of Mormon's accounts, 13-15; between Ixtlilxochitl's and Book of Mormon's teachings, 15-16; between Mesoamerican and Mediterranean cultures, 66-67; between Book of Mormon language and Hebrew, 71-72; between Mayan and Egyptian calendar systems, 94-95
Passover, 76
Periods of early American civilization, 35
Peru: history of, 58; ruins in, 58-63
Petroglyphs, 69, 73
Phoenicians: were Semitic, 64; alphabet of, 64; seafaring exploits of, 64; were great traders, 64; reasons to suspect America was reached by, 66-68; coins of, 67
Physicians, 98; types of, 98-99
Pictoglyphs, 69, 73
Pisac, Peru, 63
Pizarro, Francisco, 19-20, 58
Plato, 66
Popocatepetl, 46
Popol Vuh, 12, 13, 67
Potter's wheel, 84
Pottery, 87; of Chancays, 58; of Chimu, 60; of Mochi, 60; of Nascas, 60
Post-Classic period, 35
Pratt, Orson: on Lehi's course, 24, 25; on Jaredite landing, 24, 26; on Hill Cumorah, 24-25; on migration into North America, 26; on shipbuilding, 26; on island peoples, 26; on Christ's appearance to Nephites, 27; on Yucatan, Mexico, 28
Pre-Classic period, 35
Pre-Columbian peoples of America: definition of, vii; methods of studying, vii; were highly civilized, viii, 13, 20, 35; description of, when found by explorers, 18; customs of, 19. See also Indians
Premortal existence, 5
Prescott, William H., on Aztecs' knowledge of the Bible, 6
Priesthood, cultural parallels in, viii
Pyramid temple structures, ix; similarities between Egyptian and Mexican, 1-2; in Mexico, 42-52; in Peru, 60-63

Pyramid of the Sun, Teotihuacan, Mexico, 49

Quetzalcoatl, 10, 14, 52; Aztec conception of, 7; Temple of, 8; "bird-serpent," 8; Cortez mistaken for, 11
Quiche Maya, 13; creation legend of, 3
Quipu, 72-73
Quirigua, Guatemala, 25, 55

Recinos, Adrian, 13; on skin color, 14; on migration, 14; on creation, 16-17; on degrees in heaven, 17
Records, destruction of, 9, 97
Religious traditions of ancient Americans, 15-17, 74-76
Repentance, 17
Richards, LeGrand, story from, concerning Book of Mormon, vii
Richards, Willard, 23
River Sidon, 33, 34, 68
Roads in pre-Columbian America. See Highways
Roberts, B.H., on "revelation" of Lehi's travels, 22
Rolled stamp, 70
Roots, medicinal use of, 97
Runners, chasqui, 82-83
Ruz tomb, 67

Sacrament, partaking of, 17, 76
Sacrifice, 17, 19; among Aztecs, 35, 97-98; among Mayas, 37; in Chichen Itza, 42; among Olmecs, 47; in Kaminaljuyu, 55
Sacsahuaman, fortress of, 61
Sahagun, Bernardino de: on Quetzalcoatl, 7; on departure of Quetzalcoatl, 10; history and work of, 12-13; on banners, 13-14; on skin color, 14; on social and moral beliefs, 14; on tools, 14; on migration, 15; on anointing, 16; on baptism, 16, 74; on sacrament, 76; on physicians, 98
San Marin, General Jose de, 58
Sayil, palace of, 52
Script, Mayan, compared to Phoenician, 9
Sculpture in Copan, 57
Seer, role of, 17
Serpent: symbolism of, viii, 2, 11; feathered, various archaeological appearances of, 8
Shipbuilding, 26
Ships, Phoenician, 66
Sidonian Canaanites, letter from, 67
Sin, 17

Skin color, 14
Smith, Joseph: archaeological discovery of, vii; on archaeological findings, vii, 21-22; on Lehi's course, 22, 23; on mounds and Hill Cumorah, 24; on Tower Hill, 25; on Central America, 25; on receiving the plates, 77; finding of stone box by, 77, 78
Smith, Joseph Fielding, on location of Hill Cumorah, 25
Smith, Lucy Mack, 24, 92
Social and moral beliefs, 14
Solomon, 66
South American theory of Book of Mormon geography, 29
Southern Yucatan theory of Book of Mormon geography, 33
Spiritual testimony, importance of, vii, ix, 4
St. George, Utah, 25
Stela E, 55
Stela 5 Izapa, viii
Stelae, 55
Stephens, John L., 21-22, 56
Stone box(es): finding of, by Joseph Smith, 77; uses of, 78; finding of other, 78
Stones, precious, 19-20, 90
Surgery, 98. See also Trephination
Sword of Laban unsheathed, 77
Symbolism, cultural parallels in, viii, 2

Taylor, John, on John L. Stephens's book, 22
Teeth, care of, 14
Tehuantepec theory of Book of Mormon geography, 29
Temple of Kukulcan, Chichen Itza, 42
Temple of Niches, 47
Temple of Quetzalcoatl, Teotihuacan, Mexico, 8
Temple of the Cross, Palenque, 49
Temple of the Giant Jaguar, Tikal, Guatemala, 53
Temple of the Inscriptions, Palenque, 2, 49
Temple of the Magician, Uxmal, Mexico, 51
Temple of the Moon, Teotihuacan, Mexico, 49
Temple of the Sun: Mochi, 60; Cuzco, 63
Templs, cultural parallels in building of, ix
Tenayuca, temple of, 49
Tennessee, 4, 64, 68, 70
Tenochtitlan, Mexico, 35-36, 42, 49

Teotihuacan, Mexico, 8, 49
Testimony of Book of Mormon must be spiritual, vii, ix, 22
Tezcatlipoca, 17
Theopompus, 66
Theories concerning Book of Mormon geography, 29-34
Tiahuanaco, Peru, 63
Tierra del Fuego, 1
Tikal, Guatemala, 2, 8, 53-55
Title of the Lords of Totonicapan, 12, 13
Tlatilco, Mexico, 70
Tlaxochimaco, feast of, 14
"Tloque Nahuaque," 11, 13
Toltecs: civilization of, 39, 41; Mayan influence on, 41
Tombs, 1-2, 48, 55, 67
Tools, 14
Tower Hill, 25
Towers, 20
Toxcatl, 17
Toys, wheeled, 67, 84, 86
Tree of Life motif, viii, 2, 49, 63
Trephination: definition of, 99; techniques of, 99, 101; reasons for, 99-100; modern experiment with, 100; instruments used in, 100; anesthetic for, 100-1
Tula, Mexico, 10, 49
Tulan, arrival in, 14, 15
Tunnels, 82, 83
Turbans, ix
Turtles, House of, Uxmal, Mexico, 51
Tzintzuntzan, Mexico, 49, 51

Uhle, Max, 60, 63
Uitzilipuztli, feast of, 76
Ulcers, ancient treatment for, 98
Umbrella, use of, to indicate divinity or rank, ix
Underhill, Ruth, 4, 14; on skin color, 18
Uxmal, Mexico, 51-52

Veracruz, 47
Vikings, 64
Virachocha, 2, 8, 10, 63
Voladores, game of, 47
Volcanoes, 19, 46, 47
Votan, 67

Wall without mortar, 20
Warfare, 14, 21
Weapons, 14, 21, 60
West Virginia, tablets in, 70
Wheels: existence of, in pre-Columbian America, 83, 84-86; potter's, 84; toys with 84, 86
Whitmer, David, experience of, in meeting old man on way to Cumorah, 24
Widtsoe, John A., on geography, 22
Williams, Frederick G., 22; on Lehi's course, 22-23
Writing, ancient: destruction of, 9, 97; existence of, in early America, 69; discoveries of, 70-71

Xicolcoliuhqui, 52
Ximinez, Francisco, 13
Xlapak, 52
Xochicalco, 8, 52

Yagul, 52
Yehowa, 3
Young, Brigham: on Hill Cumorah, 24; on St. George, Utah, 25; on Manti, Utah, 25; on Joseph and Oliver returning gold plates, 77
Yucatan, Mexico, 8, 28
Yucatan theory of Book of Mormon geography, 29, 33
Yuchi Indians, 69-70

Zaculeu, 55
Zapotecs, civilization of, 41, 48
Zarahemla, 25, 28, 68; theories concerning location of land of, 29, 33, 34
Zelph, 24
Zero, Indians credited with being first to use, 1, 72
Ziggurats, ix, 42
Zitle, 47
Zodiac, signs of, 95